IMAGINING EQUALITY IN NINETEENTH-CENTURY AMERICAN LITERATURE

The theme of inequality has often dominated academic criticism, which has been concerned with identifying, analyzing, and demystifying various regimes of power and the illicit hierarchies upon which they are built. Studies of the United States in the nineteenth century have followed this trend in focusing on slavery, women's writing, and working-class activism. Kerry Larson advocates the importance of looking instead at equality as a central theme, viewing it not as an endangered ideal to strive for and protect but as an imagined social reality in its own right, one with far-reaching consequences. In this original study, he reads the literature of the pre-Civil War United States against Tocqueville's theories of equality. *Imagining Equality* tests these theories in the work of a broad array of authors and genres, both canonical and non-canonical, and in doing so discovers important new themes in Stowe, Hawthorne, Douglass, and Alcott.

KERRY LARSON is Professor of English at the University of Michigan, Ann Arbor. He is the author of *Whitman's Drama of Consensus* (1988) and of several articles on American literature and culture.

D1557398

CAMBRIDGE STUDIES IN AMERICAN LITERATURE
AND CULTURE

Editor
Ross Posnock, *Columbia University*

Founding editor
Albert Gelpi, *Stanford University*

Advisory board
Alfred Bendixen, *Texas A&M University*
Sacvan Bercovitch, *Harvard University*
Ronald Bush, *St. John's College, University of Oxford*
Wai Chee Dimock, *Yale University*
Albert Gelpi, *Stanford University*
Gordon Hutner, *University of Illinois, Urbana–Champaign*
Walter Benn Michaels, *University of Illinois, Chicago*
Kenneth Warren, *University of Chicago*

Recent books in this series

IMAGINING EQUALITY IN NINETEENTH-CENTURY AMERICAN LITERATURE

KERRY LARSON

CAMBRIDGE
UNIVERSITY PRESS

CAMBRIDGE UNIVERSITY PRESS
Cambridge, New York, Melbourne, Madrid, Cape Town,
Singapore, São Paulo, Delhi, Tokyo, Mexico City

Cambridge University Press
The Edinburgh Building, Cambridge CB2 8RU, UK

Published in the United States of America by Cambridge University Press, New York

www.cambridge.org
Information on this title: www.cambridge.org/9781107404717

First published 2008
First paperback edition 2011

A catalogue record for this publication is available from the British Library

Library of Congress Cataloguing in Publication Data
Larson, Kerry C.
Imagining equality in nineteenth-century American literature / Kerry Larson.
p.   cm. – (Cambridge studies in American literature and culture ; 156)
Includes bibliographical references.
ISBN 978-0-521-89803-4
I. American literature – 19th century – History and criticism.   2. Equality
in literature.   3. Democracy in literature.   4. Literature and society – United States –
History – 19th century.   I. Title.
PS217.E68L37 2008
810.9′3552–dc22
2008026922

ISBN 978-0-521-89803-4 Hardback
ISBN 978-1-107-40471-7 Paperback

To Matthew

Contents

Acknowledgements

I owe a great deal to many different friends and colleagues and I am grateful for the opportunity to acknowledge them here. For their response to early versions of the project as it was beginning to take shape, I would like to thank Sharon Cameron, Marjorie Levinson, Richard Poirier, and Rei Terada. Their support and advice came at a critical time. Jonathan Auerbach, Don Pease, and Xiomara Santamarina pressed me to clarify certain terms and key presuppositions in my argument, while Adela Pinch helped me think through a number of issues addressed in Part II. For their feedback on various portions of the manuscript I am grateful to Sandra Gunning, Mark Maslan, Jim McIntosh, Eliza Richards, and Michael Szalay. Gregg Crane read everything I could get to him, and was an unfailing source of good judgment and uncommon sense. Ross Posnock's interest in the project helped buoy its author and expedite its completion.

Portions of the manuscript were read at the University of Paris, Oxford University, Dartmouth College, and the University of Michigan. My thanks to the organizers of the individual conferences and the patient audiences. My thanks as well to Blackwell Publishing and *Nineteenth-Century Literature* for their permission to reprint portions of articles that appear in Chapters Three and Five.

Without the patience, humor, and absolute confidence of my wife, Lisa, this book would not have been written. Her love and support have enriched my life beyond measure. Finally, I dedicate this work to my son, Matthew, in gratitude and in love.

Introduction

For some time now literary criticism has been dominated by an interest in inequality – an interest that shows no signs of diminishing. Each day, it seems, we hear fresh reports on how inequality is mobilized, legitimized, rationalized, or naturalized. In the case of antebellum literature of the United States, considerations of race, gender, and class have so transformed the field that critical studies that do not in some way attempt to add to our knowledge in these areas will be expected to explain why. Indeed, questions relating to equality and inequality not only dominate the subject matter of literary criticism but increasingly inform how that criticism is evaluated. Thus it is not uncommon to find, say, a study of race commended for its discussion of the topic but faulted for slighting gender, or a study of gender praised for its insights but faulted for neglecting class. As scholars of nineteenth-century American literature judge the past, so are they judged in turn.[1]

Imagining Equality pursues a fundamentally different approach. Instead of treating equality as a political or social good that may be won or lost, I am interested in equality as a social norm whose presence was already well established and pervasive in the antebellum era. To think of equality in these terms is of course to follow the lead of Tocqueville's *Democracy in America*, the sheer richness of whose insights has not yet been fully exploited by students of the period. Tocqueville's great contribution was to see that "equality of conditions" produces a distinctive social psychology that permeates the beliefs and desires of citizen and non-citizen alike; in his account it emerges as a generative force that cuts across multiple domains of public and private life, modifying everything it touches. This book extrapolates some of the leading features of this psychology and makes them the theoretical framework for new interpretations of a variety of texts, both non-canonical and canonical, from the antebellum period. In essence, it consists of a series of case studies using as a point of departure arguments and key conceptual motifs from *Democracy in America* to gain new perspectives on a fundamental issue. Unsurpassed in its exploration of the sources and dynamics of inequality, contemporary academic criticism draws a blank when contemplating equality as a social reality in its own right. My book attempts to redress this imbalance.

To think of equality as a distinctively new form of social power is to stress its importance as a perceived value. Although *Democracy in America* occasionally alludes to specific material conditions that contribute to the spread of equality (in the first volume much is made, for example, of the abolition of primogeniture and other hereditary laws in the early days of the republic), it is not the existence of the real thing so much as the image of the real thing that explains its true historical significance for Tocqueville. Something less than the shared ownership of resources envisioned by socialism, his equality is something more than an abstract "right" asserted by liberal principles and protected by the state. Crossing the divide of facts and values, it is a "passion" or "immense influence" that looms before each subject as a regulatory idea or supervening fiction. It does not do away with the rich and poor, master and servant, more favored and less favored, but it does alter the relation between them. One might say that Tocqueville sees equality as a kind of ideology, except that there is no particular dominant group that it serves and therefore no set of social contradictions that it pretends to resolve. (As often as not, equality can be a *source* of contradiction in creating antithetical drives or self-conceptions that only countervailing impulses can override or hold in check.) Perhaps it would be better to say that equality as it appears in *Democracy in America* functions as a kind of democratic logos, the organizing principle that controls the horizon of social perception.[2]

It is in any case the emphasis on *imagining* equality that sets Tocqueville apart from other theorists of the time and explains his role in this study. More than any other of his contemporaries, he understood that "the democratic revolution" did not simply redistribute social power but altered its fundamental character. If under prior regimes authority assumed a form "external to the social body," as in the case of the monarchy, under democracy there is no "outside" to social power inasmuch as "society acts on itself. The only existing power is within it ... the people rules over the American political world as God rules over the universe."[3] True to his preferred method, Tocqueville leverages such insights by staging an encounter between two highly stylized, quasi-mythological entities, Aristocracy and Democracy: whereas in the first power is concrete and external to the self, in the second it is abstract and internal to the self. The opposition is overdrawn, but the point remains that the presumptive identification of the one with the many associated with a culture of equality replaces the sovereign with popular sovereignty, an abstraction that cannot be reduced to this or that individual but only arises in the imagined relation among them. Out of this projected totality a distinctively modern power is born, one that, as various commentators on Tocqueville like F. R. Ankersmit, Claude Lefort, and Sheldon Wolin have emphasized, creates a crucial indeterminacy regarding the ultimate locus of social authority.[4] The notorious looseness in Tocqueville's use of key terms, so often taken to be a sign of haste or arrogance, is no doubt in part attributable to precisely this indeterminacy. The ease with which equality can switch from a cause to an effect and back again in many of his interpretations, particularly with regard to political institutions, not to mention his confusing habit of treating equality and democracy as by turns utterly interchangeable and utterly opposed, reflects the peculiar elusiveness of modern power.[5] No more exclusively a state of society than a state of mind, equality of condition is a beguiling combination of both that strains against conventional categories of analysis.

The significance of the context-shattering nature of equality goes beyond analytic convenience, of course. In the famous introduction to *Democracy*, Tocqueville grandly reviews nine centuries of European history, portraying democracy as an inexorable, providential force that overwhelms entrenched networks of personal dependency and undermines aristocratic rule. One question he does not take up is why it is so common to conceptualize equality as an irresistible force in the first place. Why does it seem as though it is in the nature of equality to run away with itself, to be an indefinitely expandable concept? Or, to broach the same question by way of an historical anecdote, in *American Scripture* Pauline Maier relates how, in the summer of 1776, various colonies drafted constitutions whose bills of rights were so inclusive that, on further consideration, it was deemed prudent to have them revised, explained away, or dropped altogether.[6] The need for such retrenchment is obvious enough, especially in the case of a slaveholding society like Virginia, but perhaps the more interesting issue is why the need should have arisen in the first place. Evidently, there is something in the rhetoric of equality that chafes against restrictiveness: were we to declare that some are created equal we would be affirming a doctrine of inequality, not equality. Likewise, Jefferson's "self-evident truth," when taken to refer to all people, is understood to be a stirring endorsement of equality; when taken to refer to all white men, it is something else. Incipient in the concept is a movement toward ever-expanding frames of reference, a point underscored by *Democracy*'s habit of attributing to egalitarian-minded cultures an incurable fondness for abstraction and generality. Here again we find any easy distinction between reality and representation troubled: not only does democracy introduce, as we've seen, a certain confusion about the boundaries of social power – what falls inside and outside its domain – but it appears that equality carries a certain exponential logic that suggests that, abstractly, it has no objective, natural limit. Like Whitman's barbaric yawp, it is "unequal to measure itself."

To put the point this way is no more to sentimentalize democracy than to exhume the old conservative canard that the demand for social equality is at bottom irrational, nothing more than the expression of grasping resentment. The point is that if equality is for Tocqueville a collective norm organizing experience it is also something of an apparition standing beyond it, present in the here and now but also by definition incomplete and in this sense evanescent. Ever present as a social ideal, equality shrinks at the touch of the social. Perhaps *Democracy in America*'s most basic insight is that these two features do not cancel one another out but coexist and contend against one another. (Disputes as to whether Tocqueville, a near relation of Chateaubriand and lifelong student of Rousseau, ultimately sides with democracy or aristocracy have obscured a more fundamental and largely unacknowledged debt to Romanticism.) The peculiarity of democratic life is that it is organized around a norm that cannot, in principle, be present to itself. The current practice, especially pronounced in scholarship on the antebellum era, of pitting an abstract equality against the real thing thus looks past the most crucial feature of modern democratic power.[7] For it is the futility of resting with just such a distinction that most distinguishes, in Tocqueville's account, a social passion "which ever retreats before [democratic peoples] without getting quite out of sight, and as it retreats it beckons them on to pursue." To borrow another expression from Whitman used to describe "Me Myself," the democratic demiurge that embraces all people, places, and things, equality is both in and out of the game. Its homelessness, politically speaking, defines a crucial part of its social significance: "when inequality is the general rule in society, the greatest inequalities attract no attention. When everything is more or less level, the slightest variation is noted. Hence the more equal men are, the more insatiable will be their longing for equality."[8]

The overriding claim of this study is that the literature of the antebellum United States provides particularly rich ground for the exploration of such peculiarities – more so, I would suggest, than tabulations of what percentage of citizens owned what percentage of the national wealth in 1831 or data regarding the incidence of social mobility in 1848. Wary of its reckless generalizations and ingenious arguments, historians of the period have maintained a respectful distance from Tocqueville's masterpiece, but such scruples need not overawe the literary critic. This is not because literature transcends the conditions of its production but because the conditions in need of exploration – the cultural logic of equality – are so clearly a commingling of reality and fantasy. Without necessarily suggesting that literature is the privileged site for the expression of this logic, one might nonetheless hazard the opinion that at no other period in the country's history was "the great democratic God," as Melville's Ishmael earnestly puts it in apostrophizing "thou just Spirit of Equality," so visible thematically and so influential formally as in the imaginative writing of the antebellum period.[9] Arguably, the surge of democratic idealism coming out of the Jacksonian period, as notable for the intensity of its utopianism as for the bitterness of its rage, represents something of a lost world, but in *Democracy*, published in two volumes in 1835 and 1840, we have the advantage of an analysis that is more or less contemporaneous with the explosion of interest in this topic as a literary subject.

The pages that follow are grouped into three parts, each part consisting of two chapters and dedicated to a general theme extrapolated from *Democracy in America*. Part I concerns the correlation between nature and equality. Part II analyses the priority of the social whole in the imaginative life of the democratic subject. Part III takes up the topic of self-differentiation, known more loosely (and misleadingly) as individualism. The list is hardly comprehensive, which would be a decided shortcoming were this study an attempt to expound Tocqueville, which it is not. Indeed, in view of the impossibly large scope of the topic, it bears repeating that *Imagining Equality* is primarily a series of case studies in the sense that it isolates a handful of major themes without pretending to anything resembling an exhaustive examination.

Equality conforms to nature in the sense, as obvious as it is opaque, that no one is, by nature, superior to another. It's not just that equality inspires people to want to realize their own nature but that equality as such is a natural, pre-conventional value, like the state of nature imagined by theorists of the social contract. This identification of equality with nature suggests, in turn, that inequality has no such foundation, and is accordingly built on nothing more than social custom. In fact, "[d]emocracy, which destroys or obscures almost all former social conventions and eases the way to the new, causes the majority of sentiments born of convention to disappear."[10] Whether grammar, manners, literature, fashion, or family relationships, democracy gives itself the task of clearing away "all former social conventions" so that nature itself may speak. As chimerical and indeed self-defeating as this task must seem, the basic logic here should not be discounted: the more equality is taken to be apolitical, ahistorical, and indeed asocial, the more inequality stands out as a willful construction lacking a substantive identity of its own. In the antebellum era the most dramatic expression of this paradox can be found in the anti-slavery movement, where it was taken for granted that a society based on personal servitude was so contrary to nature that it could only be sustained by physical force and ideological manipulation. In the writings of David Walker, Frederick Douglass, and Hosea Easton, the subject of the first chapter, extreme attachment to equality as an absolute, otherworldly value motivates rather than deflects the attack on slavery. Examining their activism from this perspective not only helps get us past the epistemological correctness that has distorted our understanding of their rhetoric but also provides insight into the precise significance of appeals to a basic, universal equality so prevalent at the time.

It's well known, on the other hand, that Southern conservatism of the antebellum period endeavored to put inequality on a theoretical foundation. In the second chapter I try to account for why that effort failed so badly. Ironically confirming Tocqueville's sense of the pervasive influence of equality as a social norm, the pro-slavery argument was never altogether able to free itself from the logic of its anti-slavery opponent. Because the heart of that argument presumed that inequality was an inescapable by-product of all social arrangements, it echoed abolitionist appeals to a transcendent equality grounded in nature and nature's God. As developed by leading Southern ideologues such as George Fitzhugh, Henry Hughes, and others, the doctrine that would come to be known as paternalism outwardly embraces deference to rank and social hierarchy even as it sentimentalizes the plantation as an extended family of equals. On their view slavery was preferable to capitalism because it did a better job of securing mutual respect and maintaining a greater degree of equal rights for all members of society. This paradoxical and ultimately confused effort to save equality by way of inequality, crowned by the spontaneous affection between master and slave, equals in all but name, betrays the persistence of the correlation between equality and nature that Southern thought could never quite escape.

The contrast wherein the aristocratic sides with the conventional and man-made while the democratic is aligned with the natural and divine suggests a further contrast wherein the aristocratic stands for the local and particular while the democratic is drawn to the abstract and universal. Part Two, "The Many in the One," explores the antebellum investment in the concept of the social whole, a concept that is apt, Tocqueville frequently reminds us, to be an especially vivid presence in the life of the democratic subject. And indeed the very availability of an abstraction like "the democratic subject" is merely one instance of the priority of the average, the generic, and the typical, making appeals to a representative experience not only conceivable and routine but virtually normative. In the poetry of William Cullen Bryant, Lydia Sigourney, and Walt Whitman – in fact, in the earliest attempts to formulate a theory of literary nationalism – we find this idea of a representative experience so fundamental and so pervasive that interest in personal, purely subjective expression is effectively outlawed. Inheriting a tradition that began a century before with the republican campaign to democratize knowledge, antebellum literary expression tends to treat writing or authorship as an especially powerful, often excessive assertion of individual agency. Not simply were authors' legal rights associated with luxury and hereditary privilege in this period, as Meredith McGill has shown in *American Literature and the Culture of Reprinting*, but writing was specifically conceived as being tied to the part or the particular while acts of reading were taken to bear a privileged relation to the whole.[11] Tocqueville's prediction that a democratic literature would be organized around the projected responses of a mass subject or ideal-typical reader anticipates just such a development. This privileging of generic experiences and interchangeable selves, particularly as it bears upon and modifies ideas about reading and interpretation, forms the subject of Chapter Three.

The attraction of thinking that you're just like everybody else is that nobody's above you; the disadvantage is that nobody's below you. The oppressive feeling of inferiority brought on by constantly comparing yourself to a presumed equal and coming up short is another matter entirely. The observation that envy is apt to be an especially prominent phenomenon in democratic societies dates back to Aristotle, so it's no surprise to find it a recurrent topic of interest in *Democracy in America*. Its relevance to my own analysis is of course that envy affords a further if more lurid indication of the sheer immediacy of the social whole in the hearts and minds of the democratic subject. For envy presupposes the existence of perceived inequalities developing against the background of presumed equality; its outrage at departures from the norm is predicated upon an especially acute, indeed almost unbearable sense of what that norm is. With the exception of a handful of studies investigating the relation between the white working-class and their African-American counterparts, the place of envy in the literature of the antebellum United States has been neglected.[12] Chapter Four examines a prose memoir by Caroline Kirkland and novels by Nathaniel Hawthorne and Harriet Wilson to give some idea of the reach and prevalence of this particular affliction.

It's true that neither the priority of the social whole nor the conjunction of equality and nature are themes commonly associated with Tocqueville. For these one is more likely to turn to the tyranny of the majority, the revolution of rising expectations, the importance of civic voluntarism, to mention just a few of the more familiar preoccupations of *Democracy in America*. Perhaps the most hackneyed among these is the topic of individualism, a term Tocqueville is sometimes (incorrectly) said to have coined. Like other visitors to North America at the time, he was of course struck by its more crass manifestations, particularly in the obsessive pursuit of material gain, but his interest did not stop there. In lieu of treating individualism exclusively as an outgrowth of capitalism or Protestantism, the opening chapters of *Democracy in America*'s second volume explore its emergence as a by-product of egalitarian culture, an exploration that I use as a point of departure for the final section of the project. Briefly, Tocqueville's argument is that the perception of similitude on a grand scale generates a need to differentiate on a more local level; the more, that is to say, that I perceive myself to be more or less similar to everyone else, the more I will be encouraged to seek out my own distinctiveness.

The first half of Part III, "Equal but Separate," puts this simple observation to work in a series of readings of works by Emerson, Fuller, and, to a lesser extent, Thoreau. Thus, for example, the point of self-reliance is to insist that since you and I are just as good as Plato, we don't need to follow Plato's thinking but to develop our own. And the reason we know that we're just as good as Plato is that we are all attached to some greater entity (call it the Universal Mind, the Over-soul, or the Earth-Spirit) from which we all draw inspiration. As a result, by recognizing a sublime spiritual equality that renders distinctions between high and low or man and woman illusory or superficial, the mere individual is set apart from his or her peers by becoming a truly self-reliant individual, distinguished by a spirit of independent thinking and non-conformity. In effect, by drawing people together at an abstract level, equality forces them apart. The interest of Emerson and Fuller is that they articulate this logic with a startling, uncompromising clarity, so that the remote and the distant are embraced as parts of oneself (for relatedness is universal) while the near and the dear are held at arm's length or repudiated (for to take anything into the self, whether the affection of a friend or the commands of society, is to risk compromising or even corrupting that relatedness). Hence the ever-present weirdness of transcendental discourse, its beguiling habit of addressing abstractions with breathless intimacy and actual people with lofty impersonality. Beyond such idiosyncrasies, this extreme conjunction of the personal and impersonal also sheds new light on the place of social activism in the life of the democratic intellectual, a perennial, if somewhat melodramatic, topic of concern among transcendentalists and their commentators.

The final chapter examines attitudes toward work in nineteenth-century American literature, a topic that would seem to have very little to do with the syndrome just described – although it does have a lot to do with egalitarian culture. For by the antebellum period, the perception that work is to democracy as idleness is to aristocracy was of course a common-place. The source of sturdy republican virtue, work was extolled for its special relationship to democratic values. But along with this association also developed an expectation somewhat different in emphasis: work, to be truly meaningful, must also be personally expressive. If in one sense work was regarded as a distinctively democratic activity, linking all together in one common condition, in another it was seen as a vehicle for self-realization, instrumental to the worker in helping him or her actualize his or her own special self. In literature, both developments are apparent in a multitude of stories and novels chronicling the quest of a protagonist searching for his or her true place – that vocation uniquely suited to his or her true self. And yet in Hawthorne's stories, as well as texts by Louisa May Alcott and Lucy Larcom, a peculiar pattern emerges: the very urge to find work that is personally expressive only reinforces a sense of distance between the work one happens to perform and the self one is destined to be – a distance that, it turns out, is redemptive rather than demoralizing. In this respect, the logic of "same as/different from" extends beyond the realm of interpersonal relations I explore in Emerson and Fuller and governs attitudes concerning that great equalizer of the nineteenth century, work.

At one point in *The Structural Transformation of the Public Sphere*, Habermas ventures the observation that nineteenth-century liberals like Tocqueville and John Stuart Mill were prone to view majority opinion as a site of irrationality and coercion.[13] Although not altogether unfair, there is a sense in which such judgments are, at least in Tocqueville's case, somewhat beside the point. As I've been emphasizing, equality is for Tocqueville primarily a vast formalism – that indeed is its historical significance and its moral challenge. At bottom devoid of content, it is a grammar more than a language, which is to say that it is no more rational than irrational.[14] The specter of democratic despotism famously imagined in the concluding chapters of *Democracy* accordingly owes nothing to a fascination with anti-democratic ideas on the part of a benighted populace or to the ascend-ancy of state power but ultimately comes down to a matter of raw numbers. In the same way that it is more difficult to speak up in a lecture hall of 800 than in a seminar room of 8, the sheer perspicacity of the social multitude characteristic of egalitarian regimes is sufficiently imposing to make deference and docility steal insensibly over the democratic subject until such attributes become second nature. Having no discernible source nor, for that matter, any coherent object, democratic despotism as hypothesized by Tocqueville is incipient to the form that is democracy itself, so that the very sovereignty that empowers and politicizes the people also threatens to leave them isolated and weak in a post-political world of petty desires and trivial pursuits.

Tocqueville took these fears seriously enough to want to identify measures to offset and contain them. As a number of commentators have noted, throughout his analysis he underscores the importance of religious life, voluntary associations, and other sites of sociability because he was persuaded that democracy in particular needed to promote "intermediary bodies" that would span the gap between the private concerns of individual citizens and the "huge, tutelary power" of the state, executor of majority rule.[15] (And of course it is this theme that has made Tocqueville himself a tutelary presence in the communitarian critiques of US culture that continue to show up from time to time on the bestseller's lists.) Along similar lines, literature is sometimes celebrated for mediating between the interests of local or minoritized reading communities and larger publics. In what follows, however, my primary interest remains with the cultural logic of Tocqueville's as-if equality and how this is reflected in various literary texts. Instead of appraising these texts in terms of their dissent from or acceptance of this logic, I assume that all of them manifest, for better and for worse, a revolution in social perception whose reverberations are still being felt.

PART I

By nature equal

By 1835, democracy in America, according to the book of that name, had attained "an enduring and normal state."[1] It wasn't simply that a foreign visitor might find republican government "existing without contention, opposition [or] argument," its basic form "accepted as one accepts the sun's course and the succession of seasons." He might also see for himself that, comparatively speaking, the nation as a whole was "the most democratic country in the world."[2] Of course, the more than 3 million black Americans actually residing in the United States at the time, to name just one of many possible concerned parties, might have ventured a different opinion. Tocqueville was not unaware of chattel slavery in the South and racial oppression in the North, but he did elect to view their significance as primarily a local matter in the sense that they revealed more about the peculiarities of the United States than democracy more generally. (In this as in so much else he was guided by the interests and expectations of his French readers.) As a consequence, the long, rambling chapter that concludes Volume I of *Democracy* takes up the question of the three races in North America – the Native American, the African American, and the white American – from the standpoint of their likely impact on the long-term survival of the new republic. Race and the discord it excites, we are led to infer, are certainly a problem, but they are a distinctively American problem.

For some, bracketing the issue of race in this way has been taken to betray a certain evasiveness, on a par with *Democracy in America*'s silence on matters such as working-class activism, the women's rights movement, and a host of other developments that would seem to belie claims regarding "the prodigious influence" caused by "equality of conditions." Did Tocqueville overlook or refuse to recognize certain disagreeable truths in order to salvage his central thesis? Was his concept of democracy so loose and ungrounded that it allowed him to avoid coming to terms with such a question? Prominent historians of the

Jacksonian period such as Edward Pessen, Arthur Schlesinger, Jr., and Sean Wilentz have thought so.[3] Such a judgment, if correct, would seem to suggest that taking Tocqueville seriously as a guide to antebellum America means further marginalizing the already marginalized.

The point of departure for the next two chapters is to revisit Tocqueville's seemingly counterintuitive notion that "a democratic society [was] finally, firmly established" by the time he landed on American shores in 1831. Chapter One examines leading figures in the anti-slavery movement and attempts to make sense of their tendency to treat equality as a given – less a fully articulated belief than a primordial need and inescapable instinct. For it turns out that black activists, no less than Tocqueville's white citizens, accepted equality "as one accepts the sun's course and the succession of the seasons." To a degree that goes beyond polemical convenience, anti-slavery rhetoric actively dramatizes the *naturalizing* of equality as an internal presence in ways that correspond to and are clarified by Tocqueville's analysis. Put in these terms my approach may seem somewhat trivializing or beside the point when weighed against the mammoth inequalities chronicled by the slave narratives, polemics, and treatises of various African-American activists of the time. Of course I think otherwise – so much so, in fact, that I will be making the case that without a clear understanding of precisely how equality is valorized the contributions of figures like David Walker, Frederick Douglass, and Hosea Easton will continue to be misdescribed and misinterpreted.

The second chapter examines leading figures in the pro-slavery movement and attempts to make sense of their apparent *in*ability to renounce equality. Although figures like George Fitzhugh, James Henry Hammond, and other self-proclaimed aristocrats are remembered today for their theoretical defenses of slavery, their decision to uphold servitude at home by assailing capitalist inequality abroad is an odd strategy, to say the least. Slaveholding paternalism, in shunning the cruelties of the market, saw the plantation as a loving community of master and slave, who came together as equals in recognizing their common obligations to a greater good. Although Tocqueville was inclined to treat the South, like slavery, as a thing apart and therefore not relevant to his analysis, the aristocratic pretensions of the Old South were in fact shot through with sublimated appeals to the egalitarianism they otherwise professed to despise. Chapter Two concludes with a handful of novels written in response to *Uncle Tom's Cabin* where the paradoxes of paternalism stand out with unmistakable clarity.

CHAPTER ONE

Indestructible equality

THE DEFENSELESS ENEMY

In Harriet Beecher Stowe's anti-slavery epic, *Uncle Tom's Cabin*, it is easy to find examples of people who support slavery but hard to find examples of people who actually believe in it. Mr. Shelby may tell himself that it's his "*right*" (169; *his* emphasis) as a Southern gentleman to buy and sell his own "property" as he pleases, but on the day Tom is handed over to the slave-trader Haley he is so ashamed he can't bear to be present on his own farm to witness the event.[1] Haley, who is no gentleman, may boast about the "humane" treatment of his "cargo," but no amount of self-serving lies, it seems, can subdue an "uneasy conscience" (203). The same self-disgust is even more pronounced in the cases of St. Clare and Legree, two slaveholders haunted, respectively, by "a sort of chronic remorse" (306) and "slumbering moral elements" (567). Then, too, when the factory owner Mr. Wilson tries to persuade the runaway George Harris to give himself up on the grounds that slavery is sanctioned by the Bible ("we must all submit to the indications of Providence, George" [184]) and when George responds with a fiery speech on freedom and equality, Wilson almost instantly goes from urging George back to slavery to urging him onward to Canada. Likewise, Senator Bird may think that he is prepared to defend slavery's right to exist in the halls of Congress, but when confronted by a runaway slave at home his political scruples literally go out the door. Nobody really believes in slavery, St. Clare tells Miss Ophelia at one point, not even those who make it their job to uphold and defend it (331). Morally speaking, it appears that everybody in the book is pretty much on the same page.

Well, almost everybody. Marie St. Clare, for one, says of the peculiar institution, "I believe it's right" (281). Considering Africans "a degraded race," she finds the very idea of "putting them on any sort of equality with us" (268) inconceivable. Of course, Marie – narcissistic, hypochondriacal, cruel – is herself an illustration of the degrading effects of the slave system, a Southern belle groomed from birth to take her superior worth so much for granted that any "capability of affection" has long since "merged into a most intense and unconscious selfishness" (242).[2] Marie, that is to say, is an extreme case: putting it in terms more delicately than she deserves, we might say that her own moral self-representation is considerably less troubled by reality than most of the other characters in the book. For them, there does at least appear to be limits to the power of self-deception. Time after time we are invited to witness what Stowe calls, describing the backpedaling and bluster of Senator Bird when pressed by Mrs. Bird to explain his apparent tolerance of slavery, "the defenceless condition of the enemy's territory" (145). Thus for St. Clare the next worst thing to the evil that is slavery is the temptation to think that there is a principled justification for it. (His brother Alfred shares the same opinion.) Why not just come out with it, he exclaims in exasperation, and admit that "slavery is necessary to us, we can't get along without it, we should be beggared if we give it up" (281)? In other words, the scandal of thinking slavery "right" is not that it's too seductive but – just the reverse – that it's altogether threadbare. It imposes upon only foolish people like his wife. Defending the indefensible is otherwise so transparently an exercise in hypocrisy that one shouldn't even bother.

From this standpoint, *Uncle Tom's Cabin* is less an exercise in persuasion than in exposure. It is not intended to induce people, whether by logic or by emotion, into rejecting slavery. That rejection has already occurred, and the point of the novel is merely to bring it to light. "An idea of the dignity and worth of the meanest human soul" (337) is not just an idea that applies to everyone but is already implanted in everyone. This is why the killing of Tom is presented not just as an outrageous crime but also as a defiant and ultimately vain attempt by Legree to kill off those "slumbering moral elements" that have been "roused by his encounters with Tom" (567). The reference here picks up on previous allusions to "those fearful elements of woe and remorse" (535) which have been tormenting Legree ever since his abusive treatment of his dying mother; gripped in equal parts by guilt and rage – by "a fearful looking for of judgment and fiery indignation" (529) – Legree seals both in the execution of Tom, agreeing to play Satan to the latter's Christ. By the time we witness his subsequent descent into madness, the mere question as to whether slavery is defensible has long since ceased to matter as a real concern. We are instead invited to regard Legree's self-torment and eventual self-destruction as symptomatic of the social system of which he is a part, a system that is so obviously a denial of human nature that it is unsustainable. Slavery is not simply wicked. It is, at bottom, dysfunctional.

Under the circumstances, it would seem that it is really inequality, not equality, which has become unthinkable.[3] Irritated by white Northerners who would prefer their abolitionists to denounce a little less and reason a little more, Frederick Douglass caustically asks: "What point in the anti-slavery creed would you have me argue?" Approaching the subject as if it were "a matter beset with great difficulty, involving a doubtful application of the principle of justice" would only make the abolitionist look "ridiculous" and "offer an insult" to the intelligence of his audience. "Where all is plain, there is nothing to be argued … for the present, it is enough to affirm the equal manhood of the Negro race." Even the statute books of slaveholders throughout the South concur with the anti-slavery rhetoric of the North in presupposing that "the slave is a man."[4] It's not just that the time for reasoning is past but that reason itself cannot assimilate the very idea of a social system founded on unequal relations. "All the slaveholder asks of me is silence," Douglass remarks in another speech, "he does not ask me to go abroad and speak in *favor* of slavery; he does not ask anyone to do that [for] he would not say that slavery is a good thing" (409; text's emphasis). Politically, economically, and culturally, inequality is the great scourge of the land; conceptually, it can't even get off the ground. As the saying goes these days, it can't be "theorized." Consequently, for Douglass, as for Stowe, "to expose [slavery] is to kill it" (409).

At first glance, this sort of claim may seem a cunning piece of rhetorical escalation: what better way to put your opponent on the defensive than to suggest that his cause is not only unjust but unintelligible? But even if we give polemical convenience its due, the limits of this sort of approach are quickly reached. Are we to suppose that when the abolitionist (in this case Theodore Weld) declares "there is not a man on earth who does not believe that slavery is a curse,"[5] he is simply pursuing a tactical advantage? Or that when Stowe and Douglass take equality to be a presumptive norm they don't really mean it? Some may find it incredible that Douglass could insist that "the difference between abolitionists and those by whom they are opposed is not as to principles" (448), but it is even more incredible to think that he ventured such opinions for no other reason than their usefulness in advancing the anti-slavery cause. In the same way, it seems improbable that African-American delegates from a national convention in 1835 were insincere or simply confused when addressing white Americans in the following terms: "Prejudice, like slavery, cannot stand the omnipotence of Truth. It is … impossible for a bold, clear and discriminating mind that can calmly and dispassionately survey the structure upon which prejudice is founded, and the materials of which it is composed, to be chained within its grasp ..."[6] As Patrick Rael has noted, a disarming hopefulness runs through much of the literature of black protest; it's possible to come across even Martin Delany, hardly one to underestimate the ruthless tenacity of white racism, urging an increase in the number of skilled laborers in the black workforce in the expectation that it "will raise the colored class in this country, as by enchantment, from degradation to entire manhood and actual equality" with white people.[7] Again, rhetorical exigency cannot be entirely ruled out, for surely bold optimism is preferable to despairing cynicism when seeking to effect social change on so massive a scale, especially in the teeth of white antipathy and an outright disbelief in the capacity of African Americans to overcome the stigma of bondage. And yet the puzzle here is not the need to have faith in the cause but the confidence that others, even one's adversaries, cannot help but have faith in the cause. "I am of the strong opinion," declared Maria Stewart, another figure under no illusions regarding the challenges facing her people, "that on the day on which we unite, heart and soul, and turn our attention to knowledge and improvement, that day the hissing and reproach among the nations of the earth against us will cease."[8]

Naturally, not all abolitionists spoke with one voice, and in fact it's important to keep in mind that there were as many differences of opinion *within* various communities of white and black abolitionism as there were differences *between* them. Still, the presumption that inequality is an aberration and that egalitarian principles must in the end prevail cuts across a broad range of texts from the anti-slavery movement, even those where its presence may initially seem out of place or even contrary to its ostensible message. Consider, for example, David Walker's *Appeal ... to the Coloured Citizens of the World* (1829), a militant and fairly early example of black abolitionism that catalogues the many sins of white Americans in their treatment of generations of kidnapped Africans. Walker is unsparing in his depiction of white avarice, cruelty, bigotry, and sheer inhumanity; particularly intolerable is the hypocrisy of a people who, passing themselves off as good Christians and Republicans, not only retain slavery but introduce "the insupportable insult" of telling their slaves "they were not of the *human family*" but rather "descend[ed] originally from the tribes of *Monkeys* or *Orang-Outangs*."[9] And yet as the title of his pamphlet makes clear, the whites are hardly Walker's exclusive concern. In complete contrast to Stowe's sentimental politics of identification, much of the text engages in what is best described as a sustained *taunting* of the author's fellow blacks in calling attention to the complicity between white racism and their servility. As galling as Thomas Jefferson's tragically influential remarks on black inferiority are, for example, the failure of blacks to rise up and repudiate this slander is no less lamentable; in a tour de force of rhetorical invective, Walker hammers away at this theme by essentially repeating the same question for the better part of four pages (26–30) in the section entitled "Our Wretchedness in Consequence of Ignorance": "how can [our] enemies but say that we and our children are not of the HUMAN FAMILY ... [while we continue in bondage] ... [H]ow could Mr. Jefferson but say that 'the blacks ... are inferior to the whites in the endowments of both body and mind' ... when we are so submissive ... how can our [white] friends but be embarrassed ... while they are working for our emancipation [and] we are ... working against ourselves?" (26–27). And so on. From a rhetorical point of view, there is plainly nothing to be gained by declaring that to expose slavery is to kill it; on the contrary, the whole point of Walker's provocation is to insinuate that slavery makes *perfect sense* for the whites so long as it remains unopposed by the blacks. Preferring black activism to white pity – "you have to prove to the Americans and the world that we are MEN and not *brutes*" (30; emphasis in original) – Walker would therefore appear to understand equality as something to be achieved and not simply assumed. Resistance thereby becomes, in the words of one historian, "a test of human equality."[10]

But of course there is an important difference between saying that you won't be treated as an equal until you claim your right to equality and saying that someone is by nature unequal to other members of the "human family." What I have called Walker's provocation (e.g., "they love to have Masters too well!!" [64]) should be understood as just that, a provocation. This becomes clear later in the *Appeal* as Walker reflects on the ill-concealed fear of blacks in the white community, a fear that shows that the whites "know well" that "we *are* men" who "will retaliate." And indeed no amount of white perfidy or black subservience can altogether dislodge that "secret monitor in their hearts" – Walker is at this point referring to the whites – that tells them that "man, in all ages and all nations of the earth, is the same." For all their lies about racial superiority, the truths of equality, which the whites "cannot get rid of," remain intact. The result is moral paralysis – "they do not know what to do" (61). Here again, the implication is that slavery is not just reprehensible but fundamentally incoherent, producing the same kind of baffled self-division evident in Stowe's Legree or Douglass's dumb-struck slaveholders. At bottom, there can be no "test" for human equality so long as "the spirit and feeling which constitute the creature, man, can never be entirely erased from his breast, because the God who made him after his own image, planted it in his heart" (61). One can always pass or fail a test, but no one can accept or reject the presence of the *imago Dei*, guarantor of an imperishable human commonality.

Walker's image of a "secret monitor" calls to mind the idiom of moral sense theory that was prominent in Boston at the time. During this same period, for example, William Ellery Channing describes "the sense of duty" as "the inward monitor which speaks in the name of God."[11] Although it's unlikely that Walker, himself a resident of Boston at the time of the publication of his *Appeal*, was thinking of Channing or of any other contemporary in making the allusion, it is not unreasonable to suppose that he was thinking back on Jefferson's notorious judgment that blacks, while deficient in intellectual capability, were nevertheless endowed with a distinct "moral sense."[12] We know that Walker was familiar with the section of *Notes on the State of Virginia* where this judgment is made since we have already seen him discuss neighboring passages from it earlier in the *Appeal*; indeed, faithful to his own suggestion that his readers study *Notes* carefully, Walker's text is strewn with echoes and parodies of Jefferson's language (compare, for instance, Jefferson, contemplating with horror the possibility of a slave insurrection and commenting "I tremble for my country when I reflect that God is just [and] that his justice cannot sleep forever"[13] to Walker's devastating echo "but when I reflect that God is just, and that millions of my wretched brethren would meet death with glory ..." [28]). In responding to Jefferson's admission that blacks do not suffer "any depravity of the moral sense," the force of Walker's allusion is of course to return the compliment, deducing from the slaveholder's bafflement and patent equivocations over racial equality – "they do not know what to do" – the presence of a "secret monitor" that cannot be denied. Earlier Walker had joked that the whites will be "greatly offended with me" for saying so, but if "they are superior to other men, as they have represented themselves to be" (38), then that can only mean that they are beyond the reach of God's mercy. To claim superiority is to shun the soul's divinity. Hadn't Jefferson himself, while brooding over the possibility of a race war, confessed that "[t]he Almighty has no attribute which can take side with us in such a contest"?[14] Capitalizing on such concessions, Walker urges Jefferson's countrymen to heed the promptings from within as well as the warnings from without before it is too late: "I tell you Americans! That unless you speedily alter your course, *you* and your *Country are gone!!!* For God Almighty will tear up the very face of the earth!!!" (39; text's emphasis).

If equality were coveted purely as a secular good – if it was assumed to have value only in the political, social, cultural, or economic sphere – then the suggestion that inequality is at bottom unintelligible would seem fatuous or beside the point. That it did not seem so to writers such as Stowe, Walker, or Douglass suggests the need for a distinction between the pursuit of equality as a political goal and the commitment to a more basic human equality – an equality that, unlike its secular counterpart, can no more be given than taken away. Without some such distinction it becomes difficult to explain why Walker finds whites to be not just "avaricious" but "avaricious and ignorant" (66) or why Douglass feels confident in stating that "in every human breast, [the slave] has an advocate ... a man that does not recognize and approve for himself the rights and privileges contended for, in behalf of the American slave, has not yet been found" (448). Critics today tend to look through or look past this guiding attachment to a basic human equality in order to get onto the more compelling story of how the struggle for freedom and equality was fought and won or fought and lost. Overlooked in the process is the rather astonishing development whereby equality has become not simply a cause to endorse and defend but an innate endowment of the soul or "secret monitor" lodged "in every human breast." Equality of this elemental kind need not be proved. It need only be experienced.

The convergence of New Testament theology and republican ideology helped establish the terms for this internalization, making intervention on its behalf seem beyond the need of argument. Walker's evocation of the *imago Dei* and subsequent citation of the Declaration of Independence at the end of the *Appeal* set the stage for the combination of the two themes that, over the next three decades, would become a staple of anti-slavery literature.[15] To be human is to feel the call of equality as an instinctive need; not to feel this call is to risk losing membership in the human family. Thus in Walker's eyes the whites are pagans, savages, and devils not simply because of their cruelty but because, deaf to the meaning of Christianity and their own political ideals, they are in danger of becoming sub-human. Lucifer-like, they would "*dethrone* Jehovah and seat themselves upon his throne" (17; text's emphasis). Significantly, Walker never considers the possibility that black subjugation might structure the self-conception of the whites or answer, at least for them, some sort of collective psychological need. The product of "avarice and ignorance," racism is sinful. It can never be a viable way of life, for it has no role to play within the soul. In the end the whites are to be pitied for their stupidity as much as they are to be feared for their cupidity.

Walker, it is true, flirts with the idea of fixed racial differences, at one point "advanc[ing] my suspicion" as to whether the whites "*are as good by nature as we are or not*" (17; text's emphasis). But aside from the fact that this is another dig at Jefferson, who had of course used the same language to advance a similar "suspicion" regarding white superiority, it should be noted that Walker makes no secret of his ardent Anglophilia nor of his disapproval of blacks enslaving whites during the reign of the Pharoahs. Similarly, it is would be a mistake to suppose that Walker's categorical pronouncements on the sinfulness of slavery make him incapable of understanding the systemic, institutionalized, and global form of oppression we now call New World slavery. On the contrary, he delves into history in order to contrast ancient and modern forms of servitude and to establish that the "ignorance and treachery" so often attributed to African Americans were "not natural elements of the blacks, as Americans try to make us believe." Even as he conflates Christianity with equality's universalizing logic ("I believe you cannot be so wicked as to tell [our Lord Jesus Christ] that his gospel was that of *distinction*" [42; text's emphasis]), he retains a lively sense of the uses of the myth of a "natural" black servility among the whites, especially self-deceived deceivers like Jefferson. To a modern interpreter this dual emphasis would seem to work at cross-purposes, tempting one to see in Walker's unabashed universalism a limit to his otherwise trenchant demystifications of slaveholding cant and white propaganda. But perhaps this very response says more about the limits of contemporary criticism than the true workings of Walker's activism.

The concept of basic human equality espoused by Stowe, Douglass, and Walker may seem worlds apart from Tocqueville's approach to equality as a pervasive social norm, and indeed it is. And yet it's worth noting that his key premise that a culture of equality dominated and to a great extent controlled social perception is scarcely contradicted by the texts we've encountered so far, texts that find the very idea of inequality to be conceptually inadmissible. Thus when Douglass indicts slavery for overthrowing "the instinctive consciousness of the brotherhood of man,"[16] he takes for granted that this is a consciousness that is worth having and that it is indeed instinctive. That is why there is quite literally nothing to be said for inequality, why it should exist as a blank space or as nothing more than a placeholder for ignoble passions such as pride, prejudice, or avarice. The internalizing of equality as an instinctive need, along with the theoretical emptiness of its alternative, suggests that equality comes before the social in the sense that it is understood to be a pre-conventional, wholly natural value. Again, rather than pre-empting dissent, such an orientation seems to have mobilized it. Strangely, Walker's "secret monitor," like Tocqueville's "democratic revolution," leads to the suggestion that it is too late to go back, that equality has become the default position to such an extent that, as Walker would have it, the only question facing the white community is whether to repent or suffer the consequences. A force of nature, equality is imagined as Tocqueville's "providential fact," unstoppable and uncontainable.

DOUGLASS AND THE NATURE OF DEMOCRACY

In *My Bondage and My Freedom* (1855), the second of his three autobiographies, Frederick Douglass experiences a series of awakenings or epiphanies whereby "the inborn dream of my human nature" (179) is continually asserting and reasserting itself. The need for its continuous affirmation is clear enough. As Douglass explains, because slaves are "trained from the cradle up, to think and feel that their masters are superior, and invested with a sort of sacredness, there are few who can outgrow or rise above the control which that sentiment exercises" (288). Douglass has been trained to think and feel the same way; barely out of the cradle, he finds that his grandmother and "all the little children around her" refer to the " 'Old Master' ... with every mark of reverence" (143). But what elicits deference in them produces only dismay and fear in little Fred: "thus early did clouds and shadows begin to fall upon my path" (143). The point is not to charge Douglass with elitism but to note the care with which he portrays his first encounters with slavery as arousing an instinctive "disquiet" (143) – the kind of pre-verbal, inchoate, but visceral dread that recurs in scenes such as the one that finds the young Douglass overhearing the older slaves singing on their way to the great house farm and experiencing "my first glimmering conceptions of the dehumanizing character of slavery" in the "loud, long, and deep" tones that were "altogether beyond my feeble comprehension" (185). In fact, from start to finish, *My Bondage and My Freedom* goes out of its way to remind the reader of how a desire for freedom and belief in equality date from the earliest promptings of childhood, no less powerful for being inarticulate, thereby laying the basis for "that fresh and bitter condemnation of slavery, that springs from nature, unseared and unperverted" (224).

[T]here were many who could say that their fathers and mothers were stolen from Africa – forced from their homes, and compelled to serve as slaves. This, to me, was knowledge; but it was a kind of knowledge which filled me with a burning hatred of slavery ... I could not have been more than seven or eight years old when I began to make this subject my study ... I distinctly remember being, *even then*, most strongly impressed with the idea of being a freeman some day. (179; text's emphasis)

I was just as well aware of the unjust, unnatural and murderous character of slavery, when nine years old, as I am now. Without any appeal to books, to laws or authorities of any kind, it was enough to accept God as a father, to regard slavery as a crime. (209)

From my earliest recollections of serious matters, I date the entertainment of something like an ineffaceable conviction, that slavery would not always be able to hold me within its foul embrace; and this conviction, like a word of living faith, strengthened me through the darkest trials of my lot. The good spirit was from God, and to him I offer thanksgiving and praise. (213)

I was not through the first month of this, my second year with the kind and gentlemanly Mr. Freeland, before I was earnestly considering and devising plans for gaining that freedom, which, when I was but a mere child, I had ascertained to be the natural and inborn right of every member of the human family. (304)

The flight was a bold and perilous one; but here I am, in the great city of New York ... gazing upon the dazzling wonders of Broadway. The dreams of my childhood and the purposes of my manhood were now fulfilled. (349)

It is true that *My Bondage and My Freedom*, in keeping with the conventions of storytelling, also documents the author's "gradual initiation into the mysteries of slavery" (171) by citing specific incidents that "first ... opened my eyes to the cruelty and wickedness of slavery" (173). In his account of such pivotal episodes as the whipping and apparent rape of Aunt Esther, the intervention of Mr. Auld in forbidding reading and writing, or the famous battle with Covey, Douglass records his emerging awareness of slavery's barbarities and injustice. Nevertheless, it is also clear that Douglass wants us to interpret these events against the background of a more primordial and God-given understanding of freedom and equality. With each "new insight into the unnatural power to which I was subjected" (237), we find fresh confirmation of that imperishable, natural understanding. Capturing precisely this aspect of the story, James McCune Smith's Introduction marvels at "a shy old fashioned child, occasionally oppressed by what he could not well account for ... until, finally, he stumbled upon [the revelation] hidden away down in the depths of his nature ... that liberty and right, for all men, were anterior to slavery and wrong" (126).[17]

Because equality is what comes naturally and because children are closest to nature, the connection between the two is easily seen. "The equality of nature is strongly asserted in childhood" (169), Douglass remarks, echoing St. Clare's statement that "your little child is your only true democrat" (273). So deeply ingrained is the child's egalitarianism that when the seven-year-old Frederick first glimpses the Lloyd plantation, his response is to assume, against all logic and experience, that its spectacular wealth and luxury is for master and slave to share: "these all belonged to me, as well as to Col. Edward Lloyd, and for a time I greatly enjoyed them" (163). Conversely, the young "Mas' Daniel," by virtue of his "association with his father's slaves, had measurably adopted their dialect and their ideas." The truth is that "*color* makes no difference with a child" because the "wants, tastes and pursuits common to children [are] not put on, but natural" (169; text's emphasis).[18] These remarks are rather strategically inserted in the midst of a chapter otherwise devoted to an exhaustive description of the Lloyd plantation, where "the idea of rank and station was rigidly maintained" (170). Against the youth and simplicity of the "true democrat" we have the superannuated, extravagantly artificial splendor of an estate likened to "the residences of English nobility" (162) or "baronial domains" going back to "the middle ages of Europe" that are still standing, "full three hundred years behind the age, in all that relates to humanity and morals" (160).

That's not to say that "the equality of nature," so visible in youth, may not also be found in old age. "One of the most heart-saddening and humiliating scenes" in a book filled with them involves the feeble and decrepit Colonel Lloyd whipping the similarly feeble and decrepit Old Barney. What makes the scene sad – as opposed to horrific, as in the case of the brutal beating of Aunt Esther – is the spectacle of "two men, both advanced in years," the one with "silvery locks" and horsewhip in hand tottering over the other, with "bald head and toil-worn brow" (194). The pathos of the scene, Douglass's genius for the representative anecdote makes us feel, centers on how identities are virtually usurped by social roles that should no longer matter. In the same way that the innocence of youth knows nothing of the distinctions of color, the approach of death makes the division of "master and slave; superior and inferior" look all the more absurd for those who must be deemed "*equals* at the bar of God ... where all distinctions ... are blotted out forever" (194; text's emphasis). In death as in birth, democracy prevails, whatever may come between.

As equality is rooted in nature, so inequality is tied to convention. "Nature has done almost nothing to prepare men and women to be either slaves or slaveholders," Douglass says, in a typical passage, "nothing but rigid training, long persisted in, can perfect the character of one or the other" (222). The more assimilated to nature equality becomes, the stronger the predisposition to view inequality as a product of social conditioning. Thus for Sophia Auld, Douglass's new mistress in Baltimore, to regard the young author as "a child, as any other," is altogether "natural and sponta-neous," whereas to treat him as "*property*" "was a thing of conventional growth" (216; text's emphasis). (In this particular case, convention wins out, though not without considerable inner turmoil: the good Mrs. Auld, once poisoned by the exercise of power, must struggle "to justify herself *to*

herself" [223; text's emphasis], just as, Legree-like, Douglass's previous
master, depressed and irritable, is said to be "at war with his own soul"
[172].) What makes slavery unnatural has less to do with the abuses it
encourages, deplorable as the beatings, whippings, rapes, and exploitation
are held to be. Slavery's crimes should not obscure the crime that is slavery.
(As Douglass puts it, "It was *slavery* – not its mere *incidents* – that I hated"
[228; text's emphasis].) If it's necessary for Mrs. Auld to undergo "some
training, and some hardening, in the exercise of the slaveholder's prerogative" (221), that's not because she is learning how to become a sadist; as
Douglass indicates, the escalating tension in the Auld household "was not
the result of any marked cruelty in the treatment I received" (228). Rather,
Mrs. Auld requires training in order "to make her equal to forgetting my
human nature and character, and to treating me as a thing destitute of a
moral or an intellectual nature" (221). She must unlearn equality before she
can practice inequality. The first being innate, the second must be acquired.

Thus the more it is seen to exemplify the conventional, the more slavery
is bound to appear as a shamelessly transparent exercise in social engineer-
ing. Like other slave narratives of the time, *My Bondage and My Freedom*
takes note of the tremendous amount of ideological maintenance required
to keep the system running, as when Douglass pauses to ticket off, in a series
of mocking catchphrases, the propaganda of the Southern pulpit – "duty of
obedience to our masters"; "our enslavement a merciful and beneficial
arrangement"; "our hard hands and dark color … God's mark of displeas-
ure"; "relation of master and slave … one of reciprocal benefits." These and
other bromides are dispatched with one sentence: "nature laughed them to
scorn" (306).[19] To the degree that it is nature and nature alone that does the
unmasking here, the inclination to conceive of slavery as an irreducibly
social power becomes irresistible. Upon reading the *Columbian Orator*, a
popular compilation of speeches on slavery, the inspired Douglass finds "all
nature redolent" of "Liberty! The inestimable birthright of every man": "I
saw nothing without seeing it, and I heard nothing without hearing it. I do
not exaggerate, when I say, that it looked from every star, smiled in every
calm, breathed in every wind and moved in every storm" (227). Tyranny, on
the other hand, is necessarily man-made, a social construction through and
through. Its foundations may rest upon those eminently human passions,
pride and avarice (226), but of course this does not authorize its practices in
the same way that nature authorizes democracy. It is, after all, because these
are unworthy passions that propagandists like the "slaveholding priestcraft"
(306) are needed to do their work. Next to cruelty, the most common trait
of the masters tends to be trickery, cunning, covering up, evasiveness,

dissimulation. The world of slavery is a made-up world, a massive fiction. Like the fantastic, but fraudulent wealth of Colonel Lloyd's plantation, its essential feature is its artificiality.

It follows that if slavery's brutality stands any chance of escaping nature's scorn, it will need to learn how to use nature's ways to its own advantage. A case in point is the tradition of allowing slaves the dubious liberty of "drunkenness and dissipation" (291) in the week between Christmas and New Year's, another tactic designed to induce "stupid contentment" (227) among the oppressed. Described at some length by Douglass as "the holiday system," this annual practice gives the slaves just enough taste of freedom "to keep out thoughts and wishes of a more dangerous character"; its function is to serve as "conductors or safety valves to carry off the explosive elements inseparable from the human mind, when reduced to the condition of slavery" (291). Douglass's indignation at this "gross fraud," while to some degree understandable, is noticeably overwrought. He recoils at the memory of "whole multitudes … stretched out in brutal drunkenness, at once helpless and disgusting" and cryptically alludes to "scenes" that "were often scandalous and loathsome in the extreme" (292). But it is not necessarily clear why a week of "dissipation" should not *incite* rather than "carry off" that explosive wish for liberty, much less why those who do retain some "pleasures of memory" over their brief interlude of freedom should thereby find themselves beguiled of "thoughts and wishes of a more dangerous character" (291). Robert Levine has insightfully explored the debt Douglass's abolitionism owes to temperance reform, and this no doubt helps explain the horror and disgust that resonates throughout this particular section.[20] But it is also reasonable to suppose that his outrage has a further source. The "holiday system" succeeds where the "slaveholding priestcraft" fails because it recognizes the reality of the inborn yearning for freedom rather than simply denying its existence. It is the superior form of mind control because it uses just enough of nature to defeat nature.

Perhaps more than any other writer in the antebellum period, Douglass is celebrated for demystifying the fictions of power – for bringing to light those moments when, in the words of one critic, the "culturally determined" tries to pass itself off as the "naturally determined."[21] As Douglass was first making his appearance on the canonical scene more than twenty years ago, interpreters like Houston Baker and Henry Louis Gates, Jr., favoring a post-structuralist approach, portrayed the autobiographer as a literary trickster, expert in the manipulation of the masters' code and above all alert to how meaning, irreducibly "culture-bound," is always "the result of shared assumptions and conventions."[22] In the view of a number of readers since, this particular feature of Douglass's genius is displayed to best advantage in *My Bondage*: in contrast to the more terse, less reflective account issued ten years earlier in *Narrative of the Life of Frederick Douglass*, which tends to foreground scenes of physical brutality and coercion, the second autobiography more generally exhibits, according to Eric Sundquist, a deepened appreciation of "the comprehensive ideology of power" on the plantation and greater insight into "the coercion of proslavery thought."[23] Thus in the aftermath of Aunt Esther's brutal flogging, *My Bondage* goes on to describe the young Douglass brooding over the arbitrary character of racial distinctions and the patent contradiction of supposing that God could sanction torture and sadism. But these "puzzling exceptions to [the] theory of slavery" begin to be less puzzling once he realizes that "what man can make, man can unmake" (179). With this "important truth" established, it becomes self-evident that "it was not color, but crime, not God, but man that afforded the true explanation of the existence of slavery" (179). Judged in terms of contemporary accounts of Douglass, the moment is paradigmatic in pitting the slave's genius for deconstructing power and for exploiting the contingencies of meaning against the slaveholder's bid to control, fix, or master meaning. The foe of "the absolutist metaphysics of rationalist and intellectualist thought" or of "the totalizing power of universal reason held exclusively by white hands," Douglass has been repeatedly seen as deploying the subversive truths of social construction against the essentialism of his oppressors.[24]

One implication of the account I have been developing is that this familiar opposition tells just one side of the story. For it is only because equality is held to be natural, God-given, and "inborn" that exposing the constructedness of inequality can count as "knowledge quite worth possessing" (179). Slaveholders *should* fear the discovery that "what man can make, man can unmake," but this can hold no terrors for the lovers of freedom and equality, since theirs is a "birthright" granted *to* man, not made *by* him. Thus the phrase "the constructedness of inequality" is a redundant expression for the same reason that the phrase "the constructedness of equality" can only be viewed as a contradiction in terms. (Of course, today there are plenty of interpreters who take themselves to be studying the second phenomenon, but more often than not what they really mean is that they are interested in the first.) Without a belief in "the abstract logic of equality" (125), as James McCune Smith puts it in his Introduction to *My Bondage*, the anti-essentialist gesture of exposing the essentializing logic of the slaveholder would be pointless. Made nervous by Douglass's talk of inborn dreams and natural birthrights, latter-day critics play down his reliance on this abstract logic when they choose to acknowledge it at all. But what they take to *contradict* Douglass's deconstruction of power is better understood as a *source* for it.[25] Where freedom and equality are thought to be transcendent values, ingrained within all human beings but situated outside the vagaries of cultural definition, social arrangements are likely to appear more or less foundationless, more or less arbitrary. Beyond the reach of social conditioning, equality leverages social critique.

Or, as Tocqueville puts it, "equality is bound to destroy all that is purely conventional and arbitrary in forms of thought".[26] The remark comes in the context of a discussion of grammar in Jacksonian America but the larger point is that democracy, in modeling itself on nature, makes the conventionality of convention that much easier to see and, in so doing, makes the connection between the "purely conventional" and the "arbitrary" especially close. The contextualist, alert to the shifting multiplicities of meaning and the contingencies of social convention, is in this respect the offspring of the universalist, celebrant of a timeless and transcendent equality. An especially clear example of this sort of interdependency may be found in the concept of ideology and its attendant notions of false consciousness. Consider for a moment the following description of the destructive effects of ideological distortion in modern times, chosen more or less at random and every bit as eloquent, in its convoluted urgency, as anything we might encounter in the writings of Walker and Douglass.

The dominant language discredits and destroys the spontaneous political discourse of the dominated. It leaves them only silence or a borrowed language, whose logic departs from that of popular usage without becoming that of erudite usage, a deranged language, in which "fine words" are only there to mark the dignity of the expressive intention, and which, unable to express anything true, real or "felt", dispossesses the speaker of the very experience it is supposed to express. It forces recourse to spokesmen, who are themselves condemned to use the dominant language (which is sufficient to introduce a distance from the mandators and, worse, from their problems and their experience of their problems) or, at least, a routine, routinizing language which, in addition to its functions as mnemonic and a safety net, constitutes the only system of defence for those who can neither play the game nor "spoil" it, a language which never engages with reality but churns out its canonical formulae and slogans, and which dispossess the mandators of their experience a second time.[27]

Ideology is unjust because it robs people of the experience of injustice. Like Douglass's drunken carousers, its victims are denied access to the reality of their own suffering. The underlying assumption would appear to be that those who do not experience things such as mutual respect and equality will necessarily feel their absence, for if they did not feel their absence – if they yearned to forfeit their dignity or if they welcomed domination – there would be nothing for ideology to discredit, destroy, or make unreal. Thus, while the passage effectively conveys the terrible fragility of equality, there is a further sense in which it also pays tribute to its presence as a kind of baseline for human experience. There's no need to proclaim "the indestructible equality of man to man," in James McCune Smith's phrase, since that's already so deeply embedded in assumptions of the critic as to go without saying – the necessary premise for, rather than the object of, analysis. Just so, it's obvious that when Douglass indicates that "my earliest recollections are associated with the appalling thought that I was a slave," he is not inviting us to puzzle over precisely how and why he found this realization "appalling." The adjective requires no explanation since the unavoidable inference is that people are *made* to be free and equal. That's why slavery is "against nature [and] ... against the Government of God."[28]

Appeals to a universal humanity together with a powerful sense of the shaping impact of the social environment constitute, according to Patrick Rael, the "twin pillars" of black anti-slavery protest.[29] I have been arguing that it's the identification of equality with nature that makes the relation between these two impulses politically productive. Equality conforms to nature in the vague but powerful sense that nobody is, by nature, superior to another. As such, it forms the backdrop against which inequality is not only rendered visible but recognized as artifactual and, to this extent, accidental. Phrased in these terms, the point may seem innocent enough, if rather abstract. What is at stake, practically speaking, in the outlook I've described? What sort of contribution, exactly, did it make to the debate raging over slavery at the time? Because this dualism of basic equality and political equality was by no means restricted to Walker and Douglass alone, we need a clearer sense of how it structured approaches to the slavery question, pro and con, before identifying what was significant about their contribution.

THE EQUALITY OF SOULS AND THE INEQUALITY OF PERSONS

If the concept of basic human equality means anything, it must appeal to some attribute of human beings that is enduring, significant, and (in principle) universal. It asks us to stand back from the shifting contexts and local circumstances that differentiate people and to affirm an underlying, common humanity – "an abstract truth, applicable to all people and all times," in Lincoln's words.[30] It requires us to treat orderings between types or grades of human beings as purely heuristic or superficial when they are not manifestly delusional. It invokes God, nature, or some combination of both as supremely egalitarian powers that do not recognize the petty, earth-bound distinctions of master and slave or rich and poor. If on the one hand equality is an irreducibly *relational* concept (it makes no sense to say that I am equal to myself; I can only be equal to one or more others), it is also an inescapably *transcendent* one (what binds me to those others must be a Common Something that transcends time and place). For all of these reasons it's not difficult to understand why many find in affirmations of basic equality a grand emptiness whose application to anything of imme-diate consequence in the real world is at best uncertain. In a landmark essay on the topic published more than forty years ago, Bernard Williams has in fact argued that it is perfectly conceivable to imagine a highly stratified, hierarchal society that nevertheless extends a genuine regard for the basic equality of all its members. (This is precisely the position pro-slavery writers took themselves to be espousing, as we will see in the next chapter.) In any case, as Williams goes on to observe, it is evident that "the mere idea of regarding people 'from the human point of view,' while it has a good deal to do with politics, and a certain amount to do with equality, has nothing specially to do with political equality."[31]

Although our primary concern thus far has been to explore how that divide was crossed, its importance is too obvious to be discounted, all the more so once we recognize that the distinction between basic equality and political equality, far from being an abstract concern, was arguably more decisive than anything else in structuring debates on race and bondage throughout the first half of the nineteenth century in the United States. I am thinking in particular of the colonization movement, the first con-certed effort among the white leadership to frame a national policy regard-ing slavery and the immediate catalyst for the emergence of radical abolitionism in the late 1820s. David Walker devotes nearly half of his *Appeal* to a ferocious attack on "the colonizing trick" (67), while the Garrisonian wing of the anti-slavery forces, which initially recruited Douglass to the cause, first gained national recognition with its equally fierce criticisms of the American Colonization Society (ACS). Founded in 1816 by leading ministers and politicians among the white elite from above and below the Mason-Dixon line, the ACS set for itself the mission of deporting all African Americans – first free men and women of color, then slaves – "back" to Africa. Taking their cue from Jefferson's judgment that blacks and whites could never live together in harmony, the colonizationists believed that the degradations caused by slavery among the blacks and the ongoing, rooted prejudice of the whites combined to create, in effect, a feedback loop which could not be broken. Although Walker assailed colonization as a plot to perpetuate slavery and William Lloyd Garrison accused it of wanton hypocrisy in feigning benevolent concern to mask an essentially racist agenda, neither criticism was entirely fair. For one thing, this particular cause never secured a broad base of support among slave-holders; ironically, colonizationism did as much to stimulate opposition on the pro-slavery front as it galvanized abolitionist outrage to the North.[32] And while there appears to be considerable diversity of opinion regarding black "degradation," with some colonizationists believing it to be innate, others believing it to be the lamentable result of slavery and white prejudice, and still others a mixture of nature and nurture, there was general agreement that, once shipped off to West Africa, blacks would not only thrive, but become colonizers in turn, converting the continent to Christianity and republican ideals. In this spirit, Henry Clay invited members of the Colonization Society of Kentucky in 1829 to entertain "the hope, that in a period of time, not surpassing in duration, that of our own Colonial and National existence, we shall behold a confederation of Republican States on the western shores of Africa, like our own, with their Congress and annual Legislatures thundering forth in behalf of the rights of man, and making tyrants tremble on their shores."[33]

That blacks could enjoy on African soil what they were supposedly ill-equipped or unprepared to enjoy in America has less to do with muddled thinking than with a guiding assumption of the colonizationist program: abstract or basic human equality is one thing, political or social equality is another. For example, in his presidential address to the American Colonization Society in 1848, Clay explicitly rejected the pro-slavery position that the self-evident truths of Jefferson's Declaration applied to whites alone, for "as an abstract principle, there is no doubt of the truth of that declaration; and it is desirable in the original construction of society, and in organized societies, to keep it in view as a great fundamental principle."[34] Quoting at length from this same speech ten years later in his debates with Stephen Douglas, Lincoln likewise repudiated the claim that "Negroes were not included in the term 'all men' in the Declaration of Independence," arguing that such an exclusion "ha[s] a tendency to dehumanize the Negro – to take away from him the right of ever striving to be a man."[35] And yet, regarding the question of "social rights" – the question, that is, as to whether "the black man [may] ever enjoy an equality with his white neighbor in social and political rights" – the answer was clear: any such future "was out of the question."[36] This verdict comes from Clay but is made no less emphatically by Lincoln: "[t]here is a physical difference between the white and the black races which I believe will for ever forbid the two races living together on terms of social and political equality." In truth, according to Lincoln, when the authors of "that notable instrument," the Declaration of Independence, said that "all men [are] created equal – equal in certain inalienable rights ... [t]hey meant simply to declare the *right* so that the *enforcement* of it might follow as fast as circumstances should permit."[37] In short, even if "circumstances" were not propitious in 1858, that was no reason to abandon the ideals of 1776. Too precious to be surrendered as a "fundamental principle" of government, the first of the Declaration's self-evident truths was also too impractical to be actualized once it crossed racial lines.

In effect, then, the colonizationist movement formalized the disarticulation of basic human equality and political equality, making it the centerpiece of their platform, not so much burying its contradictions as encouraging a resigned acceptance of them. It did not invent this particular separation of theory and practice, of course, which is also apparent in the perennial contrast between the high-minded idealism of the Declaration's self-evident truth, sanctioned by "nature" and "nature's God" (significantly, phrases absent in Jefferson's original version) and the political expediency of the US Constitution. But colonization did give this contrast a broader scope and currency as it found its way into sermons, pamphlets, and novels throughout the antebellum period. So while it is unlikely that Stowe believed that, say, Sam and Andy, the two field hands whose buffoonery helps buy time for Eliza's escape in *Uncle Tom's Cabin*, did not share in "the dignity and worth of the meanest human soul" (337), it is also highly unlikely that she considered them entitled to a political and social equality on a par with the rest of white America. And although Stowe was a supporter of colonization (albeit a lukewarm one) even its self-avowed foes could not escape the same two-faced understanding of equality. In the case of the Garrisonians clamoring for the immediate abolition of slavery but disdaining available political channels as corrupt, the risk of indulging a sentimental egalitarianism at the cost of achieving needed reforms was real. Readers of *My Bondage and My Freedom* will recall Douglass's growing unease, as he begins to become a star on the lecture-circuit, at being instructed by Garrison and other white handlers to stick to the approved script and narrate without comment the cruelties of life on the plantation. So long as the self-educated Frederick, in other words, could play the role of the unlettered Uncle Tom, meek victim of slavery's depredations, white audiences would be happy. Apart from betraying the persistence of racism in the North, such episodes make vivid how an exclusive emphasis on moral suasion and Christian benevolence could serve to narrow the opportunities for effective intervention. From this standpoint, there doesn't appear to be much difference between the commitment to an abstract egalitarianism contemptuous of political empowerment and a commitment to political expediency severed from any immediate connection to egalitarian principles – between Garrison burning the Constitution and Lincoln grimly enforcing it. Much more than theories of racial determinism, which, up until the middle of the century, were too sporadic, vague and seemingly irreligious to command a significant degree of support, the disconnect between basic equality and political equality was the organizing framework for responses on both sides of the slavery question.

Understanding this divide places us in a better position to appreciate the contribution of figures like Walker and Douglass. Inspired by an evangelical Christianity that declares goodness to be innate and wickedness to be environmentally produced, their very commitment to equality as a decidedly transcendent value converts, as I have argued, an otherwise inert universalism into the grounds of political critique. In this respect, what had operated on two distinct registers – the equality of souls and the inequality of persons[38] – is joined together. Venerating equality as an endowment or birthright of the soul need not mean sequestering it from the earthly world. Because sameness was innate and because recognizing this made one human (recall Walker's animadversions against white devils and savages), assertions of difference that went beyond the trivial or superficial were self-evidently false or purely artificial, a product of cultural influence. Whereas figures like Lincoln may have regarded genuine equality as a beckoning, but impractical abstraction that for the time being would have to yield to the hard truths of social necessity, Walker and Douglass evoke equality as an undeniably immediate reality, always pressing against consciousness, always demanding expression, while it was inequality that belonged to the world of fiction and unreality. Ultimately this is why slavery did not require attackers to demystify it. It demystified itself.

"Nature never goes out of her limits to produce her own works; all of which are perfect," observes Hosea Easton, part-time blacksmith, clergyman, and activist whose writings, recently reprinted, afford a final and especially vivid instance of the logic I've been describing. Published eight years after Walker's *Appeal* and eight years before Douglass's *Narrative*, Easton's *Treatise on the Intellectual Character, and Civil and Political Condition of the Colored People of the U. States* (1837) begins by affirming the perfection of Nature's works as well as "the one great truth" that "God hath made of one blood all nations of men for to dwell on all the face of the earth."[39] From this it follows as a matter of course that "whatever imperfections there are in the mind, must have originated within its own sphere"(68), which is simply to say "whatever differences exist [among the children of men] are casual or accidental" (67). In the introduction to his *Treatise*, Easton associates inequality with fallenness, suggesting that "originally there was no difference of intellect, either constitutional or casual. Man was perfect, and therefore to him there was no exception" (68–69). It is only after the fall that it becomes possible to make discriminations among individuals on the basis of their intellectual development; with "the act of transgression," divine equality vanishes, replaced by a new force Easton calls "public sentiment" (69). But that is no reason to despair. Quite apart from the fact that the sheer variety produced by nature is a thing of joy and wonder, it is evident that "the mind is capable of high cultivation" even if the extent of its development "depends entirely on the means and agents employed to that end" (69). It is up to "public sentiment" to regulate such things, a power, Easton suggests, that is no less plastic and mutable than the minds of which it is composed. Indeed, next to his evocation of a blessed state of Edenic equality and reproductive abundance that dominates its opening paragraphs, Easton's introduction is most memorable for its recurrent reminders that in a post-lapsarian world differences are owing to "accidental causes" (67), "incidental circumstances" (70), or "habits of life" (80).

Easton's rigorously enforced distinction between divine or natural perfection and human mutability, in what we can now recognize as a familiar pattern, serves as the launching point for some of the most biting prose in the literature of anti-slavery protest, surpassing even Walker in its bitterness. Taking the idea that a denial of equality is a denial of nature about as far as it can go, Chapter One anatomizes what Easton calls "the lineal effects of slavery on its victims" (85). If difference is a token of sin, then sin practiced systematically and remorselessly can only be called a disease. "Slavery, in its effects, is like that of a complicated disease," writes Easton, and to illustrate the point he calls attention to "the deformities of the offspring" of slave parents: "contracted and sloped foreheads; prominent eye-balls; projecting under-jaw; certain distended muscles about the mouth, or lower parts of the face; thick lips and flat nose" (85). What we would now view as the racist iconography of the time Easton takes to be the real effect of slavery's profanation as he invites his reader to imagine a slave mother witnessing the contorted visages and wrenched forms of her fellow slaves under the lash and helplessly imprinting this suffering on the features of her unborn child. In express contrast to the reproductive beneficence of nature that had been evoked in the opening paragraphs with a Whitman-like exuberance, slavery poisons and defiles nature in the most intimate way imaginable, "despoiling her works even in her most sacred temples" (89). One could not ask for a more striking – indeed, lurid – rendering of the sheer unnaturalness of servitude.

By the same token, feminizing nature is of a piece with naturalizing equality. This helps account for the presence, once again, of a muted, but unmistakable optimism embedded in the very terms of Easton's critique. Grim as his theory of genetic imprinting may seem, it is premised on the primacy of mind over matter; it is only because the scenes of cruelty and torture all around her enter the black mother's consciousness that these disfigurements get passed on and inscribed, as it were, on the body of the child. In suggesting that slavery corrupts the very process of gestation, Easton is not succumbing to biological determinism but insisting on his claim that slavery indeed functions like a disease, so that once the monstrous cause is removed its baleful effects will likewise disappear. "One thing is certain," Easton confidently observes, "that when nature is robbed, give her a fair chance and she will repair her loss by her own operations" (88). As with Walker and Douglass, slavery is an aberration, the purest negation of nature imaginable. It has nothing to say for itself. However oppressive its "legal codes" may be, "[they] have never as yet been able to crush the aspiring principles of human nature" (103). Indeed, "the real monster slavery cannot long exist" (103) without being propped up and sustained by its auxiliary, "malignant prejudice" (99), which casts a web of illusion and self-serving lies throughout the land.

"Misapprehensions of what truth is have their beginnings and their endings," Douglass writes in "An Antislavery Tocsin," but "properly speaking, there is no such thing as *new* truth; for truth, like God, whose attribute it is, is eternal."[40] Only error has a history, only falsehood a human context. Easton makes a version of the same point when he declares that in trying to explain "intellectual differences" between people "we cannot rationally conceive the cause to originate with God, nor in nature" (68). Persuaded that nature's truth knows nothing of distinction, Easton joins Walker and Douglass in being all the more adamant (not less) in his insistence that "we have no right to go above nor below the sphere which the mind occupies" (68) when it comes to proposing theories of difference, racial or otherwise. As it takes up white justifications for hatred of blacks, the subject of the third chapter, the *Treatise* is accordingly scrupulous in keeping things down to earth. In what one historian rightly calls "the most insightful analysis of prejudice" in the antebellum era,[41] Easton prefaces his exposition by noting that those repulsed by black skin are fixated on an "imaginary cause," color being an entirely accidental property that, abstractly considered, "cannot be an efficient cause of anything" (102). Initially nothing more than an ill-concealed pretext for justifying slavery, prejudice against blackness nevertheless begins to acquire "a kind of omnipresence" and "universality" in "the public sentiment" of the whites, taking root in the "oral instruction from the nurse" and spreading to common sayings uttered by the fireside, anecdotes overheard in the tavern, and placards seen from the bookstore windows. Racism in the white community so permeates everyday life that children who misbehave are told "they will be poor or ignorant as a *nigger*, or that they will be black as a *nigger*, or have no more credit than a *nigger*, that they will have hair, lips, feet, or something of the kind, like a *nigger*." From the crude, often harrowing jeers on the street ("see *nigger's* thick lips – see his flat nose – *nigger* eye shine – that slick looking *nigger* – *nigger*, where you get so much coat – that's a nigger priest" [106; original emphasis]) to the more understated but equally pernicious bigotry that governs the seating arrangements at church, the free states of the North have enforced "[a] kind of education [that is] not only systematized but legalized" (107). Just as one can hardly do justice to both the intensity and comprehensiveness of Easton's outrage, so Easton laments his own inability to do justice to the grinding, soul-destroying effects of what it means to be black in America.

In their edition of his writings, George R. Price and James Brewer Stewart suggest that Easton's bitterness should be viewed in the context of a white backlash against abolitionism that emerged just as the movement was beginning to gather recruits to the cause through the 1830s.[42] Certainly the distance traveled in a mere eight years from Walker's *Appeal* to Easton's text is revealing: gone are the exhortations for African Americans to give the lie to the white colonizationists and prove their capacity for self-reliance and self-improvement; gone as well are any thundering prophecies of black vengeance sweeping the land or calls for slaves to overthrow their masters. One of the earliest black proponents of the so-called damage theory of New World slavery, Easton considers the effects of the peculiar institution an unmitigated disaster, as we've seen. Those held in bondage, with their contracted brows and protruding eyeballs, reflect the pain and pathologies of servitude all too literally. One infers from the *Treatise* that this ghastly mimesis precludes the possibility of slave resistance or the flourishing of a slave culture, neither of which is mentioned by Easton. And yet, as we've also seen, he assumes that the damage done by slavery is not permanent. It is a myth of the whites, Easton explains in the concluding paragraphs of the *Treatise*, to think that slaves require re-education or extensive training to cope with freedom should they be emancipated. What they need is not

de-conditioning but simple, tangible aid, most preferably of an economic
sort. Should the "pestilence" that is slavery and prejudice be one day
eradicated, the healing would commence instantly, registered on the very
countenances of the oppressed: "their narrow foreheads, which have hitherto been contracted for want of mental exercise, would begin to broaden.
Their eye balls, hitherto strained out to prominence by a frenzy excited by
the flourish of the whip, would fall back … indicative of deep penetrating
thought" (120). The socially dead would return to life, permitting nature at
last to finish her work (89).

Nothing better illustrates the logic of indestructible equality than this
combination of extreme environmentalism and its confident overthrow.
The same combination at work in Douglass's epiphany that "what man can
make, he can unmake," which simultaneously acknowledges and defies the
power of circumstance, is registered in Easton's maxim that, just as "mind
acts on matter," so "mind acts on mind" (87). The colonizationist, too,
enlisted his own brand of social constructionism, but in a way that can begin
to suggest that the power of circumstance was indeed all he could see. In his
Appeal, Walker cites Clay's opinion that the condition of the free blacks,
beaten down and blighted by generations of bondage, to say nothing of the
"unconquerable prejudices" of the whites, make "amalgamation" impossible (46), an utterly typical and not especially controversial claim on the face
of it. (It's worth noting that in its earliest stages the American Colonization
Society did count many African Americans among its number, though their
participation dwindled sharply after the first few years.) For colonizationists
such as Clay or Mr. Peyton, the benevolent master of Sarah Hale's novel,
Liberia, who sends his freed slaves to Africa after many failed attempts to
secure a home for them in the states, a coolly rational appraisal of the weight
of custom and lessons of history led irresistibly to one conclusion: the
United States was simply too hostile an environment for African
Americans to establish their independence and self-respect, both individu-
ally and collectively. To be sure, slavery was a sin, and racial animosity its
bitter fruit. But just as the current generation of whites should not bear
responsibility for crimes committed by their ancestors long ago, so they
should not blame the blacks for the degradation plainly caused by an equally
long history of oppression. Thus Hale's Mr. Peyton scoffs at the notion that
the failure of "his people" to thrive in free society has anything to do with
"an inherent defect in the character of the colored race," while her narrator
warns against "blam[ing] these ignorant beings whose mental faculties lie
almost dormant for want of exercise."[43] Unlike Hale's Philadelphia, hotbed
of working-class bigotry, condescending philanthropy, and dissensions

within the black community sown by ostracism, Africa is a place favorable for the cultivation of precisely these faculties. Talk of inborn dreams and natural birthrights was idle. It was all a matter of finding the right sort of environment for a beleaguered people.

Lincoln shocks us, in fact, with his cynical realism when, directly after commenting on the "physical differences" that supposedly separate whites and blacks, he offhandedly adds in his debate with Stephen Douglas that as long as the two races do have to live together, then "there must be the position of the superior and the inferior, and I as much as any man am in favor of having the superior position assigned to the white race."[44] Someone who thinks that social hierarchies are up for grabs in this way – who reasons that if there's got to be a superior it might as well be me – does not need to be instructed that human behavior is convention-bound and therefore subject to contingency. Although snatching a quote out of context is hardly fair to Lincoln, whose views on these matters are far too complex to be summarized here, the contrast to the other writers we've been examining is worth pursuing. If Easton imagines nature promptly restoring the slaves to health once their chains are lifted, so confident is he in "the innate principles of moral, civil and social manhood in the downtrodden colored Americans" (119), the strict environmentalism of the colonizationist could only regard any such return to health as fanciful. Ultimately his respect for the deter-mining power of custom and history pandered to a fatalism about race that was no doubt a large part of the movement's attraction. Allowing for the universal fellowship of human beings only to sever it from any political consequence, the social constructionism of figures like Clay and Lincoln served at best as a counsel of despair and at worst as an exercise in bad faith.

Affirming equality before God while upholding the legitimacy of inequality on earth has a long history. A time-honored device for containing what I earlier described as equality's inherently expansive, exponential logic, it reaches back through the centuries. Yet the slavery crisis brought new pressures to bear on this formula, and in the polemics of Walker, Douglass, and Easton we encounter a methodology that, by summoning nature and Nature's God, blurs together what had been kept apart. Indeed, it was not until the emergence of the so-called "American School" of ethnology, whose popularity gained momentum in the 1850s, that nature became program-matically enlisted in the task of marking fixed, irrevocable distinctions. By affording "objective" evidence for the multiple origins of humankind, nature itself gave the lie to the premise of a common humanity. Abolitionist rhetoric was turned against itself, with appeals to the natural equality of the human family dismissed as nothing more than a piety unable to withstand the scrutiny of science. Douglass's comparison of the anti-slavery movement to "the great forces of the physical world, fire, steam, and lightning [which] have slumbered in the bosom of nature since the world began" would come to seem, to many of his white adversaries, less danger-ous than quaint – the sentimental bluster of a bygone age.[45]

At the same time, what the white ethnologist meant by nature and what the ex-slave meant by nature were of course entirely different – as different as pouring lead shot into a skull to measure for intelligence and escaping from bondage to realize "the inborn dream of my human nature."[46] Douglass's dream was not addressed by "science," much less confuted. Rather, it was made the victim of a kind of semantic hijacking, with nature now purged of its ties to Christian Republicanism and converted to dead matter. Southern "aristocrats," of all people, seemed to be the only other party dismayed by this turn of events. The ethnologist's talk of skulls, bloodlines, and separate species was not only impious but counterproduc-tive. A culture of inequality, they had been saying for some time, was desirable for its own sake; there was no need to renounce either Christianity or Republicanism in defending bondage. The abolitionist charge that inequality was unnatural, incoherent, and unsustainable – above all that inequality could not speak for itself – could and should be met on its own terms.

CHAPTER TWO

Inequality in theory

A BENEVOLENT DESPOTISM

It may seem strange to say that inequality could not be theorized at a time when there was no lack of Southern ideologues attempting to do just that. The figure most often mentioned in this connection is George Fitzhugh, whose *Cannibals All!* (1857) is dedicated to the proposition that "domestic slavery is, in the general, a natural and necessary institution."[1] Sounding the usual themes of Tory conservatism, his book invokes Aristotle to confute Locke (CA, 71), bows before the Great Chain of Being (CA, 68), jeers at newfangled notions of human equality (CA, 87), and denounces the triumph of laissez-faire. In doing battle with this last enemy, the chief concern of the book, Fitzhugh draws freely on the discourse of socialism in pitting the "moral cannibalism" (CA, 16) of the Northern capitalist against the benign paternalism of the Southern slaveholder. On his account, the difference between those who are free and those who are enslaved comes down to a difference between two kinds of laborers – the workers of the North "who labor under all the disadvantages of slavery, and have none of the rights of slaves" (CA, 12) and the workers of the South who likewise labor under slavery but nevertheless do enjoy those rights. Sheltered from "the false, antagonistic, and competitive relations in which so-called liberty and equality place man" (CA, 36), the "negro slaves of the South are the happiest, and, in some sense, freest people in the world" (CA, 18). In its unchecked exploitation of the worker, "capital is a cruel master" (CA, 20), whereas slavery, in setting limits to this kind of exploitation, must be esteemed as "more benevolent, equitable, and natural than [any system] of the North" (CA, 260).

And yet, as this last phrase already begins to suggest, it would be a mistake to assume that Fitzhugh's defense of slavery is driven by an enthusiasm for inequality. On the contrary, the central point of his polemic is to argue that slavery is superior to capitalism because slavery does a better job of protecting the worker from exploitation, which is simply to say that it does a better job of honoring the demands of distributive justice by giving the slave a fairer return on his labor than the operative. Inequality will always be with us – "the doctrine of Human Equality," we are told from the outset, "is practically impossible, and conflicts with all ... social existence" (CA, 8) – but that doesn't mean we should allow it free rein. That's why it's better to live under the mitigated inequality of the South than the radical inequality of the North. Persuaded by the classic socialist thesis that under capitalism "democracy and liberty [i.e., laissez-faire] are antagonistic," Fitzhugh upholds the peculiar institution because it serves "to equalize advantages, by fairly dividing the burdens of life and rigidly enforcing the performance of every social duty by every member of society, according to his capacity and ability" (CA, 82) to an extent that the North can never hope to achieve. What, after all, would "a poor family of [Northern] laborers" lose by moving South and becoming slaves with masters, as opposed to slaves without masters? The answer is clear: "just nothing." In fact, by becoming slaves "they would have more liberty than now and approach nearer to equality" (CA, 223). Fancying himself a "Brother Socialist" (CA, 260) who actually lives in the communist utopia his Northern counterparts can only dream of, the "ultra-slavery man" steps forward to save freedom and equality from the clutches of capitalism's "abnormal and anomalous" hegemony.

Fitzhugh is most often remembered today as one of the South's more forceful advocates of paternalism, the view that African Americans, being incapable of caring for themselves, must be taken care of by others. And it is certainly true that a number of passages in both *Cannibals All!* and its predecessor, *Sociology for the South: Or The Failure of Free Society* (1854), leave no doubt that Fitzhugh believed that blacks were made for servitude. At the same time, Fitzhugh goes to great lengths to insist that such considerations stand to the side in his attempt to justify slavery. For that justification must be taken to a higher ground: "domestic slavery must be vindicated in the abstract, and in the general, as a normal, natural, and, *in general* necessitous element of civilized society, without regard to race or color."[2] Against abolitionists who routinely portrayed the peculiar institution as a relic of the feudal past – recall Douglass's comparison of the Lloyd estate to the "baronial domains" of medieval Europe – Fitzhugh insists that "as modern civilization advances, slavery becomes daily more necessary" (CA, 30). The only viable antidote to laissez-faire, slavery is needed by all races, not just one. This is why Fitzhugh declares that "he who justifies mere Negro slavery, and condemns other forms of slavery, does not think at all" (Faust, 277). This is why, too, it is necessary to repudiate the newly emergent racist theories of ethnologists like Nott and Gliddon, whose attempt to base a defense of slavery on the biological inferiority of the African is not only impious but tantamount "to giv[ing] up expressly the whole cause of the South" (Faust, 285). It is not enough, then, to view the "Negro slaves" of the South as "the happiest" workers in the world – they must also be deemed "the freest."

Although there is no denying that paternalism as it is commonly under-stood plays a central role in Fitzhugh's polemic, we should not fail to note that in an important sense it also poses something of an *embarrassment* to works like *Cannibals All!* Because vindicating slavery in the abstract means vindicating it for all, the question of engaging the particular needs of a particular race must be bracketed as tangential to the conversation. If the white workers of the North needed significantly less assistance, care or protection than the black workers of the South – if they were, regardless of circumstance, more independent and self-reliant by some significant margin – then Fitzhugh's thesis would fall apart. Slavery would not be superior to capitalism because the cases of the two workers would not be commensurable. It is only because these two types of workers may be treated as equals that the defense of inequality can go forward. And it is above all *types* that arguments such as Fitzhugh's require. What matters about the Northern family of so-called free laborers who travel South to find freedom in slavery or the fugitive slave who goes North to find poverty and oppression in freedom is that these be considered interchangeable cases, not distinct situations separated by race or region. (By extension, it is this same logic of interchangeable identities that suddenly makes "the Negro" a veritable citizen of the world in pro-slavery discourse, the representative whose lot is incessantly compared and contrasted to his counterparts around the globe, from the Russian serf and Chinese peasant to the Irish servant and British factory operative.)

Thus, while it is common to number Fitzhugh among those Southerners notable for "their increasing rejection of egalitarian doctrine,"[3] there is a sense in which this view, while not exactly wrong, is not exactly right either. "There certainly is in the human heart, under all circumstances," writes Fitzhugh, "a love for mankind and a yearning desire to equalize human conditions" (Faust, 293). As we have seen, this is, according to Fitzhugh, a desire best realized by slavery, for "what equality of conditions can there be in free society" (Faust, 295)? It's the market-ridden North, not the Old South, which has forsaken democratic ideals. "Free society" is worse than a contradiction in terms, since a world where all are slaves to Capital cannot be called free any more than a world where all compete against each other can be called a society. And because a regulated liberty is better than no liberty at all, a respect for hierarchy and subordination must be maintained. It seems symptomatic that for Fitzhugh this imperative is best satisfied through an idyllic communalism and not a dynastic model of inherited authority. As this proud scion of a long line of plantation owners writes in *Sociology for the South*, freely availing himself of the jargon of the utopian socialists of his day, "a southern farm is a sort of joint stock concern or social phalanstery" best suited to foster an ideal "association of labor." Domestic slavery, in fact, is "a beautiful example of communism, where each one receives not according to his labor, but according to his wants."[4]

To be sure, scoffing at "the well-sounding, but unmeaning verbiage of natural equality and inalienable rights" (Faust, 87) was a favorite pastime for Southern intellectuals like Fitzhugh. Plantation owner and leading politician James Henry Hammond of South Carolina makes short work of "the ridiculously absurd ... dogma of Mr. Jefferson" by trumping the Virginian's self-evident truth with a supposedly more powerful one of his own: "no society has ever yet existed ... without a natural variety of classes," which is to say "the rich and the poor, the educated and the ignorant" (Faust, 176). True to a conservative tradition that counsels respect for "adventitious circumstances and relations" over "the mere enunciation of abstract truths," Thomas Roderick Dew finds "maxims that 'all men are created equal'" to be "inapplicable and mischievous" when confronted by the hard realities of society (Faust, 28). Throwing up his hands in exasperation, William Harper likewise reports that he, for one, can "attach no definite idea" (Faust, 83) to the meaning of equality, an inherently airy, ahistorical concept – nothing more than "the passion of the day" (Faust, 101). The sad truth, according to Harper, is that "man was born to subjection," or at least most of them anyway: "it is in the order of nature and of God, that the being of superior faculties and knowledge, and therefore of superior power, should control and dispose of those who are inferior" (Faust, 85, 89).

It doesn't require much reflection, though, to see that universalizing slavery only succeeds in exchanging one set of empty abstractions for another. Designations like "rich and poor, educated and ignorant" are, after all, little more than blank slots that may in theory be shuffled around and occupied by anyone. Who indeed are those superior beings and what makes them different from "those who are inferior"? Because the peculiar brand of inegalitarianism favored by this school of thought forbids it from leaning on innate differences in order to justify servitude, its treatment of the roles of master and slave are inevitably vague and formalistic. Sometimes it all seems a simple matter of arithmetic. If, according to Fitzhugh, "nineteen out of twenty individuals have 'a natural and inalienable right' to be taken care of and protected," then it must be the case that "the one in twenty are as clearly born or educated or in some way fitted for command" (CA, 69). Of course, "clearly born or educated or in some way fitted" is not very clear; it appears to leave a lot of latitude. Can anyone be master? In *Cannibals All!* Fitzhugh tries to narrow the field by reasoning that since "family association" is the template for society then fathers must rule society (CA, 72). And yet the sort of father he has in mind is much more a benevolent caretaker than stern despot, a loving guardian of the weak and oppressed cut out of the same cloth as one of Stowe's matriarchs. For example, even if it is true that the "patriarchal government" of "a Cromwell or a Joe Smith" "works well, because it works naturally," it must also be acknowledged that "this success can only be temporary" since it benefits only "a society ... that wants the elements of cohesion in the natural ties that bind man to man" (CA, 72). The beauty of slavery is that, by protecting and honoring those "natural ties," it actually *restrains* patriarchal authority by embedding it within a network of mutual obligations, whereas the cruelty of capitalism is that, by renouncing any sense of civic obligation, it allows that same authority to run amok, with the capitalist exploiting not just the worker but, more particularly and more shamelessly, the female worker who "is reduced to the necessity of getting less than half price for her work" (SFS, 56). Stowe's vision of a maternal influence correcting the moral stupidity and mindless aggression of the male is replaced in this case by a paternal influence that performs very much the same function.

In the course of expounding Locke's political philosophy, Jeremy Waldron introduces a makeshift but handy distinction between two kinds of inegalitarianism, the particular and the general.[5] A theory of the divine right of kings is an example of *particular* inegalitarianism in that it singles out a specific individual as superior to other individuals. So according to this theory, it is only because Elizabeth and Elizabeth alone is directly descended from Adam that she is entitled to claim the role of Queen Elizabeth in Renaissance England. A *general* inegalitarianism, by contrast, concerns a certain type or class of individuals who are deemed to be superior to another type or class. Racism and sexism are obvious examples of general inegalitarianism: for instance, it is precisely because Elizabeth is a woman that she cannot vote or run for political office in nineteenth-century America. One of the many peculiarities of pro-slavery discourse is that it doesn't see itself following either model. That a white propertied elite should govern society seemed self-evident to most of its adherents, but slogans like Fitzhugh's "Liberty for the few and ... slavery for the masses!" (CA, 63) hardly tie privilege to specific individuals within that elite. And while no one can doubt the massive importance of racism and patriarchal authority to the Old South (or for that matter to other regions in the United States), leading proponents of slavery such as Hinton Helper, Thomas Roderick Dew, J. H. Hammond, Henry Hughes, and William Harper joined Fitzhugh in explicitly refusing to make the racism they freely acknowledged a pivotal part of their defense of bondage.[6] Preferring to make their case by emphasizing its ubiquity and inherent goodness, these writers tended to conceive of slavery in utterly abstract terms – a "timeless essence," as John Grammer says of Fitzhugh's view, disentangled from the "local particularities of nationality, region, and race."[7] Because it was viewed as a universal condition, servitude could not be upheld on account of the divisions it created, whether between individuals or between groups.

Another way of putting this is to say that once it is thought that there is nothing especially peculiar about the peculiar institution, then the identity of the master, like that of the slave, becomes, in principle, a secondary concern. This is why a text like *Cannibals All!* is reduced to bland formulations like "some are formed for higher, others for lower stations" (CA, 69). Who rules and who is ruled is at best a matter of historical circumstance. Consequently, when Fitzhugh remarks that "negro slavery has no other claims over other forms of slavery, except that from inferiority, or rather peculiarity, of race," he wants it understood that this is "a subject of temporary, but worldwide importance" (CA, 201); in the same way, when he takes note of "the general truth that master and slave should be of different national descent" (CA, 200), he means for us to see that he is doing nothing more than passing on a useful piece of advice about some tried and true methods from the past. The striking development here is not that we glimpse the specter of racism rising to the surface but that the racist needs to work so hard to fit it into his defense of slavery, so powerful is the logic that says that what is good for the one must be good for the many. Thus the hedging over "inferiority, or rather peculiarity of race" has nothing to do with guilt but emerges as a necessary concession to the requirements of a color-blind defense of slavery. In a maneuver used by some of his fellow apologists, Fitzhugh elsewhere says that Southerners should consider themselves lucky to have in their midst a people whom God and Nature so obviously intended for bondage, the implication being that the innate inferiority of the Negro, while it never can be doubted, can never be allowed to play a meaningful role in the discussion and so must be viewed as a happy accident of fate (Faust, 276).[8] Such are the contortions the Southern gentleman must endure in order to profess inequality in egalitarian times. The goodness of slavery is a goodness available to all: "How can we contend that white slavery is wrong, whilst all the great body of free laborers are starving; and slaves, white or black, throughout the world, are enjoying comfort?" (CA, 201).

By his own admission, not all of Fitzhugh's opinions found ready acceptance among his contemporaries, and Drew Gilpin Faust and others have rightly warned against overrating his representativeness.[9] And yet the project of defending inequality in the name of equality is by no means peculiar to Fitzhugh. No doubt the most egregious instance of such a project may be found in the emergence of what George Fredrickson, borrowing a phrase from Pierre van den Berghe, has called "herrenvolk" ideology, which exploits a virulent racism against blacks in order to secure a radical egalitarianism among whites. Thus for Josiah Nott, co-author of *Types of Mankind* (1854), the Enlightenment notion that differences between races could be explained in terms of acquired characteristics caused by environmental factors alone is unacceptable, both because it denies the scientific "fact" of the biological inferiority of blacks *and* because it encourages the anti-democratic assumption that the lowly white was doomed to be less capable and less gifted than the high-born white.[10] With another turn of the screw, John Van Evrie, during the 1850s and 1860s, insisted that the better whites understood the absolute racial divide that separated them from blacks, the better whites would learn to see the differences among themselves as wholly artificial, nothing more than the vestige of an aristocratic past.[11] Though the turn to an aggressive, biological racism immediately prior to the Civil War is taken to mark a new direction in racist "thought," the special appeal of counter-identification had been discovered well before Nott and Van Evrie. In a shortened version of his *Review of the Debate in the Virginia Legislatures of 1831 and 1832*, identified by Faust and other authorities in the field as setting the tone for much of the pro-slavery discourse to follow, Thomas R. Dew attempts to bolster his case against both colonization and emancipation by marveling at "the perfect spirit of equality so prevalent among the whites of all the slaveholding states." With disarming candor, Dew affirms that "no white man feels such inferiority of rank as to be unworthy of association with those around him" for the simple reason that "the menial and low offices [are] all performed by blacks" (Faust, 66), the true levers of democracy. The argument is amazing not because it was advanced but because it was so noisily proclaimed. If A and B consider themselves equal so long as they consider C inferior, then you'd think that it would be unseemly for A and B to keep pointing this out to each other. But where equality is the great desideratum, any amount of absurdity, it appears, may be indulged. Fredrickson quotes Henry Wise's infamous declaration "break down slavery and you would with the same blow break down the great democratic principle of equality," but neglects to mention that he said this on the floor of the House of Representatives, where, according to the *Congressional Globe*, it was greeted by laughter.[12]

Interpreting these invocations of freedom and equality as signs of guilt or ambivalence does not seem very plausible as a general claim. By and large, the strangeness of pro-slavery discourse has little to do with misgivings over the essential rightness of the institution. As Faust in *The Ideology of Slavery* observes, "slaveholders were less troubled about *whether* slavery was right than precisely *why* it was right and how its justice could best be demonstrated" (7–8). That the reasons for believing in slavery should lag behind a belief in slavery suggests the quandary of a discourse that, wishing to defend the cause, is compelled to draw upon a vocabulary that makes it look willfully perverse, even silly. Douglass and other abolitionists insisted, as we saw earlier, that their dispute with the slavocracy was not reducible to a matter of principle: Congressman Wise, after all, wants to protect "the great democratic principle of equality" too. It is instead the mismatch between substance and rhetoric that produces an Orwellian world where freedom has become slavery and slavery safeguards freedom. With a similar flair for the absurd, novelist Caroline Lee Hentz informs her readers, in *The Planter's Northern Bride*, that for a white person to treat a black person as his equal is to commit the double error of degrading the black and exalting the white. "I claim him as my brother," the Southern planter Moreland says, describing his relation to any one of his many bondsmen, "but he is not my equal physically or mentally, and I do not degrade him or exalt myself by this admission."[13] Somehow the standard argument *against* racism has got twisted into an argument *for* racism, so that the objection to treating the African American as an equal is that it degrades him. And in fact Eulalia, daughter of a die-hard abolitionist who has been trained by her father to regard black and white as "having only the accidental difference of colour to mark them" (192) and who is to marry Moreland, develops such a bad case of Negrophobia that she fears slave insurrections by day (191) and has nightmares of black rapists by night (108). It is left to her husband, the slaveholder, to reassure her that once she gets free of her misguided notions about racial equality "her repugnance to the African race ... born of prejudice and circumstance" (116) will be overcome. Evidently, the advantage of accepting the truth of white superiority is that it replaces the "hideous image" (108) of the Negro as a beast with the image of the Negro as "my brother," the object of "the sincerest attachment and the deepest interest"

(206). By learning to accept your racism for what it is, you will learn to see your inferior as something more than your inferior.

Obviously not all pro-slavery discourse was an exercise in sophistry. If one serious claim did dominate the genre, it was that some form of personal servitude was necessary for societies to exist and prosper.[14] This is what Hentz has in mind, for example, when proclaiming "the great commanding truth that wherever civilized man exists, there is the dividing line of the high and the low, the rich and the poor" (17). A growing refrain in the literature from the 1820s to the Civil War, the insistence that "progress, civilization, and refinement" are impossible without "the very mud-sill of society,"[15] as Senator James Henry Hammond put it in a famous speech of 1858, was arguably the cornerstone of Southern conservatism and what most justified its pretensions to considering itself to be an "aristocracy." This same identification of inequality with social necessity also underwrites Southern complaints against Northern institutions, for the objection to the radical egalitarianism of democracy was not, in the end, that this was a different way of organizing society – a rival model – but rather that such egalitarianism was the negation of the social itself. Pro-slavery theorists believed that "Human Equality … directly conflicts … with all social existence" (CA, 8) because they thought that the very possibility of "social existence" was predicated on inequality. "We deny there is a society in free countries," Fitzhugh declaims in *Sociology for the South*, "[t]hey who act each for himself, who are hostile, antagonistic, and competitive, are not social and do not constitute a society" (SFS, 62). Where everybody's on the same level, nobody's in charge, and where nobody's in charge everybody is at each other's throat. For a genuine society to get off the ground, there need to be superiors and inferiors, the latter serving as the necessary "mud-sill" upon which the edifice of society is erected.

But however opposed the aristocrat and democrat appear to be on this question, the logic they draw upon is basically the same. Saying that inequality is the price we pay for society is simply the negative version of the more positive claim that equality is a supremely natural value that transcends social definition. William Lloyd Garrison or Lydia Maria Child would no more object to the premise that social institutions are, regrettably but inevitably, dependent to some degree upon inequality than they would question the distinction drawn by one pro-slavery advocate that "the law of justice is a written rule of life" shaped in accordance with "the laws of society," while "the law of equity dwells in the heart."[16] To be sure, these same pro-slavery advocates also invoked divine or natural necessity to justify hierarchy and subordination in making their case, as the frequent appearance of tropes like the Great Chain of Being or the body politic attests. But once the concept of *social* necessity is added to the discussion the very idea of necessity is bound to appear somehow more negotiable and less binding. Thus in Hammond's "mud-sill" speech, slavery is a blessing for Africans because (a) God designed them to be "an inferior race" suited for bondage and (b) "the *status* in which we have placed them is an elevation. They are elevated from the condition in which God first created them, by being made our slaves."[17] To improve upon what God created is already to begin to suggest that God's creation is not necessarily fixed. Once it is thought that servitude is not just a matter of divine mandate but is also a product of social arrangements, what had been regarded as foreordained and immutable can start to look as though it may be alterable. Hammond of course wants it both ways: his point in underscoring "status" is to suggest that the Negro's inferiority is indeed unalterable but that there are presumably grades of inferiority such that his outward circumstances may be improved. This is on a par with the recommendation made by Hentz's slaveholder – by treating your inferior as your inferior you will make him into your brother. Every society may require its "mud-sill" but that doesn't mean that the unfortunates who compose this class are not "elevated" by the experience.

   This double gesture of upholding while seeking to rehabilitate servitude is of course what paternalist ideology is all about. Sentimentalizing unequal relations, it casts the master in the role of a humanitarian who intervenes on behalf of the weak and the helpless to improve their lot. And just as the members of the "mud-sill" are elevated by this attention, so the master himself experiences a transformation for the better. The paternalist line of defense requires the antebellum South to undergo the same development that was so often being described as occurring elsewhere in the modern world – the depatriarchalizing of family authority.[18] For all his bluster about Aristotle and the Old Testament, Fitzhugh illustrates this point perfectly. As we have seen, one of the merits he attributes to the peculiar institution is that it converts the patriarchal despot into a loving father. Writing in *De Bow's Review*, he explains that the mere presence of "smaller and weaker bodies" arouses "compassion and pity," which serves "not only to neutralize the despotism of the larger [bodies] but *to control and rule them*" (Faust, 294; my emphasis). Fatherly authority is based on a reciprocal yielding: the very submissiveness of the child, wife, and Negro before the white master compels him to submit to the responsibilities he owes to them. In effect, the lessons of New Testament morality are best exemplified on the plantation, where the very powerlessness of the weak and the helpless constitutes their power. Contriving "laws and penalties" to protect them is therefore pointless, for to say " 'I am thy slave, deprives me of the power of a master!' " Any "interpositions" that society may construct, Fitzhugh notes, are vain when compared to the "checks to power" that operate of their own accord "within the family circle," which is established "naturally [by] a tie of affection" (Faust, 295). To understand all this is, finally, to see that the common tendency to assume that the distinction between master and slave is equivalent to the distinction between superior and inferior is at bottom a misconception. Given the "tie of affection" that lays them under a "mutual obligation," both parties are "each in a broad sense equally slaves, for the superior is as much bound by law, natural feeling, self-interest, and custom, to take care of, govern, and provide for inferiors or dependents, as they to labor for him. Which is the happier condition, in general, none can determine" (Faust, 295).

Inequality may be grounded in social necessity, but equality takes its sanction from nature. A sworn believer in the first half of this proposition, Fitzhugh can't help but follow the second. Making his case for slavery on the basis of the "domestic and family affection" (Faust, 294) it nurtures and protects, he takes the further step of associating this "natural feeling" with the leveling of distinctions. An issue that should have no business entering the discussion somehow obtrudes itself: "How does slavery equalize human conditions?" (Faust, 294), Fitzhugh asks the readers of *De Bow's Review* in perfect seriousness. Were the mud-sill of society to remain nothing more than the mud-sill of society, then asking that sort of question would be worse than pointless. But once the justification for slavery proceeds from the heart and is legitimated "within the family circle," the site of unforced affection, then the issue of equality must somehow be accommodated. "[L]aw … self-interest and custom" may also regulate the master's dealings with the slave but then, as Fitzhugh has already made clear, without "natural feeling" these are mere social contrivances or "interpositions." In an important chapter from *Cannibals All!* entitled "The Strength of Weakness," he expands on this point, observing that "human law cannot beget benevolence, affection, maternal and paternal love; nor can it supply its places" (CA, 205). Instead, it is ultimately "their common humanity" and the mutual perception of "abject weakness" that binds master and slave and that accordingly renders their share of power, as Fitzhugh would have it, more or less equivalent: "the dependent exercise, because of their dependence, as much control over their superiors, in most things, as those superiors exercise over them. Thus, and thus only, can conditions be equalized. This constitutes the practical equality of rights, enforced not by human, but by divine law" (CA, 204–05).

In *Masters and Statesmen*, Kenneth S. Greenberg argues convincingly that the foremost concern among proponents of the so-called "positive good"

school of pro-slavery thought centered upon worries over the corrupting
influence of unrestrained power. Even more than the specter of black upris-
ing, the Southern intelligentsia feared, Greenberg suggests, the specter of
Simon Legree – the specter, that is to say, of the white slaveholder dehuman-
ized by the "boisterous passions" and "odious peculiarities" that absolute
power fosters.[19] The appeal of paternalism is of course that it turns this danger
on its head by insisting that the very defenselessness of the weak constitutes
their strength, thereby transforming irresponsible power into responsible
stewardship. The logic is counterintuitive to say the least, and of course in
the case of Legree himself it backfires inasmuch as Tom's passivity only serves
to fuel the master's rage. To bolster their case and show that "slavery is *not
barbarism* – is *not* despotic power – is *not* lawless might," as Louisa McCord
so emphatically puts it,[20] Southerners needed to go beyond economic self-
interest and goodwill and appeal to what amounted to their own version of a
Higher Law. Thus for Fitzhugh the chastening of patriarchal aggression
brought about by the dependence of the dependent is recognized as "a law
of nature," a reflex of compassion that is both involuntary and inscrutable.
Because "inferior and superior act and re-act on each other through agencies
and media too delicate and subtle for human apprehension," he maintains
that "man should be willing to leave to God what God only can regulate"
(CA, 205). Built into the paternalist script is the expectation that extremes
meet and touch; the superior is brought low while the inferior is lifted up. A
worrisome imbalance in power is in this way rectified. Fitzhugh's God does
not exactly preside over the erasure of all distinctions, but then He does not
exactly uphold them either. The terms of superior and inferior are retained,
but with the suggestion that these are labels of social convenience that do not
altogether reveal the true character of a relationship sanctioned by natural law
and regulated by divine supervision.

What we are left with, then, is a fundamental dualism. On the one hand,
we encounter an anti-utopian strain in Fitzhugh's thinking that tells us that
rank and privilege are sure to prevail whenever human beings gather to form
a community – that in fact the individual has no rights bequeathed to him
or her by some mythical state of nature but is from the outset "subordinate
to the good of the [social] whole" and is therefore "born its slave" (SFS, 59).
It is mostly because of such views that Fitzhugh is remembered today as the
laureate of Southern conservatism. But inasmuch as the correlation between
society and inequality only works to reinforce the correlation between
nature and equality, a utopian strain is equally pronounced (though less
noted) and is nowhere more evident than on the plantation, that commune
or "joint-stock society" where "family affection" is so profound as to make

talk about rank and privilege appear unacceptably cold and superficial. The peculiarity of Fitzhugh's writings is that this split happens to be especially glaring; what may be praised in one moment as a "police system" (CA, 29), notable for its efficiency in controlling the labor force, may in the next be celebrated as a welfare state, notable for its success as a "beautiful example" of utopian socialism and of its gospel of "passional attraction" (CA, 101).

In theory, the family is assigned the task of mediating these extremes. Both social institution and site of intimacy, it harmonizes hierarchy and compassion. In doing so it becomes hard to say where the family ends and slavery begins. The abolitionists' refrain that slavery breaks up the family was, to the Southern paternalist, worse than wrongheaded. It perversely failed to see that slavery was the family's last, best hope on earth, not its enemy. For paternalist ideology conceived Southern society at large on the model of a network of localized families, a model that was unimaginable in the North. Stowe's sanctification of the home as a retreat from the loveless impersonality of public life demonstrated as much; there was no need for any such retreat in the South, at least not in theory, since by caring for the weak and helpless the peculiar institution made the division between domestic and public space much harder to see. Fitzhugh's enthusiasm for the commune, the association, or the phalanstery, often seen as an eccentricity, merely reflected a longstanding view that plantation society was ideally situated between the twin extremes of massive urban centers, with their pauperism and crime, and the confines of the bourgeois home and its tightly bound nuclear family so lovingly evoked by Stowe. The plantation and its "people," each with his or her appointed role, achieved an ideal balance between power and sociality, interest and affection. The police state and the welfare state would be merged and reconciled within the holy circle of the family. And at the center of it all would be the patriarch exercising his "despotic discretion" (CA, 248).

The self-serving character of this fantasy is no doubt obvious enough, perhaps even more so than the strange idea that the chattel slavery of the South somehow offered an alternative to capitalist practices, as opposed to being in fact utterly dependent upon them. No small part of paternalism's appeal would have been the implication that hierarchy, once cast in terms of familial roles and obligations, was reversible – that if pressed far enough it would mutate into a sort of subliminal equality. Political economy may have required distinguishing between superior and inferior, but the psychic economy of the family took such distinctions to be merely the outward sign of a social role, beneath which subsisted a web of interlocking interests and affective ties. Only the mean-spirited Yankee or the vulgar ethnologist could think the Negro sub-human; the slaveholder recognized him as a family member in need and not a beast to be despised. The father's relation to his children, both black and white, was unequal by definition, but this was an inequality of a uniquely furtive, even self-cancelling kind. According to Louisa McCord, in a metaphor that simultaneously alludes to and yet deflects the realities of bondage, "such human links as exist between the races under this system are, necessarily, all of a softening character." Groping for a terminology that might walk the line between affirming too much distance between master and slave and too little, McCord goes on to assert that "the natural antipathies of race are checked, and almost obliterated, by the peculiar relation which, at once, unites and separates the races, acting in social life like the disjunctive conjunction in grammar, linking, yet severing so distinctly, that there is no possibility of confusion among the objects thus connected."[21] "Peculiar relation" marks the place where social necessity and loving bonds commingle, producing a baffling but somehow beautiful harmony of conjunctions nestled within disjunctions, of intimacies within hierarchies.

Needless to say, the mere fact that a condition of mutual dependence subsists between two or more human beings does not, in itself, mean that all hierarchies between them have been removed. Interdependence and equality are not the same thing. But as I've been emphasizing, this is a distinction that the Southern apologist has trouble holding onto. And this is no less true when that same apologist turns away from the family and pursues other lines of defense. Consider, for example, the question of consent, another subject that one would think has no business entering a discourse devoted to the proposition that all are created unequal. Curiously, Fitzhugh's talk of the master ruling the servant and the servant ruling the master often comes close to sounding like a bargain is being struck; the two parties come together and reach an agreement. Just as the master's compassion serves to raise the "status" of the slave, so the slave's submission will soften and humanize the master's authority. Each needs the other to avoid enslavement of a truly degrading kind, one to ignorance and the other to passion. "Let it be regarded," James Henry Hammond similarly writes of Southern bondage, "as a compact between the master and the slave, and I assert that no saner or more just agreement was ever made working to the mutual benefit of both."[22] Expanding upon the widespread perception that blacks, too, possess immortal souls and are therefore moral beings, this conception of slavery as the outcome of a contractual agreement insinuates the further assumption that blacks are rational agents capable of independent thought – assumptions loudly derided elsewhere by Southern conservatives, who also derided, for that matter, social contract theory. In the case of the *Treatise on Sociology*, another key document of pro-slavery paternalism, Henry Hughes goes so far as to replace the terms master and slave with "warrantors" and "warrantees," a flourish of legal jargon typical of a work that, in exhaustively codifying the roles and responsibilities of both parties, reads more like an extended description of a contract than an effort to defend the practice of one human being enslaving another. In effect, with its overriding message that under slavery "reciprocity is absolute" (Faust, 239), the definition of slavery as a perfectly sensible accord between freely contracting parties, though it draws upon an entirely different vocabulary from the sentimental rhetoric of the family, nevertheless ends up affirming the same message.

Still, it might be objected that these and other instances of a creeping egalitarianism in pro-slavery thought signify little more than a mere excrescence – the unpurged residue of an unwelcome ideology. Should we regard the specter of equality in these writings as more rhetorical than real? That would be a mistake. For in the end the dispute between the friends and foes of slavery comes down to a question of which side could best honor the tenets of basic human equality. (Certainly, the question of honoring political or social equality never emerged as a serious matter of contention, for neither side was prepared to concede *that*.) To the charge that slavery was responsible for turning a person into a thing, the pro-slavery propagandist retorted that it was in fact the abolitionist who de-personalized the Aunts, Uncles, and Daddies of the plantation, that it was the hypocritical reformer who could not get past the superficial title of slave and see, as Hentz puts it, "the loving heart through the black and sooty skin" (293). In the same way, when Henry Hughes affirms that slavery, in "its essentials," is "necessary," he is careful to stipulate that "this necessity is not political and economic only: it is a moral necessity" (Faust, 241). A society that cannot care for its own violates the "existence-rights" of its members, for "existence is the right of all" (Faust, 253). Under capitalism, the "economic system" is constantly at war with the "political system," whereas under personal servitude this antagonism disappears, allowing "the fundamental duty of [slaveholders to tend to] the subsistence of all" (Faust, 251). Like other proponents of the "positive good" school of thought, Hughes abhors amalgamation but treats race as an "accidental" consideration in the sense that, as regards "the sovereignty of one race and the sub-sovereignty of the other," the "restriction of this power is accidental" (Faust, 262). As in Fitzhugh, the social roles of superior and inferior are considered circumstantial, a matter of historical contingency, while slavery is championed for its success in answering the demands of a common humanity. As in Fitzhugh, too, telling the master apart from the slave is ultimately a vain exercise since "the warrantor [master] is the political servant of the warrantee [slave]" no less than the other way around. The final upshot of Hughes's text is familiar enough: capitalism chases the mirage of political and social equality while neglecting justice and equity; slavery repudiates the mirage while assuring justice and equity for all. But of course in retailing this line Hughes and his associates also project a mirage of their own with the suggestion that subordination and interdependency beget a fellowship so profound as to make political and social equality look like a thin and substanceless imitation of the real thing.

Polemicists such as Fitzhugh, Hughes, and others did not need to confront the possible complications in this message, much less its frequent departures from reality. Such, after all, are the advantages of being a polemicist. Others who took up the cause did not always enjoy the same exemption, especially those who, in the aftermath of the publication of *Uncle Tom's Cabin*, turned to fiction to issue their own defense of the peculiar institution. Goaded especially by Stowe's portrayal of slavery's destructive effects on the family, Southern novelists, many of them women, relied heavily on paternalist themes in foregrounding the domestic virtues of the peculiar institution. In the course of doing so they did not succeed in confuting Stowe so much as the doctrines they thought they were defending. In particular, the extreme idealization of the family as the site where hierarchy and compassion are reconciled, to say nothing of the sadomasochistic subtext that sees feminine helplessness disarming masculine aggression, constitute the volatile raw materials of paternalist ideology that, once dramatized in the narratives of writers such as Caroline Lee Hentz, Maria McIntosh and others, assume an increasingly unmanageable shape that can often make upholding the peculiar institution indistinguishable from condemning it. Precisely because these narratives adhere so faithfully to the principles of Southern conservatism, they provide a fitting sequel to the writers we've been examining. The outward features of Fitzhugh's prose style – its flamboyant paradoxes, lurid sentimentality, and preening erudition – already suggest the incipient absurdity of a position that Fitzhugh himself would recant with the onset of the Civil War. Just how absurd this attempt at upholding inequality was, can only be truly appreciated, however, once we turn to the fiction that it inspired.

THE FICTION OF SOUTHERN PATERNALISM

Although George Eliot famously credited Stowe with the invention of the "Negro novel," one might with equal justice note that Stowe's influence was also instrumental in the emergence of another, albeit much more short-lived, tradition in American letters. The roughly three dozen novels composed between the publication of *Uncle Tom's Cabin* and the firing on Fort Sumter and framed, with varying degrees of explicitness, as fictional replies to Stowe's bestseller constitute something of a sub-genre, incorporating elements of the plantation novel but also moving in directions that a prior generation of Southern novelists would have found extreme and perhaps even distasteful.[23] Pastoral excursions like *The Valley of the Shenandoah* (1824) and *Swallow Barn* (1832), really more a string of sketches than fully developed narratives, celebrate the charms of the Old South in a self-consciously whimsical, nostalgic fashion; in recounting the picaresque misadventures of youth along with the foibles of old age, these early examples of the plantation novel pointedly shy away from controversy, relegating slavery to the scenic background. In launching their counterattacks, producers of anti-*Tom* fare required more potent ammunition – something more timely, more state of the art, as it were. The prominence of paternalist thinking in this fiction must be considered inevitable if for no other reason than it so perfectly honors the methods of sentimental reformism while reversing its conclusions. Finding compassion in what Stowe took to be cruelty and cruelty in what she considered compassion, slaveholding paternalism could not only answer Stowe but beat her at her own game.

Indeed, pursuing this last point, we might begin by noting that there is an important sense in which the very term pro-slavery fiction can be more than a little misleading. For in order to be in favor of something, one must, at a minimum, be prepared to acknowledge that it exists, a requirement that is not always met in these texts. For example, in the opening pages of Martha Haines Butt's *Antifanaticism: A Tale of the South* (1853), a slave by the name of Rufus is offered his freedom by a Northern visitor who happens to be an abolitionist, an offer that Rufus promptly declines. In the discussion between the abolitionist and a fellow Northerner that promptly ensues, the author goes to some lengths to establish that Rufus is not only a contented slave but that his contentment is utterly genuine, untainted by the least hint of coercion or self-deception.[24] Of course, one case does not prove much of anything, which is no doubt why *Antifanaticism* eventually offers freedom to all its major black characters, an offer that is sometimes declined and sometimes accepted but either way is always received with the blessing of a benevolent master. Here bondage may be upheld as a positive good just so long as it doesn't conform to anything resembling real bondage. Texts such as *Antifanaticism* are, that is to say, so zealous in meeting the criticisms of their anti-slavery opponents that they are left with nothing to defend; a world where slaves are at liberty to choose to come and go as they please is a world where slavery reigns in name only. In such cases the effort to vindicate the peculiar institution is over before it begins. (It's revealing that Stowe felt called upon to comment briefly on only one of these novels, J. Thornton Randolph's *The Cabin and the Parlor*, in *A Key to Uncle Tom's Cabin*, the latter a book which, in exhaustively canvassing all manner of documents critical of the novel, can hardly be accused of failing to take notice of its many detractors.)

Another way of failing to disagree with Stowe is to expand the scope of her critique, as opposed to, say, taking issue with it. In the unrelenting catalogue of horrors that makes up Caroline Rush's *The North and South: Or, Slavery and its Contrasts* (1852), the sons and daughters of the impoverished Harley family are bound out to service, whipped, beaten, denied schooling, shut up in closets filled with rats and human skeletons, tortured, and starved to death. Systematically matching the abuses alleged on the plantation with those visited upon a poor family in Philadelphia, Rush is forever rebuking the abolitionist for overlooking the evils done to whites at home while magnifying their effects on blacks far away. In what may well be a literary first for the time, she invites us to weigh the history of suffering in each of the two groups, to compare their disabling legacies, and to award our sympathy on the basis of which can demonstrate the greater degree of victimization: "we shall see whether 'the broad-chested, powerful negro'," Rush's narrator promises, quoting Stowe's description of Tom, "or the fragile, delicate girl, with her pure white face, is most entitled to your sympathy and tears."[25] As might be expected, it's not much of a contest: except for a brief sojourn in Mississippi, Rush never even bothers to take us below the Mason-Dixon line, much less include any black characters to speak of. As harrowing as her portrayals of "white slavery" can be – the sheer sadism of Rush's white matrons is equaled only by Harriet Wilson's unforgettable depiction of the diseased Mrs. Bellmont in *Our Nig* – and as unflattering as her picture of Northern philanthropy is, the aim of *The North and South* is not to defend slavery but to pre-empt the need for any such undertaking. It is essentially indifferent to slavery, both as an economic institution and a way of life. In this respect, it, too, may be recognized as an extended non sequitur.

The same cannot be said of Hentz's *The Planter's Northern Bride* (1854), reportedly one of the more accomplished works of fiction written in response to *Uncle Tom's Cabin* and, unlike many of its companions, deserving of a more extended response.[26] Not content with limiting itself to stereotypes of the happy slave and benevolent master, the novel is fairly clever in turning the standard features of anti-slavery rhetoric to its own advantage. So it is the Southern plantation owner Russell Moreland who, at the outset of the book, must patiently endure prejudice, intolerance, and even open contempt as he travels through New England, while it is the fanatical abolitionist at the end of the book who, in fomenting a slave rebellion, is possessed by an uncontrollable and utterly unprincipled desire to impose his will on others. Or it's Moreland's own family that suffers the trials of separation when his daughter is kidnapped, while it is the hypocritical, "Quaker-like" (155) Softlys from the North who seduce the slave Crissy into forsaking her husband and child and running away for no good reason. And whereas Stowe appeals directly to the women among her readership to feel sympathy for the slave, Hentz makes the same direct address to the women in her audience, asking them to have sympathy for all the young men doomed to perish on the battlefield should war between the states break out owing to the reckless misrepresentations of agitators like Mrs. Stowe (137). Naturally, Hentz sees herself as rising above mere partisanship and embracing "our *national* honor" (3; text's emphasis), one reason why *The Planter's Northern Bride*, in telling the story of the marriage of a Southern slaveholder to the daughter of a Northern abolitionist, describes, near the end of the book, the fruit of their union as having "the blood of the North and the South ... blended in its veins," the living "representative of the reunion of these now too divided parties" (315).

For all its emphasis on sectional reconciliation, however, the novel itself is divided over how best to vindicate "plantation life" (3). On the one hand, Hentz advances an essentially class-based defense of slavery, taking frequent breaks from the storyline to mock "the free hirelings" (17) of the factory or "the nominally free but literally and practically enslaved poor" (171) of Great Britain or "Russia's forty millions of slaves" (195). Closer to home, among Moreland's first acquaintances in his travels is Nancy Brown, who has been dismissed by her employer after an illness and lives on the outskirts of a small New England village with her destitute and dying mother, both shackled to the "bondage of poverty" (15) and both unquestionably worse off than the African Americans of Moreland's plantation, who are "watched over as kindly as if born of a fairer race" (29). No less than those African Americans who run away from the plantation and beg to be taken back, Nancy "wished she could breathe [the] balm" of servitude as she daydreams of "the soft, mild atmosphere that bowed around those children of toil" (29). Later on, at the conclusion of a lengthy description of British textile workers – "that pale and ghastly and multitudinous band of females imprisoned within close and narrow walls" – Hentz goes so far as to implore the "God of the white man, as well as the black" to give both races "bondage and chains" in lieu of an empty freedom to "work or starve; work or die; work or sell themselves to the demon of temptation" (138). The false choices offered by freedom under capitalism are simply indicative of the meaninglessness of the concept in the first place. "We wonder who is really free in this great prison-house the world," the narrator muses, "ask him who sits in the White Palace, chief of this great republic, filling the grandest station in the world, – if he is free! Are you free? Are we?" (195).

On the other hand, even if "we" are all in some sense slaves, it clearly does matter that the occupant of the "White Palace" be white. By treating personal servitude as a universal norm that benefits all of humanity, Fitzhugh, as we have seen, tries to finesse increasingly entrenched beliefs about racial difference among his compatriots by treating the alleged inferiority of the black as a matter of serendipity and nothing more – as indeed he must if his account is to escape the "thousand absurdities and contradictions" that he thought plagued "the defence of mere Negro slavery" (Faust, 286). But Hentz, who is writing a novel and not a polemic, can afford to be somewhat less scrupulous in her claims about the universal goodness of slavery, even to the point of having her Southern planter, when called upon to justify the peculiar institution, protest rather defensively that "we had no more to do with its existence than our own. We are not responsible for it" (47). Taking himself to be more of a missionary than a slaveholder, "appointed by heaven for the good of a benighted race" (85), Moreland does not hesitate to affirm that "God has not made all men equal, though wiser men than God would have it so" (175). Judy, who has the misfortune, as the novel sees it, of being a free black woman living in the North, agrees: "Talk 'bout us being on a 'quality with white folks, no such ting. De Lord never made us look like them. We mustn't be angry wid de Lord, for all dat" (154). So even as the white pauper Nancy longs for the protective embrace of slavery or as the Irish maid Betsy concedes that she is "ten times more of a slave this minute" (100) than the genuine article – indeed, even as Hentz's narrator assails the very concept of freedom as essentially an illusion – the novel is equally emphatic in pressing the point that the sons and daughters of "poor, degraded Africa" are slaves by nature who will never learn to cope with the demands of a free society.

Going back and forth between universalizing slavery and racializing it produces peculiar results. If in certain moments the narrator, faithful to the pieties of plantation fiction, can get choked up over the bonds the master shares with his bondsmen – "a sable filament was twisted in every cord that bound him to the past" (289) – in others she can have the same character

shudder in disgust at the idea that a black man once fingered the same
cutlery as his beloved fiancée (23). The alternation between benevolent
paternalist and virulent racist is especially stark in this novel. Of his slaves
Moreland says "they are entwined with my affections as well as my interests," adding that "they are as much incorporated with my being as the trees
which have shaded my infancy and childhood" (175). By the same token,
equally "entwined, like conscience" as "an inherent principle of the human
breast," is a universal "horror" of "amalgamation" supposedly shared by
both races; the white person who "professes to look upon [a black person] as
his equal and his friend" is, according to Moreland, fooling no one but
himself, for the fact is that "he would sooner see a son or daughter perish
beneath the stroke of the assassin than wedded to the African" (117). The
black is inextricably part of the white (e.g., "I never dreamed, when a boy,
that it was possible to separate my existence from theirs" [175]); the black
can never be a part of the white (e.g., "[God] has created a barrier between
his race and ours, which no one can pass over without incurring the ban of
society" [117]).

One reason for thinking that this stark dualism is more than a passing
curiosity is that the novel goes out of its way to encourage the suggestion
that Moreland himself has passed over the barrier that God has created. For
the true interest of *The Planter's Northern Bride* is not its story of the
courtship and marriage of a Southerner to a Northerner, which in any
case functions as little more than a pretext for Hentz's editorializing. Rather,
what keeps the narrative going is the buried story of Moreland's previous
marriage to a Southern belle named Claudia who is presumably white but is
insistently made to seem black. "The daughter of Italian parents," Claudia
leads a "wild, gipsy life" (215) until she is purchased by a wealthy widow in "a
Southern city" (216) and is in time married to Moreland. But "the taint was
in Claudia's blood" (217): "the slave of her own wild passions" (198), she
courts "the fellowship of gay, unprincipled men" (216–17) and even receives
one of their company "clandestinely at home" (217), all the while neglecting
her duties as wife and mother. Like the fugitive slaves of the novel who do
not know what to do with freedom once they get it, Claudia squanders the
fortune bequeathed to her by her adopted mother; with her signature "large,
black, resplendent, yet repelling eyes" (209) veiled by "black lace drapery"
and "raven black hair" (210), she succumbs to the same "unlicensed liberty"
and "wild excesses of sin" that Hentz's narrator elsewhere describes as
befalling the British West Indies or St. Domingo once freedom converts
docile subjects into a "lawless and degenerate people" (170–71). The tie
between Claudia and slave revolts is in fact more than just incidental. With

what seems full deliberation, Hentz devotes a long chapter to narrating Claudia's death and then shifts immediately in the succeeding chapter to a scene that shows the unraveling of the plot to overtake Moreland's plantation by a party of slaves corrupted by abolitionist propaganda. Finally, true to his assertion that a white parent would sooner see a son or daughter perish than see either "wedded to the African," Moreland, playing the double role of transgressor and censor, is repelled by the presence of his infant daughter and so "shun[s] its sight and shrink[s] involuntarily from its innocent caresses" (118).

If there were ever a literary work that confirms the presence of a political unconscious, *The Planter's Northern Bride* would have to be it. A full-blown assault on abolitionist sanctimony and irresponsibility, the novel comes close to echoing abolitionist attacks on Southern patriarchy for its sexual criminality and hypocrisy. With due allowance for the stock figure of the "dark seductress" drawn from the pages of Sir Walter Scott, to say nothing of her formulaic sacrifice for the sake of social harmony, something more is clearly at stake than deference to generic convention. Interpreting its not so subtle hints of miscegenation as a veiled criticism of plantation society, Betina Entzminger conjectures that Hentz's status as a Southern writer born and raised in the North may have something to do with the combination of attraction and repulsion that governs Claudia's characterization.[27] Certainly the dissociation of sensibility is extreme: the presence of Claudia is not simply a source of embarrassment for the slaveholder ("so dark a cloud has rested on my home" [118] is his rueful description) and of humiliation and pain for his wife ("It was exquisitely painful to her to think that Moreland had ever loved such a being" [215]). Her presence also makes a mockery of categorical pronouncements from Moreland like "there is no such thing as irresponsible power at the South" (118) and converts standard pro-slavery fare into something disturbing and perverse, as when Moreland reassures his fiancée that in the North "the Negro" may be "an isolated, degraded being, without caste or respectability – a single black line running through a web of whiteness," but in the South she is "surrounded with the socialities of life" (119).

Of course, there is a further sense in which Hentz may not be critiquing plantation society so much as taking its premises to their natural conclusion. "Family government, from its nature, has ever been despotic" (SFS, 105), writes Fitzhugh, a statement that makes brothers and sisters of the slaves at the same time that it makes slaves of the wives. For "marriage is too much like slavery not to be involved in its fate" (SFS, 206) – or, as Claudia puts it, "I thought I married a lover! He turned into my master, my tyrant! He wanted me to cringe to his will, like the slaves in the kitchen and I spurned his authority" (211). The paternalist fantasy of one happy family has obviously gone too far; if the master can't tell the difference between a wife and a slave, that's not just because of unbridled lust. In a rather surreal way, the novel keeps suggesting that an insistence on hierarchy leads to a wholesale erosion of social distinctions – which of course is just what paternalist ideology promises. When the black Claudia taunts the white Eulalia, contemptuously referring to her as "the daughter of a Northern clime … who may wear the yoke without feeling it, and yield the will without knowing it," the planter's bride, otherwise so submissive, is seized by a "sudden storm of passion rising and surging within" (211–12), momentarily forsaking "the angel of consideration" and crossing over to the "dark and sultry" (214) resentment of the slave. More powerfully still, the novelist most likely did not intend (but her reader can't help but infer) a certain irony when the slaveholder, whom we first encounter "two years after his legal emancipation from the[ ] unhallowed bonds" (217) of matrimony, assures his slaves that he'd gladly give them freedom but that they would only squander it in dissoluteness and vice. This is probably not what Hentz had in mind when having her hero boast that he finds it impossible "to separate my existence from theirs" (175).

"The slaveholder is like other men," Fitzhugh remarks in *Sociology for the South*, meaning to be reassuring but not quite pulling it off, "the ready submission of the slave, nine times out of ten, disarms his wrath even when the slave has offended" (SFS, 247). However much it may mystify or cloak patriarchal violence, paternalism necessarily presupposes its existence. At one point Hentz has Moreland exclaim over his wife's power to "bind [his anger] with a silken thread" as he recalls a fairy tale heard in his boyhood about "a holy virgin going on a pilgrimage through the wilderness, and the wild beasts hushed their howlings, and crouched submissively at her feet" (177). But this is indeed only a fairy tale; the novel never actually dramatizes the wild beast tamed by his "sweet, confiding, angelic" (177) spouse. This is not to say that the contest between helpless innocence and savage fury disappears. It is, rather, located elsewhere. In Hentz's novel, that is to say, the tensions of a benevolent despotism are displaced from the white patriarch and relocated within the African and the wife. I have already noted how the portrayal of "the Negro [as] degraded, benighted, and imbruted … in his native land, plunged in the lowest depths of sensuality and heathenism" (258) alternates with images of "the Negro [who] would twist his dark fingers in [Moreland's] childish locks, and pray God Almighty to bless him and make him a blessing to mankind" (289). The angry passion in the master that is subdued by the trust of the weak and helpless is never altogether dispelled in the weak and helpless. In one of the novel's most powerful scenes, Moreland unveils his newborn son to his "people" and their awe elicits in turn the narrator's reverential description: "the admiration, love, and devotion which the Negro feels for the children of a beloved master, is one of the strongest, most unselfish passions the human heart is capable of cherishing" (293). It is at such moments that "the partition wall of colour is broken down [and] the sable arms are privileged to wreathe the neck of snow, the dusky lips to press soft kisses on the cheek of living roses" (293). As if on cue a handful of sentences later we find the narrator calling to mind "St. Domingo, Jamaica, and the other emancipated islands" and brooding upon "the emancipation of brute force; the reign of animal passion and power; the wisdom of eighteen centuries buried under waves of barbarism" (294). Reversing the parable of wild beasts tamed by holy virgins, the unnerving closeness of "unselfish passions" to "animal passion and power" – the ease with which one may trade places with the other – makes vivid the instability of the paternalist script.

By extension, the same dualism is recapitulated in the master's two wives, one a paragon of forbearance and blind obedience who not only accepts Moreland's despised daughter but "transfuse[s] a portion of her angelic sweetness" (268) into her, the other "the humiliated victim of her own unmastered passion" (272) who dies unrepentant. Features so perfectly synthesized in the person of the master – the fearful exercise of power and its pleasurable surrender – become, in the case of the wife no less than the slave, an unstable compound of warring elements. It is as though those characteristics reserved for the slaveholder have been reassigned to his various dependents in exaggerated, distorted form – as though, indeed, the basic features of paternalism could not be assembled in narrative form without beginning to stray and fall apart.

Eugene Genovese and other historians have frequently reminded us that paternalism, more than simply a mythology concocted by Southern intellectuals, did in fact have a far-reaching impact on the life of the plantation.[28] But *The Planter's Northern Bride*, fictionalizing a body of material that already was verging on self-parody, makes this reminder difficult to keep in mind. One way of appreciating the extremity of the case it makes (and of making sense, more particularly, of its treatment of the slaveholder's "dark" past) is to compare it to another novel written in response to Stowe, Maria McIntosh's *The Lofty and the Lowly*, published one year earlier in 1853. Although it too has its share of wicked abolitionists conniving to lure slaves into freedom, McIntosh's novel takes the theme of sectional reconciliation much more seriously than *The Planter's Northern Bride*, whose idea of peacemaking appears to consist in fulminations against Northern intolerance and arrogance. (Reversing Hentz's trajectory as a native of Massachusetts who relocated to the South, McIntosh was a Georgian-born resident of New York at the time she wrote her novel.) Chronicling the intersecting fate of two families, the slaveholding Montroses and the mercantile Brownes, the novel stitches together regional connections by marrying Southern daughters to Northern sons and Southern sons to Northern daughters. This use of marriage is of course entirely conventional, as is the stereotypical juxtaposition of the Cavalier and the Yankee, here represented on one side by Colonel Montrose, contemptuous of "everyone who dwelt north of the Potomac" on account of "their meanness, avarice, and low cunning," and on the other side by Thomas Browne, who "regarded his southern fellow-citizens as an indolent and prodigal race, in comparison to himself but half civilized, and far better acquainted with the sword and the pistol than with any more useful implements."[29] The novel begins with the news that the Colonel's brother, who is married to Browne's sister, has recently died up North; predictably, the Colonel insists on taking in the widow at Montrose Hall, where she and her children "shall have no need to labor while I have a home for them" (I, 17), while the merchant brother insists that she will be better off finding employment rather than "liv[ing] the life of an idler and the humble dependent on the house of another" (I, 26).

But rather than favoring Southern magnaminity over Northern thrift, McIntosh is worried that the options have become too polarized. The scion of the house of Montrose, Donald, is a spoiled idler who, deeming labor "ignoble" (I, 153) and "degrading" (I, 154), gambles away the family fortune. The son of the Northern merchant fares no better: George Browne is a financial speculator, ultimately the villain of the tale, whose dealings make it difficult to say where business ends and extortion and thievery begin. Each personifies the decadence of an economic system that, it's implied, has too long existed in isolation. As the novel's subtitle suggests, *Good in All and None All-Good*, neither capitalism nor chattel slavery are in a position to claim moral superiority. Too long dependent on slave labor, Donald can no more discipline his desires than his finances; when he impetuously presses marriage on his cousin Alice, it is made clear by both the narrator and the other characters that his quasi-incestuous passion is both unseemly and overwrought. Too long dependent on himself, Robert Grahame, self-made millionaire industrialist and eventual hero of the story, is on the other hand portrayed as a workaholic who suffers from too little impulsiveness instead of too much; when it comes time for him to propose matrimony to Alice he can barely muster the presence of mind to pull it off (II, 277). In the best manner of a wise mediator, McIntosh suggests there is plenty of blame to go around, but not so much so that the excesses peculiar to one region might not offset and correct the excesses of the other if judiciously brought together.

The Lofty and the Lowly contains, to be sure, the usual assortment of proslavery motifs: the slaves rejoicing at the return of the master and mistress (I, 197); Southerners regarding with disbelief anti-slavery reports of cruelty and torment on the plantation (II, 162); abolitionists trampling over the rights and wishes of servant and master alike (II, 98, 167–70), and so forth. But protracted and bitter debates among whites over the peculiar institution are avoided altogether by McIntosh, just as sustained evocations of a deeply felt emotional bond between white and black are minimized. In this respect, the book follows the precedent of the plantation novel, preferring to keep slavery on a comparatively low profile. One apparent exception arises when "Daddy" Cato, faithful to a fault, travels from Georgia to Boston to assist his mistress when she leaves the plantation after the Colonel's death. But aside from the fact that Cato has been freed by the Colonel and is therefore no slave, his voluntarism and initiative set him apart from the rest of "the unconscious, innocent people" (II, 118) he leaves behind at Montrose Hall. Hiring himself out as a laborer to help Alice and her mother, Cato affords McIntosh the opportunity to detail the indignities of Northern racism (II, 69). By shifting attention away from the "indissoluble bonds" between master and servant, the novel tends to defuse the erotic tensions in the relationship between races, relegating these instead to the crisscrossing courtships that will culminate in the marriages of the novel's four major characters.

Hentz, on the other hand, marries off her planter to his Northern bride within the first ten chapters of the narrative. This satisfies the novel's declared goal of sectional reconciliation while leaving plenty of room to accomplish a further, unspoken aim, namely, the elimination of "the dark cloud" hovering over the Moreland estate with the installation of his incomparably white Northern bride. The contrast to McIntosh is symptomatic: in order to overcome the division between North and South Hentz is finally compelled to go beyond matrimony and appeal to the differences between white and black. This strategy gives us the true explanation why *The Planter's Northern Bride* flirts with the theme of miscegenation in the coupling of the slaveholder and the gypsy Claudia. It assigns to Eulalia, the white woman of the North, the role of cleansing the stain of patriarchal indiscretion. Forging the bond between the slave states and free on the altar of racial purity, Hentz tacitly abandons the color-blind defense of slavery such as espoused by Fitzhugh and other proponents of the positive good school of thought. In so doing she also confirms their worst fears; the novel's physical revulsion at the sights and smell of blacks – Eulalia's "shudder of inexpressible loathing" makes the Negrophobia of Stowe's Ophelia look almost refined by comparison, while Hentz's diatribes on African cannibalism and others forms of savagery represent, in one historian's judgment, "the worst descriptions of Africa by any Southern writer" – evoke all too clearly the ascendancy of ungovernable passion and unhinged contempt that paternalism was expressly designed to tame and correct.[30]

But if *The Planter's Northern Bride* differs from other anti-*Tom* productions in terms of its treatment of race, there is nothing unique about its insinuations regarding the sins of the slaveholder. Like Russell Moreland, Graham Mildmay of T. B. Thorpe's *The Master's House* is presented as a paragon of Southern gentility who marries a Northern bride and brings her to his plantation in Louisiana. But where Moreland is haunted by a "dark cloud" from his past, Mildmay's tragedy does not come to fruition until the very end of the story when, against his better judgment, he slays his neighbor in a duel and so mortifies his wife that she, too, is struck dead. It's instructive that this duel is the only action of any real significance performed by the otherwise mild-mannered, aptly named slaveholder in a novel mostly concerned with depraved slave-traders, corrupt overseers, and the buffoonery of poor whites. "In spite of our civilization," Mildmay tells his wife as he departs for what she's been led to believe is a hunting trip, "there is enough of the savage life in us ... to make the sports of the field sometimes agreeable."[31] Predictably, if not melodramatically, once the savagery of the Southern gentleman is exposed and gives the lie to his placid exterior, the wife suffers the consequence. Upon hearing the news of the duel, Annie Mildmay instantly "turn[ed] deadly pale, and rising straight up from her seat, she fell toward him, as stiff and cold as if she had been marble." Consumed by "the never-dying worm of remorse" and "stunned beyond recovery," the dishonored widower of Heritage House is last seen on the novel's final page grieving at the grave of his Northern bride, himself "enshrouded" in "the thick darkness of a starless night."[32]

One may well ask what any of this has to do with answering *Uncle Tom's Cabin*, a question that is very much to the point. The theme of male improvidence, irresponsibility, and loss of self-control overpowers the proslavery novel, at times threatening to eclipse its ostensible mission altogether. Rush's *The North and South* spends more time berating husbands than it does Mrs. Stowe: "those lords of creation, who hold our destiny in their hands," fumes the narrator, "just give them a chance over the weak and the helpless, and they will rejoice to find an extremity of torture, to make their power felt" (162–63). Before marriage men may appear "the very perfection of all goodness," but "once in possession of that magical word, power," they "display to view tempers and passions more worthy of fiends than men" (164). Never mind that this is a far better description of the white women in the novel, whose sadism drives their servants to suicide and infanticide; never mind, too, that the husbands of these sadists are portrayed as impotent bystanders too cowardly to intervene. "But where in the world am I going to?" (165), Rush's narrator interrupts herself at the end of one of her lectures on male perfidy, as if in recognition of their somewhat compulsive nature. Though she whimsically reproaches herself for having "wandered off" from her story, what seems a digression is in reality the novel's true object of interest. It is not hard to see why.

In underwriting claims that the peculiar institution is above all a benevolent institution, paternalism makes male aggression a problem in need of a solution. More often than not, the pro-slavery novel is so preoccupied by the problem that it forgets about the prescribed remedy. Thus the inescapable refrain common to all these texts that "a planter's wife is the greatest slave that exists," as Thorpe puts it *The Master's House*,[33] is not meant to affirm a power made available to the wife by virtue of her helplessness; pieties about "the strength of weakness" such as we find in *Cannibals All!* are notably absent in the pro-slavery novel. In the course of being deployed to justify bondage, paternalism does something more – it serves as a lightning rod for an assertive, at times caustic feminism, as in Rush's contention that "if you want to see slavery in its worst form – the slavery that trammels mind and body, and holds in life-long chains its wretched victims, you have only to visit the homes of many married people" (164). Works of fiction created to rebut the libels of Stowe somehow metamorphose into attacks on male tyranny so radical that even Stowe would have balked: when Mary Eastman, author of *Aunt Phillis's Cabin*, quotes a sentence from *Uncle Tom's Cabin* ("Is man *ever* a creature ever to be trusted with wholly irresponsible power?"), she takes the liberty of italicizing the second word and of inviting her reader to consider that "although [Stowe] is speaking of slavery politically, can you not apply it to matrimony in this miserable country of ours?"[34] Many women had of course been doing precisely that, but they lived in the North and bore names like Margaret Fuller and Lydia Maria Child. That the author of *Aunt Phillis's Cabin* should take the author of *Uncle Tom's Cabin* to task for failing to honor "women's rights" as fervently as the rights of African Americans must be counted one of the more bizarre ironies of literary history. "This is the era of mental and bodily emancipation," Eastman writes, momentarily forgetting, it would seem, her sketches of "little darkies" (244) happily cavorting on the plantation grounds, "[t]ake advantage of it, wives and Negroes! But, alas for the former! There is no society formed for *their* benefit; their day of deliverance has not yet dawned, and until its first gleamings arise in the *east*, they must wear their chains" (111).

Like the elements of egalitarianism that cling to Fitzhugh's discourse, this sort of consciousness-raising hovers in a peculiar limbo, something less than a fully integrated, articulate position and something more than a matter of polemical expedience. What little plot there is to *Aunt Phillis's Cabin* centers, after all, upon the breaking of Alice Weston, who must renounce her love for one man and learn the art of submission in acceding to her mother's insistence that she become another's bride. So even as Eastman includes scenes we might expect to find on the pages of *The Liberator* (e.g., a bondswoman, discovering her five daughters and two sons sold one day, dreams of killing her master; a slaveholder, beyond the power of self-control, beats an old servant until his outraged wife intervenes and puts a stop to it [43; 241–42]), she narrates the tale of a young white woman who, overcoming her attachment to an impecunious suitor in order to placate her uncle and mother, eventually accepts her role as a planter's wife. This sense of antithetical narratives operating on separate tracks that never intersect, obvious enough in *The Planter's Northern Bride* and *Aunt Phillis's Cabin*, is even more blatant in *The North and South*, where animadversions on male tyranny alternate with panegyrics on the saintly Mrs. Harley, who endures without complaint the humiliation and neglect that come with supporting an alcoholic husband. (Not that the poor wife, whose obedience to her spouse "amid all the horror of adversity" [119] verges on the fanatical, is a total pushover; she does draw the line when Mr. Harley, in the throes of despair, orders her to gather the children so the family can all commit suicide together.)

Those who find it important to sort through the hegemonic and counter-hegemonic implications of literary texts will have their hands full with the pro-slavery novel. What's to be done with a text (in this case *The Ebony Idol* by G. M. Flanders) that imagines a recent convert to abolitionism so condescending in his sanctimony that his offended wife herself becomes converted to the view that "men ... do not hesitate to exercise this oppressive vigilance, and [so] many an active, high-spirited girl degenerates into a hackneyed, humdrum housekeeper"?[35] Or with a novel (in this case *The Master's House*, on a somewhat different topic) that describes in the most harrowing terms imaginable the spiritual crisis of a slave-trader who agonizes over his many sins only to be rescued by the soothing platitudes of a pro-slavery preacher? Doubtless the reductio ad absurdum of this brand of ideological dissociation may be found in *Aunt Phillis's Cabin*, which begins with the observation that all true

Christians must know that slavery is sanctioned by Holy Writ (much is made of Noah's curse) and ends with the confession on the part of the narrator that "I have no wish to uphold slavery. I would that every human being that God made were free … free bodily, free spiritually – 'free indeed!' " (277). This is of a piece with a book that enthuses over all the blessings slavery confers upon the helpless Negro and what a cruel fate mere freedom would be, but that also includes the kindly planter Mr. Weston granting freedom to Aunt Phillis's children on her deathbed in recognition of her services not as a slave but as "a friend and nurse to my wife and a mother to my only child" (258). "Sometimes," adds Mr. Weston, confiding to his cousin and sister, "I have almost reproached myself that I have retained a woman like Phillis as a slave" (253). No wonder one reviewer asked with some perplexity "was it written by a friend or foe of slavery?"[36]

The true fiction of Southern paternalism is of course its suggestion that one might be both. It has become a commonplace to say that pro-slavery attitudes over the first fifty years of the nineteenth century evolved from ill-concealed defensiveness to enthusiastic endorsement – or, in historian Michael O'Brien's assessment – "from a bleak sense of human limitation to a quasi-millenial vision."[37] Like many commonplaces, this one is worth revisiting. For at the heart of appeals on behalf of the peculiar institution as a positive good lay the ongoing recognition that it was also a necessary evil; when Eastman's narrator tells us "I would that every human being that God made were free" (277), she is saying that God has *not* made every human being free *and* registering her regret that this should be so. And in fact following Hentz's invocation of the "great commanding truth" that there will always be the rich and the poor, Hammond's references to "the mud-sill of society," or Fitzhugh's insistence that to live in the social realm is inevitably to live with inequality, Eastman adds her voice to the chorus, noting that were we to follow the leveling doctrines of the abolitionists, "the foundations of society would be shaken, nay, destroyed" (19). Those espousing such "arguments" were no more foes of slavery than its friends; they were, rather, attempting to be both at the same time. "Though an evil, it is one that cannot be dispensed with," we read in the Preface to *Aunt Phillis's Cabin*, the best-selling of all the anti-*Tom* novels, "how long it will continue, or whether it will ever cease, the Almighty Ruler of the universe can alone determine" (21, 24). Perhaps one day the Lord will come around, but for the time being those willing to entertain the possibility of being against slavery must remain for it.

In *A Key to Uncle Tom's Cabin*, Stowe defines the aristocrat as "he who, though he may be just, generous, and humane to those he considers his equals, is entirely insensible to the wants, and sufferings, and common humanity, of those whom he considers the lower orders. The sufferings of the countess would make him weep, the sufferings of a seamstress a quite another matter."[38] On this definition, there are no aristocrats in the South. Inasmuch as "his whole life is spent in providing for the minutest wants of others, in taking care of them in sickness and in health," Fitzhugh's slave-holder is a consummate humanitarian, easily outperforming, in his reach of empathy, those hypocritical "votaries of Liberty and Equality" to the North (SFS, 247–48, 251). The wishful merger of two opposed belief systems, paternalism undertakes to raise an edifice of inequality on egalitarian foundations. In the case of the pro-slavery novel this project barely gets off the ground before it is sidetracked by other pursuits that involve every-thing from demonizing blacks to assailing white male privilege or anato-mizing class inequities. Although we think of Southern paternalism as embodying something like the very quintessence of ideology – the happy slave the textbook case of false consciousness – in point of fact the pro-slavery novel can barely rise to the accusation of distorting reality, so undisguised are its conflicting imperatives and so muddled its final message. A popular sentiment on both sides of the sectional divide in the antebellum United States held that slavery, if left to its own devices, would die of its own accord. It's one of the curiosities of literary history that the pro-slavery novel is the literary enactment of the same belief.

THE DUMB-STRUCK SLAVEHOLDER

Political theorist Robert Dahl has argued that all serious alternatives to democratic rule may be reduced to one of two schools of thought, namely, anarchism or guardianship.[39] Anarchism disputes the right of anyone to exercise power over others, even the people, whereas guardianship, doubt-ing the wisdom of even the people to rule themselves, entrusts power to a select few, like Plato's philosopher-kings or Lenin's revolutionary vanguard. Southern conservatives obviously understood themselves to be pursuing the second path, though just as obviously failed to see how far they strayed from it. For if the whole point of guardianship is, as Dahl notes, that the rulers are *exempt* from the defects of those they rule, this is precisely what the paternalism of the antebellum South, with its appeals to the chastening power of the weak and helpless to subdue the strong, does not provide. In the end that is why the Southern theory of class is in reality no theory at all, unless the affirmation that somebody needs to rule and others need to be ruled counts as a theory. The family would seem a more promising

candidate for sanctioning the hierarchies the pro-slavery argument wished
to uphold, but even here equality slips through the back door, so to speak,
for the point where social necessity ends and loving bonds begin is the point
where the discourse of inequality gets alchemized into the discourse of
equality.

None of which means that inequality, especially as manifested along
racial lines, didn't exist in the antebellum United States. The observation
that "the Negro has no rights which the white man is bound to respect"
came, after all, from the Chief Justice of the highest court in the land. Even
here, though, it's important to note that Justice Taney's remark illustrates,
in its callousness, just the mentality that writers such as Fitzhugh and
Hughes were anxious to disavow and that the novelists we've been discussing saw all too plainly. From this standpoint, Genovese may be under-
stating the case when he suggests "planters as well as yeomen all across the
South found it almost impossible to surrender the rhetoric, although not
necessarily the substance of [an] ostensibly Jeffersonian egalitarianism."[40]
For if the strange career of paternalist thought is any indication, the
combined gesture of endeavoring to renounce the substance while retaining
the rhetoric of egalitarianism produced truly dysfunctional results. The
disconnection between rhetoric and substance that made pro-slavery arguments run in circles, appearing to lack the means of articulation, takes us
back to Douglass's portrayal of the dumb-struck slaveholder, rendered mute
by a cause that will not allow itself to be spoken. And if the ex-slave's point
that the enormity of the sin of slavery defies any attempt at apology is not
quite my point, the inability of the slaveholder to get equality out of his
mind nevertheless had its own role to play as well in his defense of the
peculiar institution.

PART II

The many in the one

One point of departure for many of the analyses in the second volume of Tocqueville's *Democracy in America* concerns the way in which equality alters the relationship between part and whole. The "nearly equal, roughly similar citizens of democracy," precisely because they regard each other as nearly equal and roughly similar, inevitably come to see themselves as more or less interchangeable on many different dimensions. Thus "in democratic societies, where all men are very small and very much alike, each man, as he looks at himself, sees his fellows at the same time."[1] Within every part may be discerned the whole; within the one may be seen the many. There is of course nothing mystical about democracy's power to facilitate this instant connection. It seems to follow almost trivially from the standard idea that equality places people side by side, revealing a common tie.

As we might expect, Tocqueville teases out the importance of this development by painting a vivid, highly simplified picture of the opposite condition. In aristocratic times, he suggests, "each man was conscious of only another man, whom he was bound to obey. Through that personage he was linked, without realizing it, to all the rest." Though it may be true that "aristocracy links everybody, from peasant to king, in one long chain," without a special effort of the imagination neither is necessarily aware of this fact. A dim and furtive abstraction, a "general conception of human fellowship" does not come naturally to the aristocratic subject.[2] Even as someone like Hobbes, writing nearly two centuries before Tocqueville, had thought it self-evident that "he that is to govern a whole Nation, must read in himself, not this or that particular man; but Man-kind," it was equally obvious that the sovereign would need special assistance in discharging this duty, which is why, as he explains in the introduction to the text, Hobbes decided to write *Leviathan*.[3] But what must be learned in times of inequality becomes automatic and indeed unavoidable in times of equality.

"In all people I see myself, none more and not one a barleycorn less," chants the "kosmos" of a poem that would come to be known as "Song of Myself." Tocqueville's question is to ask what happens when everyone can say this – when claims to representativeness cease being the sovereign's prerogative and become a common condition. If the famous frontispiece to *Leviathan* had shown the king literally composed of the bodies of his subjects, here each of these subjects would likewise contain multitudes. Judging from the second volume of *Democracy in America*, this development has multiple and sometimes contradictory consequences: it invests majority opinion with unprecedented immediacy, even to the point where it may take the form of an intolerable "weight" that "presses down" on the individual; it makes sympathy for strangers more inclusive, more instantaneous, and therefore more superficial; it helps account for why the conversation of Americans should broach the most familiar and even intimate topics imaginable with a bombastic and impersonal formality. And so on.

In this universalizing of representativeness literature has its own role to play. Although interchangeable selves and generic souls are nowadays likely to call to mind the dystopian landscapes of postmodern fiction, the relation between such constructs and the literary imagination need not be purely adversarial. The next chapter explores the influence of the social whole – the many in the one – in a somewhat more formative sense, beginning with the figure of the common reader. By definition a composite of many different individuals, the common reader of course stands for the general, the typical, the average, the conventional – in sum, the anticipated or projected response of that imagined totality. With the idea of reading, particularly as it relates to works of the imagination, thought to bear a privileged relation to the whole, acts of writing are in contrast linked to the part – to something less than the whole. Using this basic division as an organizing framework, what follows is a condensed literary history of sorts that cuts across domains not customarily brought together, beginning with the discourse of literary nationalism, moving on to sentimental poetry, and concluding with Whitman's *Leaves of Grass*. To the degree that "poets in democracies can never take a particular man as the subject of their poetry,"[4] the development of a literary egalitarianism in the United States is primarily a story of what might be called the de-individualizing of experience.

In lieu of simply debunking claims to representativeness, then, I want to take them seriously enough to explore their consequences.

Chapter Four engages the topic of envy, where such claims are simultaneously assumed and contested. With the envious, that is to say, appeals to a social norm of some kind are both crucial and tendentious; the presence of the many in the one is a source of anguish and outrage. Starting with Tocqueville's observations on the ubiquity of this emotion in cultures organized around the idea of equality, it canvasses works by Caroline Kirkland, Nathaniel Hawthorne, and Harriet Wilson to understand the attractions of this distinctively democratic vice.

CHAPTER THREE

The precise spirit of the average mass

In the inaugural issue of the *North American Review*, soon to establish itself as the country's leading voice of literary nationalism, there appeared an admiring notice of a volume entitled *Moral Pieces in Prose and Verse* (1815) by one Lydia Huntley. After commending the "considerable merit" of the poetry and quoting several passages at some length, the unnamed critic takes the opportunity of urging "Miss Huntley" to pursue more native themes in the future. "We have in the way of subjects," the reviewer grandly declares, in the manner of a salesman showcasing the company wares, "a rich and varied mine that has hardly been opened." Considering what "the genius of Scott" was able to do with the utterly "rude materials" of petty feuds and tribal warfare on the Scottish highlands, there is no reason why the American artist should not take advantage of much more attractive features closer to home. The countless stirring events surrounding two relatively recent revolutions, one against the French and the other against British, the legends of Indian history, the exploits of the early colonists, and the Puritan past are among the unexplored treasures "furnish[ing] materials at once interesting and grand ... that might be rendered highly poetical." In addition to "the magnificence of the scenery" waiting to be quarried and brought to the page in all its "diversified, animated, and picturesque glory," there are "the many romantick adventures of individuals" such as "the polished French nobleman from the court of Lewis XIV, the dignified British governour, the hardy American colonist, and the chiefs of the Six Nations" that beckon, each worthy of the notice of any aspiring poet or novelist.[1]

Within a few years Miss Huntley became Lydia Huntley Sigourney, who would go on, as "the Sweet Singer of Hartford," to produce nearly sixty works of poetry and prose over the course of a long career. A dominant force in the literary marketplace of antebellum America, she is inevitably (if unkindly) remembered as the Emmeline Grangerford of her day, churning out child elegies and various other forms of sentimental commemoration. Her poetry is hard to think about. Open her *Select Poems* at random and you will likely

come upon a poem on the death of a close relation – mostly infants, sometimes mothers, and occasionally daughters, sons, and fathers – written in
stately, curiously aloof blank verse. On the subject of her consolation verse,
Nina Baym comments forthrightly: "today's trained reader will repudiate this
poetry in part because such open emotionality is scorned; and in part because
its vocabulary and imagery are severely impersonal. Sigourney makes no
attempt to bring the events home to her own experience, and does not seek
wording that will bestow the significance of uniqueness on the recounted
event."[2] In veering from open emotionality to severe impersonality,
Sigourney's poetry makes vivid sentimentalism's scandalous paradox: the
spectacle of feeling that is not felt – emotion that is not "brought home"
and made genuine, so that "the merely personal is sifted out and the inward
grief becomes externalized in standard turns of speech."[3]

But if today's trained reader is troubled by the jarring combination of raw
experience and artificial convention, yesterday's reviewer apparently was
not. For next to its rather silly tone perhaps the most striking thing about
the notice from the *North American Review* is its assumption that artistic
achievement above all involves making use of the right associations, the
more "poetical" and "romantick" the better. As we are told, the reason why
some objects are more suitable for literary representation than others – why,
say, the sounding cataract or the Indian lament is preferable to a swamp or
the harangue of a local politician – is because some objects are more
evocative of emotions – awe or melancholy, for example – thought to be
distinctly aesthetic in nature. Literary pleasure, in other words, works by
capitalizing upon a collection of pre-existing, utterly repeatable responses.
Thus the point about "the genius of Scott" is not that America, too, requires
its own unique voice to transcend tawdry reality, which is not at all what the
reviewer has in mind. In the same way that ticketing off types like the
polished French nobleman or the dignified English governor indicates that
what literature most demands are indeed types, not distinct individuals, so
the conceit of riches waiting to be mined suggests that literary "materials"
need only be unearthed in order to be appreciated. In short, if "today's
trained reader" expects a unique voice unaware of an audience, yesterday's
critic looked for an aesthetic wholly organized around the anticipated
responses of a typical reader.

What would a literature look like that explicitly privileges the collective over
the individual in this way? What would be the consequences of treating
experience deductively, as proceeding from the whole – the representative,
the generic, or the typical – instead of the part? And how would this preference
affect ideas about authorship, interpretation, and meaning? Recent

developments in the scholarship are beginning to help us think past the opposition whereby the general and abstract is taken to signify nothing more than an effort to mask the interests of the particular and concrete.[4] In reversing this familiar script for reading inequality, I draw and expand upon these developments in exploring one branch of literary egalitarianism. I start with the discourse of literary nationalism and its reliance on the aesthetic theory known as associationism, which, as Theo Davis has demonstrated in an important study, offers us a useful way of thinking about the primacy of typical experience in American letters. Nationalism's interest in valorizing experience patterned after the hypothetical response of a generic listener sets the context for my discussion of Sigourney's child elegies, where reading virtually becomes its own ideology, particularly in its determination to level the difference between author and reader. A reconsideration of Whitman's "Song of Myself," exemplary in pressing this same ideology to the limit, concludes the discussion.

THE ENCHANTMENT OF THE MULTITUDE

In its earliest stages, the discourse of literary nationalism desired to build American letters literally from the ground up. "It is best to connect our best intellectual associations with places in our own land," John Knapp wrote in 1818, again in the *North American Review*: "[W]e love our country because our minds seem to have been furnished from its surface, and because our most natural and vivid ideas are inseparable from pictures which have it for their groundwork."[5] Knapp loves his country the same way that someone loves the pond on her uncle's farm where she spent so many summers growing up; and because her acquaintance with, say, serenity, was originally derived from her experiences of that pond, the mere picture of it will be sure to give rise to a "natural and vivid" idea of serenity. Taking its lead from empiricist epistemology and treating ideas as built up from simple, discrete bits of sense impressions, literary nationalism takes it for granted that the building blocks for any literature must be a storehouse of objects, each stamped, as it were, with readily identified and commonly shared emotions. This is why "the stranger" from another country "is only alarmed or disgusted by the hoarse and wild musick of your forests and sea-shore," says Edward Tyrell Channing in 1816, referring to the productions of the American muse. For "strangers are not expected to feel the beauty of your old poetical language, depending as it does on early and tender associations … and inspiring an inward and inexplicable joy, like a tale of childhood."[6] The "nativeness" of a literature is only secondarily about choice of a theme – honoring democracy, celebrating Columbia, and so on. Nor is it reducible simply to evoking American landscapes. "Nativeness" is possible only when the artist can tap into a pre-established fund of emotions grounded in certain objects which, when strung together, produce an aesthetic bliss of a peculiarly intense, special character.

By implication, then, the success or failure of a national literature has ultimately less to do with the skill of the author than with the conditions of reception. Producing lively images of a pond may be done well or ill, but the execution is moot if there are not enough readers in place who share the requisite collection of "early and tender associations." And then again, to cite a still more common worry, the pond itself may turn out to be an unworthy candidate for "poetic material," too prosaic or banal and so another case of what some commentators were starting to fear was a "poverty of association" in the New World. Getting the jump on Henry James and his lament about the "missing things" in American life, Channing wonders how a novelist like Charles Brockden Brown can possibly succeed, considering the "want in his readers of romantic associations with the scenes and persons he must set before us, if he makes a strictly domestic story."[7] But even as worries mounted in the 1820s over standards of taste in the United States, there was never any doubt that there was such a thing as a standard, average reader who could be an object of interest and concern. As Robert Streeter pointed out some time ago, reviewers like Knapp and Channing found it necessary to posit the existence of "a typical American mind" in their speculations.[8] Even when evidence to the contrary might arise, this construct remains a constant presence in nationalist discourse. In a review of Catharine Maria Sedgwick's *Redwood*, for instance, William Cullen Bryant dismisses suspicions that American soil is too barren to support a literature of its own by reminding his readers of the rich diversity of regional, religious, and occupational differences throughout the continent, all of which may be taken "to show what copious and valuable materials the private lives and daily habits of our countrymen offer to the writer of genius."[9] At no point does it occur to Bryant that these very differences might work against the presumption of a shared vocabulary of response his nationalism demands. Instead, by assuming "the imagination of the reader is always ready with its favorable effects," Bryant's chief concern is to sharpen the responsiveness of that imagination. If associations triggered by scenes and pictures that are too familiar leave no opportunity for "the reader to heighten the interest of such a narrative," those that are too exotic run the risk of failing to stir the imagination at all.[10] Such an outlook is prepared to acknowledge that taste is context-dependent, but only so long as this insight serves the overriding commitment "to incite to action the onlooker's or reader's mind," as Streeter puts it.[11] Much more concerned with respondents than creators, literary nationalism's interest in articulating the right sorts of associations required for literary distinction makes its postulation of this generic mind a conceptual necessity, however much it may have been an historical absurdity. For better or worse, then, "the reader" would remain "the reader."

But nationalism does more than construct a hypothetical reader. Its underlying logic is such that it renders the difference between authors and readers hard to see. The root idea of associationist theory is perhaps best captured on the first page of Lord Kames's (Henry Home) *Elements of Criticism* (1762), the founding text for a school of thought whose popularity continued well after the colonies secured their independence. In the book's opening paragraphs Kames observes that the perceptions and ideas passing through our minds in any given moment are not controlled by our will but are instead governed by "the relation by which things are linked together."[12] Now it is a short step from treating the will as a passive spectator of perceptions and ideas unfolding before it to regarding the author as more or less in the same position. If a text, painting, or piece of music operates, that is to say, by setting in motion a pleasing chain of associations, each one building upon the other and creating a momentum of its own, then the chief responsibility of the artist is to get out of the way. Like a stage manager standing in the wings, his or her task is to cue the right emotion and then let "the relation by which things are linked together" run its course. The creator does not create so much as prompt. True, artists can and should exercise some discretionary power; they can err, for instance, by making associations too familiar or too exotic, as we've seen Bryant warn. But even in such cases it's clear that the author is to think of himself or herself as a proxy for the reader, calculating likely effects, anticipating the expected response. At the heart of associationist theory is a resistance to dividing the world between originators and receivers, creators and respondents. By thinking of the "relation" between thoughts and feelings as a self-governing force, moving in accordance with its own special logic, it makes such designations appear to be of secondary or of superficial importance.

In connection with this last point and in an account to which I am much indebted, Theo Davis has written incisively on how the writings of Kames and his followers collectively reflect "a foundational belief that experience might be an aesthetically coherent object of spectatorship," which is to say that "they held that we may regard our own thoughts and emotions as we view a painting or read a novel." Davis is especially astute in pointing out that Scottish aesthetics, in looking at literature wholly in terms of the effects it produces on a hypothetical reader, inevitably takes experience itself to be detachable from the individual subject and therefore something that becomes "abstracted, emptied, impersonal."[13] Logically, this detachment of experience from agency should apply to readers as much as authors; politically, however, it is the author who is much more commonly singled out as the figure who betrays the sin of an excessive subjectivity. As William Charvat documented more than fifty years ago, even in that Federalist bastion of conservatism, the *North American Review*, a recurring impatience with authorial intrusiveness sets the terms of critical response:

In Burns, Cowper, and Thompson, we see woods and fields and streams with precisely those emotions and associations which the objects themselves produce; in Byron we are always reminded that we are looking through a medium and are assuming the impressions of another ...[14]

Notice that "we" don't want to see the woods and fields and streams through Byron's eyes or anyone else's, not even our own. Rather, we want to see these ordinary objects from the standpoint of those "emotions and associations" that these objects may be said, generally speaking, to inspire. Nevertheless it is pointedly the author who needs to stand aside, not stand out, a lesson that upstarts like Southey and Wordsworth might also take to heart, for, according to another reviewer, both give off

a disinclination to consult the precise intellectual tone and spirit of the average mass to whom their works are presented ... [T]heirs is a poetry of soliloquy. They write apart from and above the world. Their original object seems to be the employment of their faculties and the gratification of their poetical propensities.[15]

On the other hand, a local talent like William Cullen Bryant is praised for delineating natural objects in a way to suggest that a "common property has come into his hands to be invested with qualities, uses, associations ... [without] the slightest attempt to force upon it unnatural virtues or relations, or to connect it with feelings to which it could not have given birth."[16] To accomplish this it is best for the author to abandon himself or herself to the flow of perceptions as they course through the mind. As Bryant himself puts it,

To us there is something exceedingly delightful in the reckless intoxication with which this author surrenders himself to the enchantment of that multitude of glorious and beautiful images that come crowding upon his mind, and that infinity of analogies and relations between the natural objects, and again between these and the moral world, which seem to lie before him wherever he turns his eyes. The writings of no poet seem to be more the involuntary overflowing of his mind.[17]

Even as Bryant here alludes to Wordsworth's famous definition of poetry as "the spontaneous overflow of powerful feeling recollected in tranquility," we see the difference in emphasis. Where Wordsworth is interested in the flow of feeling as part of the composition of the self, Bryant is interested in the overflow – that alone is what matters. No more concerned with natural objects in themselves than with the poet's developing relationship to nature, Bryant is captivated by the cascading rush of images that make every author into another spectator. From this standpoint, it seems fitting that one of the country's first acclaimed poems, Bryant's own "Thanatopsis," should be so intent on taking an inventory of people's various, stock responses to nature that outside of a handful of perfunctory epithets – "venerable woods," "complaining brooks," meadows green" – it has no real interest in describing the landscape itself, much less in disclosing the author's personal connection to it.

> To him who in the love of Nature holds
> Communion with her visible forms, she speaks
> A various language; for his gayer hours
> She has a voice of gladness, and a smile
> And eloquence of beauty, and she glides
> Into his darker musings, with a mild
> And healing sympathy, that steals away
> Their sharpness ere he is aware ...[18]

Pondering the "public benefit" conferred by literature, Bryant writes in his review of *Redwood*: "it is as if one were to discover to us rich ores and gems lying in the common earth about us."[19] The image of gems lying upon the ground, produced by no one's labor but simply there, is literary nationalism's equivalent of that procession of "perceptions and ideas" unfolding in the mind that first intrigued Kames and that writers like Bryant attempt to recreate on the page.

In "Some Sources of Poetic Inspiration" from *Democracy in America*, Tocqueville spells out the political impulses behind this aversion to personal expressiveness. He starts by suggesting that "none of the single, nearly equal, roughly similar citizens of a democracy will do as a subject for poetry, but the nation itself calls for poetic treatment. The very likeness of individuals, which rules them out as subjects for poetry on their own, helps the poet to group them in imagination and make a coherent picture of the nation as a whole."[20] Because perceived likenesses among individuals preclude a poetic interest in any one of them, democratic expression takes as its subject the group – "the spirit of the average mass." And this of course is what literary nationalism seeks to do. Its quest to locate objects rich in association is an attempt to "make a coherent picture" of the feelings of a mass subject. Associationist theory proves congenial to the nationalist not only because it offers a lexicon for codifying the experience of converging perception but because it affirms that this convergence may in itself be a source of aesthetic pleasure. Essentially hostile to authorial subjectivity, it is, at least in principle, equally indifferent to the subjectivity of the reader, though, as I've been suggesting, it is significant that authorial aggrandizement occasioned much more concern than the possibility of wayward or undisciplined responses in the reader. By implication acts of writing are aligned with the part or individual unit; they bear the impress of agency that must be suppressed or transcended. Acts of reading, in turn, encompass the whole; they lend themselves to the general, abstract, or universal. Sensing precisely this development, Tocqueville predicts that the democratic poet, in forsaking a preoccupation with "external appearance" that characterized the productions of his aristocratic forbears, will turn to "the dark corners of the human heart," albeit in a manner that, paradoxically enough, does not concern "the actions of an individual." For in the same way that the purpose of literature for the nationalist is not to express my feelings or your feelings but the feeling that most would be likely to have, Tocqueville's democratic poet aspires to "glimpse the soul itself."[21]

Indeed, the same mistrust of experience that cannot be generalized ultimately applies to objects as well. As Charvat says of the theories of Kames and disciples like Hugh Blair and Archibald Alison, "description is a means, not an end," which is simply to say that the object itself, like Whitman's blade of grass or Melville's doubloon, serves as the point of departure for "that infinity of analogies and relation between the natural objects," before which "the author surrenders himself."[22] So while the literary nationalist requires an assortment of ready-made emblems, types, and touchstones connected to a particular place and a particular time, it is their suggestiveness that is most coveted. "The view of the house where one was born, of the school where one was educated, and where the gay years of infancy were passed" may initially be of interest only to those involved, but as Alison points out, over time "they lead altogether to so long a train of feelings and recollections that [they] ... raise emotions for which we cannot well account; and which, though perhaps very indifferent in themselves, still continue, from this association, and from the variety of conceptions which they kindle in our minds, to be our favorites through life."[23] This sort of journey from an object world fixed in space and time (home, school, years of infancy) to the haze of inscrutable association resembles Channing's dual insistence that a foreign visitor could not possibly understand American settings *and* that Americans who do understand these settings will find themselves carried away by "an inward and inexplicable joy, like a tale of childhood." In each case, a condition of charmed bafflement takes hold of the perceiver and serves to confirm the extravagance, as Thoreau might call it, of association – its wandering away from subject and object alike.

Conceivably, this progressive distancing of experience from its ostensible source could, unchecked, lead to a string of "feelings and recollections" sustained entirely by their own internal momentum, cut loose from any specifiable referent. In the early years of the nineteenth century, the paradigmatic case of this sort of free-floating affect would invariably concern loss and mourning. "For," as Archibald Alison adds at the end of the passage cited a moment ago, seeking to describe the quintessentially evocative moment, "we are somehow affected by those very places in which we behold the footsteps of those whom we love and admire." Mute traces of a departed, beloved object that "somehow affect" us, giving rise to a chain of conventional associations: perhaps it's not surprising that associationist principles, with their frequent allusions to childhood and the domestic circle, should lead us to the doorstep of the sentimental lyric.

SIGOURNEY'S TWILIGHT MUSING

"They're here, in this turf-bed – those tender forms," read the opening lines of Sigourney's "Burial of Two Young Sisters," "So kindly cherished and so fondly lov'd, / *They're here*" (text's emphasis).[24] They're forms, the sisters, presumably because in dying so young – "how quick the transit to the silent tomb" – their souls have gone straight "to that better land." But they are also forms, here on the page, a procession of poeticisms and figures of speech (e.g., "fair buds," "blooming ones," "your treasures") that leaves the reader with the vague impression that the act of describing has lost touch with its ostensible purpose, the description of two young sisters. And indeed even in life they barely come alive, so abstract and generic is the narrator's language: "I do remember them, their pleasant brows / So mark'd with pure affection, and the glance / Of their mild eyes." If Bryant begins "Thanatopsis" by giving us an account not of nature's "visible forms" but of people's responses to them, Sigourney can appear to take such a practice a step further by evoking figures who already seem the distillation of such responses, self-consciously encrypted "forms" of convention.

Admittedly, poets like Sigourney would seem, at first glance, poor candidates for illustrating Tocqueville's thesis about democratic art and its

alleged antipathy to personal expressiveness – to the idea, more exactly, that
thoughts and feelings must belong to the whole and not the part. Isn't
Sigourney regularly scolded for an excessive interest in the purely "private
and personal?" Doesn't she emerge from a tradition that "tended to narrow
poetry's authority to the fields of personal or interpersonal emotions?"[25] But
as we've seen with Baym's characterization of this verse, an exclusive
emphasis on the personal can quickly turn impersonal, leading one to ask
where its true interests lie. Adopting a tone of heightened reserve that runs
counter to common assumptions about self-indulgent emotionality, her
consolation verse, with its iconography of polished brows, tinted cheeks,
and fervid limbs, resolutely keeps us on the outside. "Sigourney's aesthetic
was impersonal by design," writes Eliza Richards, in the best short account
of the poet we have, "[she] presided over an emotional transmission
between readers and poems which preferred immediate and complete
understanding."[26] No doubt it is this kind of transparency that stands
behind the otherwise inexplicable fact that Sigourney's writing was so
often singled out for praise by her contemporaries on account of its "entire
freedom from artificiality."[27] In giving us instantly recognizable pictures
charged with visceral emotion, her vignettes of domestic sorrow suggest that
all we need do is perceive the image to be touched by it. The alleged
hegemony of the "merely" personal in Sigourney is in this respect somewhat
misleading.

More to the point, perhaps, Sigourney works from a finite, well-defined,
and stable stock of recurring images and highly stereotyped scenarios.
Inevitably, the constant recycling of themes and motifs creates an impression of interchangeable parts; her practice of quarrying poems from previously published books and recombining them into separate volumes
dedicated to a specific topic like temperance (*Water-Drops*, 1848), ships at
sea (*Poetry for Seamen*, 1845), flowers (*The Voice of Flowers*, 1848), or famous
American places (*Scenes of My Native Land*, 1843) simply instances on a
larger scale a procedure that can be seen at work in the composition of
individual poems. Inevitably, too, as one reads of infants cloaked in floral
imagery and of flowers suffering an early death, the reader cannot avoid
forming the impression of an ur-Sigourney lyric, a hidden template from
which variations are spun off. And indeed the sheer breadth of topics
covered by Sigourney is in large part owing to its underlying uniformity
of manner: apostrophes to a cactus, "Pelicans on the Lake of Galilee," the
heroes of Bunker Hill, a goose, Western homesteaders, "African Mothers at
their Daughters' Grave," a dead canary; satires on "Gregory Brandon
(Executioner of Charles the First)" or Napoleon; celebrations of the

admission of Michigan to the Union, Shakespeare, a shred of linen, a clock in Versailles, "Moravian Missions to Greenland"; retellings of Noah's Ark or Pocahantas – it seems that anything that caught her eye or her fancy got written down. As she writes of the Muse in a poem of that name, "at home or abroad, on the land or the sea, / Wherever it came, it was welcome to me."[28] Her ambitious reach no doubt reflects the pride and determination of a gardener's daughter who, while fortunate to win the favor of a wealthy patron early in her career, was entirely self-taught. The omnivorous, apparently indiscriminate receptivity of her verse calls to mind another autodidact, a carpenter's son, who loved to mix the lofty and the mundane in his own work.

Nothing better illustrates the principle of interchangeability in Sigourney's writing than the dead or dying infant or child. For, not to be too crude about it, in the baby we have the prototypical type, a human being who is not yet fully a person, a presence devoid of, well, presence. Judged according to the needs of a truly democratic literature, the infant makes a natural fit, capable of generating volumes of feeling while retaining no real identity. Whatever experience we may ascribe to the child is largely prospective and therefore hypothetical; like the gems of the literary nationalist that are strewn about or immediately underneath the ground, it is experience that has not yet been claimed. Since there is no psychology to penetrate, no essence to distill, no separateness to overcome, the dead child seems the very emblem of an impersonal, generalized subject. Whereas the children depicted in the writings of Goethe, Wordsworth, or Freud typically serve to project a rich and compelling inwardness, a widespread theme whose evolution Carolyn Steedman has so richly brought to light, Sigourney's aesthetic is notable for moving precisely in the opposite direction.[29]

The lingua franca of middlebrow culture for much of the nineteenth century, the child elegy was arguably the first manifestation of a legitimately democratic taste in the United States. As much at home on the prairie as in the literary salon, in the local newspaper as in the expensive gift books of the antebellum period, written by professors at Harvard and native women on the reservation, collected and circulated among family members on the farm and in the city, it forged, with its quaint diction, lockstep rhythm, and stilted mannerisms, a common literary idiom that cut across lines of gender, class, race, and region. Here was a theme, as Whitman might say, that was creative and had vista. In Sigourney's case, this particular aesthetic opportunity is exploited to its fullest extent, for in her elegies the grieving mother above all emerges as an exemplary beholder transfixed by the otherworldly sublimity of her relationship to the "cherish'd babe." This latter figure is valorized not (or not only) for its moral purity but for its fecundity as a "fount of thought" that does not itself think and as a source of images that does not itself imagine. Although the following lines from "Death of an Infant in Its Mother's Arms" begin by speaking of the mother charming the son, the general emphasis appears to flow in the opposite direction, with the mother described by the narrator as intently taking in a "daily lesson" whose content is left unspecified:

> Full was thy lot of blessing,
>   To charm his cradle-hours,
> To touch his sparkling fount of thought,
>   And breathe his breath of flowers,
> And take thy daily lesson
>   From the smile that beam'd so free,
> Of what in holier, brighter realms,
>   The pure in heart must be.
>
> No more thy twilight musing
>   May with his image shine,
> When in the lonely hour of love
>   He laid his cheek to thine;
> So still and so confiding
>   That cherish'd babe would be,
> So like a sinless guest from heaven,
>   And yet a part of thee.[30]

"[A] part of thee," the infant also stands apart, a figure of primal blessedness. Trailing clouds of glory, his heart is "pure" not just in the sense of being uncorrupted but in being a virtual, virginal text: to "touch" his thought and "breathe" his breath is to act as the enraptured medium for inarticulate, because as yet unlived, experience. Altogether the child seems less an object of love than wonder. His primary role, it would seem, is to act as a figure that stimulates the mother's imaginings.

In this way the child serves much the same purpose as the remembered landscape or resonant object. True, we do not necessarily witness him generating that "multitude of glorious and beautiful images that come crowding upon [the] mind" described by Bryant, but even so it remains striking that Sigourney's stricken infants become the focal point for a kind of speculative musing as much as for outright dread and anxiety. (This is indeed transparently the case in a certain type of poem – "Filial Claims" or "The Little Hand" are good examples – where the speaker daydreams at length over the multiple possible futures her [living] child might have.) So marked is this speculative tone that it often becomes apparent that the more the mother contemplates the child, the more the two identities begin to mirror one another until they appear interchangeable, one no less impressionable than the other. As "The Sick Child" unfolds, for instance, it becomes increasingly difficult to tell the experience of the mourner apart from that of the mourned. The poem begins:

> Thy fever'd arms around me,
>   My little, suffering boy –
> Tis better thus with thee to watch,
>   Than share in fashion's joy. (SP, 91)

The mother, oddly, is not watching the boy, but watching with him, as if the two, perfect equals, were jointly engaged in the same activity. But perhaps this is nothing more than a stray impression – perhaps we are simply meant to infer that the mother, happy to be with her son especially in his distress, is keeping a watch on his condition. But after three stanzas expatiating on the emptiness of "fashion's joy," the poem begins to suggest that this peculiar construction of watching with the boy may be of some importance after all:

> I knew not half how precious
>   The cup of life might be,
> Till o'er thy cradle bed I knelt,
>   And learn'd to dream of thee;
>
> Till at the midnight hour I found
>   Thy head upon my arm,
> And saw thy full eye fix'd on mine,
>   A strong, mysterious charm;
>
> Till at thy first faint lisping
>   That tear of rapture stole,
> Which ever as a pearl had slept
>   Deep in the secret soul. (SP, 92)

Kneeling over the cradle containing her sleeping boy, the mother learns to dream; gazing upon her child, the mother finds his gaze already fixed on her; hearing the child's first furtive attempts at language, the mother tries to articulate what the rapture that steals into her consciousness feels like. The pattern of doubling reverses Wordsworth's iconic image of the infant imbibing or "drinking in" the mother's presence, for here it's the mother who has been bewitched and transfixed by "a strong, mysterious charm" associated with the child.

The succession of dream, charm, and rapture makes it seem as though the mother's joy in her son is on a par with a spectator's delight in a work of art. This is not quite the same thing as saying that the mother "aestheticizes" the sick child, for to do that the mother would actually need to see the boy. It seems preferable to say that the child offers an incitement to the mother to engage in a kind of reverie – that rather than being an object you look at or watch, he is something you "watch with" – a vehicle that moves the beholder into a state of abstraction, leading her "deep in the secret soul." What lies "deep in the secret soul" is of course no more the mother's experience than the child's but the primal affection that mesmerizes both. Since it is in the nature of this "strong, mysterious charm" to lift both mother and son out of their identities, the boundaries between each break down. Thus, while it may seem as though the remaining five stanzas of the poem basically forget the child, that's because he has become so thoroughly absorbed into the mother, who herself begins, in turn, more and more to resemble the child. Abruptly startled from her daydreaming by "that start, that cry, that struggle" of the child who of course has likewise awakened from his slumber, the mother shifts the poem's term of address from "my little, suffering boy" to "my God," and implores the latter to "send forth thy strength to gird me." The boy's previously described fevered, feeble, and utterly vulnerable state is now transferred to the mother as she portrays herself as "but clay" and "a bruised reed" who needs divine strength "to wring out sorrow's dregs," as if sorrow were a fever that needed to be purged from her system. The final line, addressed to the heavenly father, "Oh! Not my will but thine" (SP, 93) crowns this development by making the mother another helpless dependent. The degree to which the child sets off in the mother a chain of identifications is so pronounced that by the end of the poem it is impossible to say for sure if the child has in fact died or if the mother is in the grip of a fantasy that cannot be shaken.

The reverie-inducing power of the boy in the first half of "The Sick Child" is merely a local instance of a more diffuse style adopted in many of Sigourney's best and most memorable poems, written mostly in blank verse and in a self-consciously dreamlike manner. "The Mourning Lover," "Death Among the Trees," "Twilight," "Dream of the Dead," and a number of other meditations conjure a dreamscape occupying a borderland between the real and the imaginary. A staple of antebellum literary expression prominently featured in the short stories of Irving, the early sketches of Hawthorne, or in Bryant's and Poe's verse, the reverie profiles an individual observer whose plotless musings are set forth in an invariably brooding, vaguely melancholy tone. Sigourney's adaptation of this mode, in evoking the talismanic power of maternal love, sometimes produces a state of absorption so intense that it cannot be broken; more often, of course, the spell is indulged only to be shattered by the intrusion of the "spoiler," death. The result, especially in the latter case, can be wrenching, producing its own kind of strange beauty. A fine example may be found in "The Lost Darling," which starts by outlining an idyllic past that we already know is doomed to be short-lived.

> She was my idol. Night and day, to scan
> The fine expansion of her form, and mark
> The unfolding mind, like vernal rose-bud, start
> To sudden beauty, was my chief delight.
> To find her fairy footsteps following mine,
> Her hand upon my garments, or her lip
> Long sealed to mine, and in the watch of night
> The quiet breath of innocence to feel
> Soft on my cheek, was such a full content
> Of happiness, as none but mothers know.
>   Her voice was like some tiny harp that yields
> To the slight fingered breeze, and as it held
> Brief converse with her doll, or playful soothed
> The moaning kitten, or with patient care
> Conned o'er the alphabet – but most of all,
> Its tender cadence in her evening prayer
> Thrilled on the ear like some ethereal tone
> Heard in sweet dreams. (SP, 150)

The speaker's rapt attention, focused not just on the child's past existence but on the future she will not be allowed to enjoy, creates the impression of someone musing over an object, lost in the "full content / Of happiness." Appropriately, the child is all activity and motion, expanding, "unfolding," "start[ing]," "following," "convers[ing]," "sooth[ing]," and so on, while the mother portrays herself as so engrossed in "delight" as to "find," as if in a dream, "footsteps following mine" and a "hand upon my garments." And indeed the footsteps are not just footsteps but "fairy footsteps," the implication being, of course, that the child is not just a delicate, fragile "form" but that as an "idol" of the mother's heart she is already crossing over into a realm of fantasy. The child, or more exactly the child's unclaimed experience, her future life, is manifestly a text that is there for the mother "to scan" and "mark."

Thus, even as we are told that "none but mothers know" the bliss here described, it's important to note that the significance of the mother is not to nurture or to form the child's identity. The significance of the mother is to behold, to serve as a proxy for the reader – any reader. Her trance-like passivity in the opening lines (e.g., it is the child's "lip / Long sealed to mine" and not the other way around, the peculiar self-distancing in the description of "The quiet breath of innocence ... Soft on my cheek") anticipates her role as an unseen presence who eavesdrops upon the child absorbed in her daily activities. Once again we see how the mother is less a privileged creator of life than an enthralled witness to its bringing forth. It's not just that Sigourney eliminates from the scene all other presences – father, sisters, brothers, and so on. Interaction between mother and daughter is itself pared away, superseded by the bond between mother and reader as both are lost in the contemplation of a vanished object rich in remembered associations.

In due time, of course, a third party does intervene. The pathos of the poem consists in the mother's attempts to sustain her "twilight musing" in the face of God and his overly controlling designs. As in "The Sick Child," the crisscrossing identities are noteworthy: just as the child is portrayed, endearingly, engaged in adult-like activities – conversing with her doll, consoling her kitten, saying her evening prayers – the speaker portrays herself in the second half of the poem as, tragically, playing at the role of mother, clinging to a role that can only be mimicked. And just as her identification with the child is made transparent with parallelisms such as that between the wish to quiet the child ("Hush thee, dearest") and the need to calm herself (e.g., "Be still, my heart!"), equally obvious is the anger that must be suppressed even if it can't be ignored.

> But now alone I sit,
> Musing of her, and dew with mournful tears
> Her little robes, that once with woman's pride
> I wrought, as if there were a need to deck
> What God hath made so beautiful. I start,
> Half fancying from her empty crib there comes
> A restless sound, and breathe the accustomed words
> "Hush! Hush thee, dearest." Then I bend and weep –
> As though it were a sin to speak to one
> Whose home is with the angels.

> Gone to God!
> And yet I wish I had not seen the pang
> That wrung her features, nor the ghastly white
> Settling around her lips. I would that Heaven
> Had taken its own, like some transplanted flower
> Blooming in all its freshness.

> Gone to God!
> Be still, my heart! what could a mother's prayer,

In all the wildest ecstasies of hope,
Ask for its darling like the bliss of Heaven? (SP, 151)

The repetition of the exclamation "Gone to God!" is of course a giveaway
that the speaker continues in a state of shock, whatever pieties she may find
herself mouthing. Her efforts at self-persuasion call to mind some of Emily
Dickinson's dramatic monologues where angry young women endeavor,
with mixed results, to reason their way out of disillusion, anger, or outright
cynicism. Sigourney does not go this far – in the end she wants to underscore rather than question the need to render back to God what rightfully
belongs to him. Even so, it's clear that the very intensity of the reverie
sustaining the daughter's image only makes divine judgment look all the
more petty and appropriative.

The least eschatological of poets, Sigourney's verse is essentially indifferent to questions about the afterlife and its mysteries. Indeed, given the pre-
packaged moralizing that dominates so much of her writing, it can perhaps
go without saying that she never sees her verse as a place for moral
deliberation, much less the working out of moral conflict. With respect to
her child elegies in particular, she may characterize her doomed infant as a
"sinless guest from heaven" and the mother as in touch with "holier,
brighter realms," but the actual state of one's soul never emerges as much
of a concern. (Thus the anger of the speaker against God appearing at
the end of a poem like "The Lost Darling" is something that may be
acknowledged but not pursued.) From the standpoint of critics like Ann
Douglas, this lack of theological seriousness is the root of the evil that is
sentimentalism.[31] On this still very widespread and powerful view, anti-
intellectualism, commodification, a weakness for easy vicarious pleasures,
and various other sins of self-indulgence associated with sentimental
culture – all may be traced back to a failure of spiritual rigor and honesty.
Judged against the poems we've been attending to, this notion of an
unpardonable moral slackness in the sentimentalist is, even if tendentious,
not altogether wrong. Toned down, there is clearly something to be said for
the view that moral concerns play a marginal or token role in Sigourney's
verse, however much she has come to be regarded as purveyor of middle-
class moralism, especially as regards the incorruptible purity of mothers.
The crass, almost offhanded brutality of the Lord's behavior in a poem like
"The Cheerful Giver," for example (espying a "tender flower," the "Father
Supreme" [SP, 27] demands it; the mother balks, whereupon Father
Supreme reproaches her, irritably reminding her that "He, who asked of
thee, loveth a *cheerful giver*" [SP, 28; original emphasis]), is so cartoon-like as

to suggest less a cunningly veiled critique of patriarchy than the diffidence of a writer whose willingness to confront difficult moral issues is more perfunctory than real. Because the moralist's mask, in other words, is so obviously put on, it cannot but seem disposable.

To sharpen our sense of what is at stake here and cast it in a somewhat less judgmental light, it is worth shifting the topic slightly and looking at a strain of commentary fairly prominent in the literature of the child in this period. Readers familiar with *Lyrical Ballads* will recall any number of poems ("We are Seven," "Anecdote for Fathers," "The Thorn" are among the most memorable) dramatizing the cognitive violence done to children by overweening, insecure adults anxious to impose their understanding on the innocent. In the same vein, recent scholars investigating the social construction of childhood have documented the many ways in which children are manipulated and coerced by various forms of ideological control.[32] The common concern of these critiques, nothing if not moral, is the failure of one consciousness to respect the sanctity of another's. Sigourney does not share this concern. She is not interested in a sick child, she's interested in "The Sick Child" – like the reviewer who wants to see the French nobleman, English governor, or Indian chief she is interested in types – "The Mourning Lover," for example, or "The Mourning Daughter," or "The Consumptive Girl," or "The Mother." Worries over one consciousness encroaching upon another have little purchase in a world that sets so little store in the propriety or boundedness of mental constructs. Thus in "Thought" she expresses a fear of thought – a fear that has nothing to do with the content of any particular thought and still less to do with scruples over intellectual aggression. Instead, the reason to "beware of thought" is that thought, a vagrant, impalpable, and utterly impersonal force, is wont to affix itself to a particular subject. As it turns out, the culprit responsible for this is God himself.

> Stay, winged thought! I fain would question thee;
> Though thy bright pinion is less palpable
> Than filmy gossamer, more swift in flight
> Than light's transmitted ray.
>
> Art thou a friend?
> Thou wilt not answer me. Thou hast no voice
> For mortal ear. Thy language is with God.
> – I fear thee. Thou'rt a subtle husbandman,
> Sowing thy little seed, of good or ill,
> In the moist, unsunn'd surface of the heart.
> But what thou there in secrecy dost plant

Stands with its ripe fruit at the judgment-day.
– What hast thou dared to leave within my breast? (SP, 84)

With lighthearted earnestness, Sigourney sexualizes the associationist view that feelings and ideas operate by a will of their own, leaving the agent a baffled bystander. Turning the tables on the conventional wisdom that says a woman can never be too careful, the analogizing of thought to seed is used to suggest that choosing "good" thoughts over "ill" is simply beside the point. Rather, the mere fact that thought finds a host, takes on bodily form, and thereby becomes attached to a subject is enough to provoke consternation. Strange as it seems to put the two names in one sentence, Sigourney here captures what Nietzsche, a few decades later, would spend a great deal of time expounding – that morality requires an accountable agent capable of taking ownership of its beliefs and desires. It's typical of Sigourney that she should treat this demand for individuation as an unsettling development: "Beware of thoughts. They whisper to the heavens. / Though mute to thee, they prompt the diamond pen / Of the recording angel" (SP, 85). Whereas Wordsworth fears the violation of one individual consciousness by another, "Thought" implies that we should equate the emergence of the individual as such with a violation. Discovering oneself to be the author of one's own thought (whatever that thought may signify) is experienced retroactively as a transgression – indeed, a kind of rape.

Accusing the sentimentalist of moral shiftlessness thus begs the question of what kind of morality makes an appearance in her pages and why. And in fact it is worth asking whether it's not the technology that accompanies moral assessment, as opposed to morality itself, that's really at issue here. In our prior discussion of literary nationalism we saw a tendency to conceive of writing in terms of the individual unit or the part, a correlation which in turn suggests that writing, like the "diamond pen" of "the recording angel," is above all concerned with acts of particularizing, discriminating, and ranking. Correspondingly, the God who appears in Sigourney's elegies is a figure of authorial intrusion who is responsible for shattering the mournful reveries of the mother and for holding errant thought to account. "Heaven records … [E]ach deed that shuns the light / Each word that melted into air," she writes in "The Past."[33] The exact antithesis to the reverie, divine judgment hunts down every stray thought and rather obsessively insists on attaching it to an agent: "The very thoughts that in their birth / Sank motionless and dead, / All have their impress on that page / Which at God's bar is read." Perfectly conventional as the notion that God remembers everything is, one cannot miss the implication that a mindless rigor informs

His writing. The labor involved is nothing short of superhuman. Conversely, when Sigourney tells us in her preface to *Select Poems* that what lies within the volume are purely "extemporaneous productions" composed during "short periods of time," her point is that their very brevity may be taken as a sign of their artlessness, of their distance from a controlling will. If the disavowal of authorship is an enabling fiction for the poet (the same preface goes on to compare her compositions to "wild flowers" that "sprang up wherever the path of life chanced to lead" and that she has "gathered" [SP, 9]), no such fiction may be countenanced in heaven, where even the most fleeting and stillborn of thoughts must be tagged and taken to the grave.[34]

By now it will be obvious that the appeal of the poetic reverie is that it is a mode of discourse that blurs the difference between an organizing will and objects of perception, so much so that, in Sigourney's case, the objects themselves start to lose their salience. Bryant, as we've seen, reserves his highest praise for the author who "surrenders himself" to "the enchantment" of a "multitude" of images as they cascade through the mind, a way of speaking about literature he picked up from his study of Alison's writings, which are filled with effusions over those "trains of imagery" in which "no labor of thought, or habits of attention are required; they rise spontaneously to the mind ... and lead it almost insensibly along, in a kind of bewitching reverie, through all its store of pleasing and interesting conceptions."[35] Almost by definition, indistinctness is a hallmark of the self-effacing style demanded by the poetic reverie, as can be seen in the incessant use of the word "form" in Sigourney's verse – "those gentle forms / Of faithful friendship and maternal love" ("Dream of the Dead" [SP, 302]). The moment of crisis, on the other hand, looms when objects become overly distinct, when their "form" begins to look as though they might indeed have a form. In "The Mourning Lover," this moment arrives when the poem's eponymous heroine, resolved to cherish the memory of her beloved's "noble form" by remaining forever celibate, is startled to find him intruding too visibly into the scene at one point in her musings. Pleasure, said to have "lost its essence" for the young woman with his early death, momentarily takes on an unmistakably masculine shape, thereby breaking the spell.

> She sought devotion's balm,
> And, with a gentle sadness, turned her soul
> From gaiety and song. Pleasure, for her,
> Had lost its essence, and the viol's voice
> Gave but a sorrowing sound. Even her loved plants
> Breathed too distinctly of the form that bent

With hers to watch their budding. 'Mid their flowers,
And through the twining of their pensile stems,
The semblance of a cold, dead hand would rise,
Until she bade them droop and pass away
With him she mourned. (SP, 295)

Merely the part of a part, the "cold, dead hand" of the lover is no sooner glimpsed than dismissed, and so melts back into the scenery.

Suffused in a verbal wash of melancholy, a poem like "The Mourning Lover" leads the reader insensibly along, so that merely to pause and note, say, the phallic overtones of the lover's momentary appearance seems an impertinence. Victorian propriety aside, what's objectionable would not be the obvious eroticism but the idea that one object might stand out and be elevated (so to speak) above the others. Although it has become common-place to note sentimental culture's notorious fixation on objects, the dis-tribution of regard in these poems does more to thwart fetishism than encourage it. In "The Mourning Lover" the sheer profusion of images and scenes of blossoming, budding, ripening, and twining, used indiffer-ently to characterize "bright boyhood's charms," "manly beauty," the young woman's desolation (e.g., "blighted blossoms"), her "secret sorrow" and even her seemingly erotic musings, becomes an all-purpose signifier through which disparate bits of information are channeled and made interconnected. Because imputations of significance are thereby flattened or leveled out, the interpreter is left, as it were, with no choice. Even when Sigourney introduces that sentimental keepsake par excellence, a lock of hair from the departed, she does so in a way that embeds it in the expected complex of images, so that rather than denoting the grip of an imaginative obsession, the lock of hair seems to be called into being by its association with adjacent images, and therefore becomes merely one more item in a procession of things that materialize momentarily but can't stay separate for long:

One mild eve,
When on the foreheads of the sleeping flowers
The loving spring-dews hung their diamond-wreaths,
She from her casket drew a raven curl,
Which once had clustered on her loved one's brow,
And press'd it to her lips … (SP, 296)

As "the sleeping flowers," their "foreheads" kissed by the "loving" dew, dissolve into the image of "a raven curl," once "clustered" on the lover's "brow" and now kissed in turn, we see how a poetics of association, in working against the very idea of individuation, produces a web of connections that may go on indefinitely, overriding any temptation to dwell on one part at the expense of the rest.

This fluidity of association has its corollary in a stasis of character. Because Sigourney is very interested in types and not at all interested in the way individuals escape being typed, her characters cannot change. Stricken witnesses all, they do not act so much as exemplify. To say that the Mourning Lover bids the twining stems to "droop and pass away" or that she presses the beloved's lock of hair to her lips is simply to say that she is the Mourning Lover. Figures like the grieving mothers in "The Sick Child" or "The Lost Darling" seem closer to quasi-allegorical personae like Faith, Prudence, or Charity than actual characters that have preferences and make decisions. Now and then, as we've had occasion to note, a sense of psychological depth may be intimated, but this is hardly Sigourney's main interest. Neither, as a consequence, is moral judgment: if it's true that personal choice is more or less non-existent in her consolation verse, then it follows that the opportunity for moral evaluation, whether on the part of the author or the reader, is duly circumscribed. The point of a poem like "The Lost Darling" is, after all, neither to praise nor condemn the mother devastated by the loss of her daughter, any more than the point of "The Mourning Lover" is to praise or condemn a woman who spends a lifetime cherishing a secret sorrow. Even to say that these figures are meant to elicit our sympathy seems a mistake. To the extent that we are meant to identify with something, it is most obviously with a mood or an affect. Rather than a soul we glimpse, as Tocqueville puts it, "the soul itself" (486). We identify, as it were, with the spirit of identification.

From this standpoint, complaints about the ahistorical or apolitical nature of Sigourney's consolation verse could use some refining. It's not so much that a larger perspective or more encompassing context is missing or suppressed (for that's pretty much what such complaints, in all their vagueness, come down to), for just the opposite is the case. The bigger picture is all we have. The sick child has no name, no age, no past because the sick child is a part that has already been surrendered to the whole – to a transpersonal circuit of feeling that, like Emerson's Over-soul, is no respecter of persons. It's not, then, the withdrawal of an external context that's notable but the way in which the poem is drawn to totalize this idea. "I love everybody": Sigourney's reported last words, so often taken as a parody of sentimental fatuity, may also be taken as a token of the nearness of the social whole, where everybody has become a somebody that is more real and more important than anybody who might figure in the poem.[36] To be sure, stating the case in this manner may seem, here as indeed at various points throughout this section, as though I have simply seized upon older terms of opprobrium – the poet's unoriginality, her pandering to a mass public, her lack of emotional depth – and dressed it up in positive language. Be that as it may, my assumption has been that there is a coherent sensibility and consistent aesthetic at work in Sigourney's lyrics that can lead to a more informed appreciation of her artistic achievement once these features are brought to light.

BRINGING EQUALITY TO THE PAGE: "SONG OF MYSELF"

One can only guess at the bafflement of someone chancing upon a slim volume with a handsomely designed cover called *Leaves of Grass* when it was first published in the summer of 1855. Within he or she would have found a dozen untitled offerings of uncertain description (poems? chants? songs?) with nothing but a page break to separate them. Prefacing these productions was an essay in double columns that seemed neither prose nor poetry but a crazy hybrid of each. What would eventually be known as "Song of Myself," the longest stretch of writing in the collection, carried no numbered sections nor, for that matter, any readily discernible principle of development that might guide the reader from a beginning to a middle and an end. (The same could be said about the volume as a whole.) Aside from what could be deduced from the copyright page and gleaned from a quick and seemingly flippant reference within the text, there was no mention of an author. Improprieties of diction, grammar, syntax, prosody, and modes of address, to say nothing of a shocking candor about everything from armpits to foo foos, round out the picture of eccentricity and willful innovation.

The idea that *Leaves of Grass* forged an entirely new poetics goes back to Whitman himself, who once explained that early in his career he arrived at the realization that in order to do justice to a truly democratic society there needed to be "a readjustment of the whole theory and nature of poetry."[37] Since then it has become commonplace to say "Whitman invented poetic forms that honored a more egalitarian democracy"; that he engineered "a new participatory poetics [that not only] challenged boundaries between [speaker and listener] but tried to demolish such boundaries altogether"; and that he "revise[d] readerly subjectivity in the direction of a heightened, transforming sense of the constructedness and hence the dense politicality of all bodily experience, erotic and otherwise."[38] The organizing, explicit principle behind this revisionism is equality. As we are informed in the 1855 Preface, "the messages of great poets to each man and woman, are Come to us on equal terms. Only then can you understand us. We are no better than you."[39] By the turn of the century, it was common for figures such as Oscar Wilde and various other artists on the other side of the Atlantic to hail Whitman as "the herald to a new era ... the precursor of a fresh type."[40]

And yet one might, with equal justice, view *Leaves of Grass* as coming at the end rather than at the beginning of a long tradition in American letters. Without gainsaying either his genius or his originality, it's obvious that many of the features we take to be distinctively Whitman's – the privileging of the reader as a vital interlocutor, the muting of overt authorial judgment or invidious comparison, the use of rhetorical indeterminacy to blur differences between speaker and listener, the hostility to unduly idiosyncratic, non-generalizable experience – all had a long foreground somewhere. More pointedly, seeing Whitman as coming at the end of a tradition helps us account for what can only be called the peculiar *extremism* of his literary egalitarianism, a characteristic most notable in the determination of his verse not simply to affirm but to perform equality – to somehow actualize it on the page. "I shall be even with you and you shall be even with me" is the promise of a bard who likes to style himself "the equalizer of his land and age," and who invites us to think of his text as a sacrosanct space where inequalities among people, places, and things may be acknowledged but are also "averaged." ("I swear they are averaged now," says the speaker of "The Sleepers," "one is no better than the other" [133].) If there is an obvious sense in which Whitman has every right to claim his place beside the other immortals in F. O. Matthiessen's American Renaissance, that is not because the presuppositions and aesthetic aspirations underpinning *Leaves of Grass* are noticeably different from those of his immediate predecessors.

Not least of these presuppositions is, as we've seen, the notion of literature as a common property. Bryant's image of gems laying scattered about the ground or Sigourney's image of flowers randomly collected on the hillside have their counterpart in Whitman's picture of a table equally set, with no one slighted or turned away. For the same reason that a typical experience by definition cannot be limited to anyone's particular experience, meaning must be detached from subjects and made a common possession. And of course from the outset of "Song of Myself," his longest and most ambitious poem, Whitman is very particular about establishing the importance of these "equal terms," not only explaining that what belongs to us as good belongs to him but also giving fair warning that those who pride themselves on *mastering* meaning will only be wasting their time:

Have you reckoned a thousand acres much?
Have you reckoned the earth much?

Have you practiced so long to read?
Have you felt so proud to get at the meaning of poems?
Stop this day and night with me and you shall possess the origin of all poems,
You shall possess the good of the earth and sun ... there are millions of suns left,
You shall no longer take things at second or third hand ... nor look through the
    eyes of the dead ... nor feed on the spectres in books,
You shall not look through my eyes either, nor take things from me,
You shall listen to all sides and filter them from yourself. (26)

Casting aside the division of labor whereby the reader dutifully decodes the author's intent represents a crucial first step in the lessons of democratic hermeneutics. The poet does not settle upon, fix, master, demarcate, or stipulate meaning. Interestingly, this outlook produces a curious double-mindedness with respect to interpretation. Inasmuch as we are to take nothing on faith but "listen to all sides and filter them from [ourselves]," interpretation is a positive, empowering activity, an instrument for self-possession. On the other hand, inasmuch as the ultimate effect of encountering this text is to transcend it, interpretation is superfluous. For "the origin of all poems" is presumably no poem at all and thus something that neither reader nor author is in a position to possess exclusively, anymore than either is in a position to possess exclusively the earth and the sun. That archetype or ur-poem instead appears to connote or hint at something that surpasses textual representation, like the "lull" or the "hum" of the soul's "valved voice" described two sections later (28).

Conceivably, then, to "possess the origin of all poems" is to enjoy the charms of interactivity itself, the radical equality of speaker and listener anterior to the establishment of sense and the assignment of fixed roles. And indeed what organizes a text like "Song of Myself" is not a theme or even a cluster of themes so much as the ongoing pursuit by the reader of the poet, that shape-shifting, hectoring, seductive figure who begins with the invitation to "Stop this day and night with me" and concludes with the teasing assurance "I stop some where waiting for you" (86). It is not, in other words, meaning that drives the poem forward and gives it coherence. As has long been recognized, Whitman's poetic is largely organized around the suspension of sense, with his signature syntax of present participles and uncoiling sequences of nouns and adjectives serving to generate, as Angus Fletcher has most recently observed, "an impressionistic effect because the style uses unconnected ingredients, touches of color, [and] a general suppression of the superordinate control." "Song of Myself" thrives, that is to say, on the intransitive or what Fletcher calls "the pure verb, the verb before it is locked down into predication."[41] Resisting the pull of subject-verb-object,

Whitman's floating participles refuse to shut in and enclose thought. "You will hardly know who I am or what I mean," the bard writes, encouraging the reader to continue the pursuit beyond the bounds of the text, "[B]ut I shall be good health to you nevertheless" (86). The "good health" promised, like "the good of the sun and the earth," is expressly that which cannot be *meant*. Made vivid by virtue of Whitman's attempts to circumvent it, the connection between authorial meaning and coercion could not be more striking.

The full significance of this last point shall emerge shortly, but for the moment it's worth noting how the poet's compositional method adapts certain features of the associationist programme described earlier. In writing "Song of Myself" Whitman eschews both lyrical and dramatic formats, however much he may, from time to time, make use of them. More often than not he is drawn to contemplate a general experience, theme, or rubric and then go on to fill in its particular manifestations: here are some of the things I see and feel when thinking about harvest-time (Section 9); this is what I find myself imagining when I do nothing but listen (Section 27); these are some of the divinities that come to mind when I think of honoring all modes of worship (Section 43). This practice of exemplification alternates with statements of a more didactic, syntactically forthright nature (e.g., "I can resist anything better than my own diversity"), statements that are best described as sound bites rather than attempts to formulate a full-fledged poetic argument. This alternating rhythm is established from the outset of the poem, where the declarative pronouncements of Section 1 shift quickly into a leisurely unfolding of stray impressions and sensory experiences recounted in Section 2. The most famous instance of listing various associations brought to mind by a simple object occurs in the meditation on the grass in Section 6, where the poet abandons himself to the drift of its connotations while expressly inviting the reader to do the same:

A child said, What is the grass? fetching it to me with full hands;
How could I answer the child? ... I do not know what it is any more than he.

I guess it must be the flag of my disposition, out of hopeful green stuff woven.

Or I guess it is the handkerchief of the Lord,
A scented gift and remembrancer designedly dropped,
Bearing the owner's name someway in the corners, that we may see and remark, and say Whose?

Or I guess the grass itself is a child ... the produced babe of the vegetation.

Or I guess it is a uniform hieroglyphic,
And it means, Sprouting alike in broad zones and narrow zones,
Growing among black folks as among white,
Kanuck, Tuckahoe, Congressman, Cuff, I give them the same, I receive them the
    same.

And now it seems to me the beautiful uncut hair of graves. (29–30)

In sampling different possible meanings of the grass, the poet disarms the
wish to settle upon any one of them. With the beautiful reverie on the
"uncut hair of graves" that immediately follows this passage and that
concludes with the wish to "translate the hints" of the dead, he places
himself beside the reader, another interpreter of the text's mysteries.

Reflecting the same convergence of nationalist pride and associationist
principle we've been tracing throughout this chapter, Whitman makes
indeterminacy a pivotal feature of his new language of democracy.
Uncertainty liberates. "The expression of the American poet," he writes in
the 1855 Preface, "is to be transcendent and new," which is to say "it is to be
indirect and not direct or descriptive or epic" (8). If relics from the feudal
past like the epic or the pastoral are direct, the leaves of the bard, rich with
implication, are not. The aristocratic poet stipulates, the democratic bard
suggests. As inequality stands to the direct and the determinate, equality
stands to the indirect and the indeterminate. The less sure we are of the
poet's meaning, the more freedom we may claim as our own; the more
freedom we may claim as our own, the less likely we will view the author as
the sole arbiter and source of meaning. This of course is what critics like
David Reynolds, cited previously, have in mind in paying tribute to
Whitman's "participatory poetics" and what we can recognize as the codi-
fication of premises in circulation well before Whitman's appearance on the
scene. Because the essence of "the greatest poet [is] less a marked style" than
his becoming "the free channel of himself", understanding that "the
indirect is always as great and as real as the direct" is indispensable.[42]

Admiration for the poem's "indeterminate openness to experience" has
been a fixture in academic criticism for fifty years and more, although the
logic connecting "indeterminate" to "openness" is more often assumed than
analyzed.[43] In his influential account of Whitman's sexual politics, Michael
Moon expands upon essentially the same logic by opposing the "more
firmly grounded and determinate discourses of embodiment abroad in his
culture" to the poet's vision of the body as embracing "a range of
ungrounded possibilities standing in indeterminate relation" to these dominant discourses. Whereas Whitman's "cultural context," we are told,

"overwhelmingly privilege[d] the solid, the stable, the fixed, the restricted, and the reserved," *Leaves of Grass* asserts the primacy of "'fluidity' in the social, political, and 'natural' realms." The special distinction of his verse is to appropriate the fixed discourses of sexual embodiment of the time and "render the referents of those discourses indeterminate and fluid."[44] A case in point is the famous vignette of the twenty-ninth bather (Section 11 of "Song of Myself"), in which a "lady," gazing upon "twenty-eight young men [who] bathe by the shore," is swept away by the force, it would seem, of her own erotic daydreaming:

> Dancing and laughing along the beach came the twenty-ninth bather,
> The rest did not see her, but she saw them and loved them.
>
> The beards of the young men glistened with wet, it ran from their long hair,
> Little streams passed all over their bodies.
>
> An unseen hand also passed over their bodies,
> It descended tremblingly from their temples and ribs.
>
> The young men float on their backs, their white bellies swell to
>   the sun ... they do not ask who seizes fast to them,
> They do not know who puffs and declines with pendant and bending arch,
> They do not think whom they souse with spray. (34)

Taking issue with past readings that view this scene as representing either a thwarted female sexuality that bears no connection to the rest of "Song of Myself" or a thinly disguised homoerotic fantasy that makes the lady a proxy for the poet's own longings, Moon argues that both accounts artificially divide what Whitman seeks to merge and complicate. On his account, male homoeroticism and feminine sexuality are much more blurred than distinct, the whole point of the vignette being to project "a utopian space" that "effectively destabilizes the genders" of both the lady and the young men. Properly interpreted, for example, the "unseen hand" no more belongs to the woman than to the men but is in fact "a figure of intense indeterminacy" to the degree that it encompasses both and even extends to the "hand" of the poet himself. Just as the grass is a composite of many different meanings in one figure, so in the twenty-ninth bather we see Whitman "merging without excluding" a rich array of sexual identities.[45]

Such readings show clearly enough how the simple act of multiplying meaning may be considered to advance the project of realizing equality. Indeterminacy acquires a political significance because it *diffuses* authority so that the very idea of settling upon one meaning at the expense of another begins to look like an arbitrary imposition. In contemplating the array of significances evoked by the text, the interpreter is free to choose not to choose. If the female is equal to the male, then it is indeed a mistake to choose – a mistake to think, that is, that Section 11 is "about" male or female sexuality when it is in fact about both and neither. And if the reader and poet are equals, then it is of course a mistake to think that the poet shall dictate what the reader shall think. In this respect, critics like Moon are surely right to view "the exemplary indeterminacy fundamental to Whitman's writing" as a thoroughly political gesture responsive to the historical pressures of his time and calculated to alter certain attitudes in the dominant culture.[46]

But putting the point this way also suggests a certain irony. If the poet wants us to see that there are many meanings to the grass, then that intention is every bit as clear and as determinate as any other. If he wishes to fuse and confuse male and female desire to the point where they are hard to tell apart, then that too is a stable, fixed, and certain intention. If, in other words, Whitman's writing were as indeterminate as his critics make it out to be, then there would be no grounds for thinking that the grass has many meanings and not just one, no reason to believe that male and female desire have been joined in order to create a "utopian space." Of all the conceivable differences between Whitman's beliefs about the body and his culture's beliefs about the body, the one thing that *cannot* divide them is the notion that one belief is more or less indeterminate than the other. They must be determinate in different ways. From this standpoint, the "exemplary indeterminacy fundamental to Whitman's writing" must be a feigned indeterminacy. It is a picturesque notion, of a piece with the sentimentality that says that the poet breaks down the "boundaries" between speaker and listener or that he creates a "space" in which the reader is "no longer disturbed with doubts about his or her own subordinate position."[47]

So perhaps the real question regarding Whitman's attempt to democratize meaning is not how or whether he pulls it off but why he should wish to do so in the first place. Why, in particular, is it so important that we approach the poet on "equal terms"? The answer most commonly given just rephrases the question: the poet wants to establish a non-hierarchical relationship between author and reader – he wants to bring to bear the ideals of equality on the interpretive process itself. But, again, why should he wish to do that? Although many people can see the point of striving for political or economic or social equality, the point of striving for hermeneutic equality is harder to see. Obviously considerations of equality are important when it comes to adjudicating matters such as access, fair exchange, or competing models of rationality, as Habermas has argued, but this is not really what

Whitman has in mind. His objection to taking things at second or third hand or seeing things through his eyes is not, for example, aimed at protecting an "ideal speech situation" whose participants agree by prior accord neither to dominate nor deceive one another.[48] It is not the tyranny of any one interlocutor that concerns him but rather the tyranny of meaning itself. This is why the poet, in his role as "the free channel of himself," is "no arguer ... he is judgment" (13, 9). It's not that his propositions are wrong or right but rather that he has none to offer, for "he judges not as a judge judges but as the sun falling around a helpless thing" (9).

It may begin to seem, then, as though equality has been imported into an area where it has no meaningful role to play. Whereas a Shakespeare or Milton might worry about inequality in the real world, only the democratic bard, it seems, feels compelled to take on the added burden of worrying about it on the page. True, Whitman can often turn the very absurdity of this endeavor to advantage; when he intones "I shall be even with you and you shall be even with me" (88), part of the charm comes from our mutual awareness that he cannot be taken seriously.[49] At the same time, his determination not just to celebrate equality but to level the interpretive playing field is evidently taken seriously enough to lead, as we have seen, many of his readers to see it as the point of departure for a radical politics. But if this attempt to bring equality to the page amounts, ultimately, to nothing more than a category mistake (for I am no more oppressed by your meaning if it is transparent and well-grounded than I am freed from your meaning if it is opaque and ungrounded), then it would seem that Whitman's new language of equality, in undertaking to protect us against a tyranny that does not exist, merely ends up inventing a new form of inequality for us to fear.

Obviously Whitman's "barbaric yawp" (85) does much more than that, and it might be objected that I have slighted other features of the poem in pursuing the seemingly esoteric topic of hermeneutic equality. Have I forgotten the poet's boast that "I am large ... I contain multitudes" (85)? And yet it is precisely this determination to encompass the whole that accounts for the ban against meaning. We need to be protected against the inference that the bard means some particular thing by the grass because we need to stay with the whole, the true source of democratic art's legitimacy. Meaning, irreducibly individual, partial, private, infringes on that wholeness. It betrays the presence of a single, possessive will. This is why "Song of Myself" supplements the suggestion that it conveys a lot of different meanings for us to "guess at" with the more radical idea that the poem is essentially indifferent to meaning, especially as a token held out for us to "possess" or "get at." And indeed the wonder of that poem is that it succeeds so well, for stretches at a time, in producing the illusion of author and reader as bystanders witnessing the procession of people, places, and things, both parties watching and wondering at it, confident that everything has its place and its meaning but equally confident that any attempt to extrapolate a meaning would be wrongheaded. "O I perceive after all so many uttering tongues!" exclaims the poet as he continues to muse over "the beautiful uncut hair of graves" in Section 6, "And I perceive they do not come from the roofs of mouths for nothing" (30). He expresses the wish to "translate the hints" of these presences, but it is no surprise to discover that, like the bard himself ("I too am not a bit tamed ... I too am untranslatable" [85]), they remain unfathomable. Uttering tongues drifting away from any discernible body, voices cut loose from any signifying intent: to write equality is to honor its radical senselessness.

Inheriting a body of thought that privileges literary expression as a site where meaning circulates freely, untouched by the imposition of authorial will and guided by the experiences of a common, typical reader, the author of "Song of Myself" casts himself as a medium for common experience while luring the reader onstage as a quester in search of the poet's "faint clews and indirections" (14). Taking to heart Emerson's judgment that the poet is to "apprise us not of his wealth but of the commonwealth,"[50] his poem applies an unprecedented rigor to the concept of literary egalitarianism. "They shall not be careful of riches and privilege," says Whitman, describing "American bards" in the 1855 Preface, "they shall be riches and privilege" (14). In such moments, the idea that the poet means many different things by representing an object is replaced by the idea that he *becomes* the object, dispensing with the need for representation altogether. "[I] send no agent or medium... and offer no representative of value," proclaims the poet of "A Song for Occupations," which directly follows "Song of Myself" in the 1855 edition of *Leaves of Grass*. Rather, "[I] offer the value itself" (89). To offer the value itself is like reading, not a poem, but "the origin of all poems" (26), not a discourse, but the rudiments out of which a discourse might be built.

Ultimately it's difficult to avoid the suspicion that something like envy plays a role in the logic that equates the intent to mean with a wish to tyrannize. When Emerson tells us "the great poet makes us feel our own wealth, and then we think less of his compositions" – that "his best communication to our mind is to teach us to despise all that he has done" – it may seem as though literary theory had indeed become an exercise in *ressentiment*.[51] If, as we've seen, the perception that the authorial will is prone to cognitive imperialism, out of touch with the spirit of the average mass and betraying, ultimately, the estrangement of the one from the many, belongs to the earliest stages of US literary history, the refinement to this logic offered by figures such as Emerson and Whitman is to suggest that marking the very limits of that authorial will should help set the reader free. From this standpoint, Whitman's "participial thinking" or "participatory poetics," so far from offering an alternative to the notion that authorship is inherently autocratic and hierarchical, is nothing if not the purest possible tribute to the ongoing power of such associations.

CHAPTER FOUR

Comparatively speaking

In *Democracy in America*, envy is a recurrent theme. Called at one point "the democratic sentiment," it is distinguished from a "legitimate passion for equality which rouses in all men a desire to be strong and respected."[1] With the spread of democracy, envy progresses from an infirmity confined to one's own rank or caste to a genuinely public menace. Two salient features of democratic life, equality and mobility, are the perfect ingredients to insure its diffusion, for while an egalitarian culture renders comparisons among one's peers easy to make, the loosening of longstanding barriers to social mobility associated with the onset of equality also makes departures from the norm easy to see. "In democracies," Tocqueville explains, "private citizens see men rising from their ranks and attaining wealth and power in a few years; that spectacle excites their astonishment and their envy; they wonder how he who was their equal yesterday has the right to command them today." To ward off humiliation, the envious must concoct a plausible story to explain away the success of their rival: "[t]o attribute his rise to his talents or his virtues is inconvenient, for it means admitting that they are less virtuous or capable than he. They therefore regard some of his vices as the main cause thereof" (221). The reader of *Democracy in America* is likely to run across envy's submerged but pervasive influence in any number of domains, whether it be in the unmistakable mediocrity of the nation's elected officials (199), the contempt visited upon free blacks in Northern cities (355), or the intolerance of nonconformity in a country that supposedly prides itself on it (436).

Tocqueville never does isolate the phenomenon as such and examine it in a sustained way, perhaps for good reason. Because no one, then or now, has succeeded in coming up with a reliable method for establishing the difference between a "legitimate passion for equality" and an illegitimate one, attributions of envy are bound to be highly contested. It is a polarizing topic. For every partisan of the Right who tells horror stories of the mean-spirited have-nots dragging down the virtuous haves, we find partisans on the Left reluctant to concede that envy might be something more than a crutch for capitalist apologists bent upon trivializing the grievances of the downtrodden. Experts hoping to cross this divide meet with limited success: reading John Rawls's attempts to differentiate "excusable" envy from its more inexcusable counterparts or following the intricate guidelines surrounding Ronald Dworkin's "envy test" calls to mind Wallace Stevens's line about the helpless philosophers who still say helpful things.[2] Tocqueville, himself a French aristocrat, can often fall into the trap of using envy to pathologize working-class discontent, as when he tosses off generalizations about "this secret instinct leading the lower classes to keep their superiors as far as possible from the direction of affairs" (198). On the other hand, his interest in the structural closeness of democratic aspiration (it could be me) to embittered resentment (it should have been me) does point to a way of understanding envy's centrality as part of a larger dialectic rather than a mere reflex of "private dissatisfactions."[3] Indeed, when at one point he offers the observation that "in America I never met a citizen too poor to cast a glance of hope and envy towards the pleasures of the rich or whose imagination did not snatch in anticipation good things that fate obstinately refused to him" (531), we see in his phrasing the ease with which the two terms, hope and envy, can be made to appear as though they were interchangeable.

Beyond the controversies involved in simply *identifying* envy, then, there is the further complication of understanding its significance when thinking about the social whole. For envy is, at bottom, resentment triggered by departures from an undeclared norm. It wraps itself in the mantle of the typical, the average, or the normal, punishing those who stray from the fold. As Frances Ferguson has pointed out, whereas the other vices like gluttony or avarice or lust presuppose the existence of food or gold or bodies, one of envy's many peculiarities is that it doesn't appear to be centered upon objects in this way.[4] The affliction of the envious seems more general, their malice bound up, ultimately, not with this or that object but with their standing within the larger social field. If, as we saw in the previous chapter, the priority of the whole over the part exercises a formative influence on the imagination of poets like Sigourney and Whitman, here the same influence may be observed to a more destructive and more far-reaching effect. Envy may be regarded as a flashpoint where the instantaneous identification of the part with the whole that Tocqueville thought endemic to egalitarian cultures seizes up – where the individual's relation to cultural desire becomes an obsession that cannot get itself unstuck. As "concealed admiration," in Kierkegaard's memorable formulation, envy is "unhappy self-assertion."[5] To derive some sense of the many different guises this perversion of the social norm assumes in the literature of this period, the three texts forming the substance of this chapter approach "the democratic sentiment" from three distinctly different points of view. As we shall see, the first, *A New Home, Who'll Follow?* (1839), is written from the perspective of the envied; the second, *The House of the Seven Gables* (1851), from the perspective of the envious; and the third, *Our Nig* (1859), from the perspective of someone caught in between.

PRIDE AND PREJUDICE ON THE FRONTIER

In *A New Home, Who'll Follow?* (1839) Caroline Kirkland, writing under the pseudonym of Mary Clavers, recounts the innumerable hazards of settling in "the remote and lonely regions" of Michigan in the late 1830s.[6] Everything from mud-holes to rattlesnakes, rampant alcoholism to unscrupulous speculators, prairie fires to poisoned wells, makes life on the frontier a perilous proposition. Yet among these ordeals none is so harrowing as the prevalence of raw envy. Lured from New York by the availability of cheap land to the West, it does not take long for the Clavers' family to run up against this familiar vice. Touchy democrats, with their "air of insulted dignity" (47) and "jealous pride" (52), abound on the frontier, ready to take offense at the slightest provocation. Meeting her new neighbors, Kirkland finds, to her dismay, that each countenance wears a defiant expression proclaiming "they are 'as good as you are'" (53). Here on "the outskirts of civilization," where "the habits of society allow the maid and her mistress to do the honours in complete equality" (4), the least hint of standing out or standing apart counts as an unforgivable offense. Here in the wilderness, in other words, where society has barely taken hold, the most social of the seven deadly sins flourishes unchecked, the by-product of "an absolute democracy" that makes "the over-bearing pride and haughty distinctions of the old world" (139, 140) appear innocuous by comparison.

Somehow Kirkland never lets on that the mistrust of the local population might have something to do with her husband's status as the sole proprietor and chief landowner of the newly founded village of Montacute, the fictional name of the real-life Pinckney, Michigan. But if she stops short of drawing the obvious connection perhaps that is owing less to bad faith than to the necessity of *"wearing around"* local prejudices (52; original emphasis). As the narrator explains toward the end of the book, "the denizens of the crowded alleys and swarming lofts of the city" may now and then catch glimpses of "the lofty mansions [and] splendid equipages of the wealthy," but "the extreme width of the great gulf between" them serves as "almost a barrier, even to all-reaching envy." In the "ruder stages of society," however, differences in creature comforts may be comparatively slight but considerably magnified. In a word, "inequalities in the distribution of the gifts of fortune are not greater in the country than in town, but the contrary; yet circumstances render them more offensive to the less-favored class" (186). Needless to say, considering the "circumstances," one can never be too careful when speaking of one's possessions, especially when, as a matter of historical record, they comprise 1,300 acres of land and not a mere 200, which is the figure cited in the text.

Envy-avoidance is in fact a dominant theme in *A New Home*. Mary Clavers learns its lessons the hard way when her family is stricken by rheumatic fever and nobody in the area comes to their aid (61). Soon thereafter she vows to do everything she can "to live down the impression that I felt *above* my neighbours" (65; original emphasis), even if this means putting up with (male) guests who use the chimney as if it were a handkerchief or (female) guests who drop in uninvited, smoke in her home without asking permission, and then accuse the hostess of snobbery when she confesses that the practice makes her uncomfortable (53, 56). It's not altogether clear whether these "sins against Chesterfield" (65) are the product of simple ignorance or are calculated transgressions meant to break the eastern lady who recoils at the "brusquerie" (138) of her uncouth neighbors. Certainly stepping around "pride, that most terrific bug-bear of the woods" (53) is no easy task; when Clavers corrects the newly elected sheriff, whose legal notices bear the inscription "Justas of Piece," he reddens, adopts a "swelling air," and delivers a lecture on the limited uses of "book-learning" (172). To get on the wrong side of "the sovereign people" (120) is in reality no laughing matter: not only do the primitive living conditions make reliance on other villagers a matter of life and death, but it's also unpleasant to return to your home to find that your dog has been hung from the gate post or your pig thrown into the well (119). It's not that Clavers thinks that "feeling above" her neighbors is wrong or that in her view there's no justification for it – this is, after all, a community whose idea of entertainment is to tie a turkey to a post and stone it to death at twenty-five cents a throw. Rather, one must "look on the rational side of the thing" (66). Failing to appreciate this, more genteel acquaintances such as "Mrs. B" commit the fatal error of "allowing her neighbors to discover that she considered them far beneath her" (74), thus condemning her and her starving family to an existence of "absolute wretchedness" (75).[7]

For residents such as Mary Clavers, looking on the rational side of things above all means adopting as a rule of thumb the maxim "grant graciously what you cannot refuse safely" (67). In Montacute, the time-honored rural custom of borrowing needful things is taken to comical extremes, so that it's not only various kitchen utensils that issue from the Clavers' household and circulate through the village but shawls, shoes, shaving gear, and pantaloons. "But the cream of the joke lies in the manner of the thing," the narrator ruefully adds, for the neighbors "do not think it necessary even to *ask* a loan, but take it for granted" (68, 67; original emphasis). That they return the borrowed items worse for wear or destroyed altogether only serves to underscore the destructive urge traditionally associated with envy. This lack of respect for private property (which, as the narrator subsequently insinuates, is pretty much limited to the Clavers' private property [186]), apparently extends to privacy more generally, for "whoever exhibits any desire for privacy is set down as 'praoud,' or something worse; no matter how inoffensive" (139). The best gloss on such behavior may be found in Tocqueville's often-cited comment that what the envious most require of the envied "is not the sacrifice of their money but of their pride" (512), a claim rather starkly dramatized in Kirkland's account, which leaves us with the strong impression that the "involuntary loans" (68) she describes amount to little more than a form of extortion. To grant graciously what cannot be refused safely is in effect to pay deference to the power wielded by the community. Likewise, when Mary Clavers resolves to be as "impartial" as possible in her "visiting habits" and when she urges the genteel Mrs. Rivers to overcome her repugnance and do the same (65), the motive is plainly not to make new friends but to make a show of their submission. This too conforms to Tocqueville's sense that in the United States the more prosperous citizens "are at pains not to get isolated from the people" (511), knowing perfectly well that holding themselves aloof would only inflame their vindictiveness. "Equality, perfect and practical," Kirkland writes, describing "this model village of ours" (177), "is the sine qua non; and any appearance of a desire to avoid this rather trying fraternization, is invariably met by a fierce and indignant resistance" (183–84).

In *A New Home* envy-avoidance consequently becomes something of an art that requires keen delicacy of judgment. Knowing how best to pander to the people's pride and prejudice without stirring suspicion can present special challenges. Mulling over what to wear for the wedding of the cooper's daughter, for example, Mrs. Rivers selects an "ordinary neat home-dress" lest she be accused of "a desire to outshine" (66). Under normal circumstances and for all the obvious reasons this would seem to be a sound decision. In the opinion of the more experienced Mrs. Clavers, however, the only thing worse than betraying a wish to "outshine" one's neighbors is tipping one's hand and betraying a wish *not* to do so, which is why she chooses a dress "considered here as the extreme of festal elegance" (65). Wearing "ordinary" attire to a wedding may be, in other words, one way of living down the reputation of feeling above people, but not if the people suspect they are being humored. In that event, the two women would risk incurring the "far more dangerous suspicion of undervaluing our rustic neighbors" (66). It is not enough, then, simply to sacrifice one's pride. One must work hard at not disturbing the self-deception so indispensable to those whose lives are ruled by resentment. Not merely a powerful instrument of social cohesion that keeps the more genteel in line and communal harmony intact, the prevalence of envy also demands from figures like Kirkland's Mary Clavers a certain critical empathy that allows her to know the preferences of the envious better than they know themselves. To stay one step ahead of resentment, it is important to adopt the frame of mind of the resentful.

The significance of identifying with the envious goes beyond simple practicality, however. For it is not just "the wary pumpkin-eaters" (139), as the narrator rather uncharitably puts it, who are prone to "sour discontent" (140). Self-styled aristocrats, who project "something of a high-bred air," journey West in search of instant fortune only to encounter disappointment and eventually fall prey to "reckless self-indulgence," "fierce discontent," and "determined indolence" (75). Like their supposedly more "vulgar" male counterparts such as the ne'er do well Mr. Fenwick, who uses election day as an excuse for an extended debauch, or the quondam schoolteacher Mr. Whicher who "has made a vow against honest industry" (182), the more refined gentlemen who emigrate from the east or from England and settle in the middle of nowhere are also described as feckless idlers, just a notch above the "land-shark[s]" (83) who have duped them. "Finding themselves growing poorer and poorer," the once wealthy but now impecunious family members of the aforementioned Mrs. B thus "persuade themselves that all who thrive, do so by dishonest gains, or by mean sacrifices" (76). Scorning their lowly, uncouth neighbors, the family ends up resembling them in the process of becoming utterly consumed by "the bitter feelings which spring from ... mortified, yet indomitable pride" (75). The contagion of "all-reaching envy" is such that the resented have themselves become resentful, a reversal that is matched by the equally paradoxical spectacle of humble folk vying with each other for the distinction of who can be the most humble. Like the ubiquitous bogs, marshes, swamps, and mud-holes that threaten to waylay the traveler, the presumption of entitlement has spread through the region to such an extent that it appears to constitute, paradoxically, the only common thread that ties together "the mingled mass of our country population" (145). In Montacute and its environs, the Jacksonian opposition of humble producers nobly working the land and haughty aristocrats who sponge off them has reached such a point of self-parody that it collapses under the weight of its own absurdity.

But it is really in connection with Kirkland's own point of view as a narrator and particularly her relation to the reader that the importance of this erosion of the boundary between the envious and the envied is most keenly felt. At first glance there would seem to be little question about the book's intended audience: conceived as "a sort of 'Emigrant's Guide'" written for "the courteous reader" (1) *A New Home* records "peculiar features of Western life" (3) for the amusement and instruction of "any fashionable reader" (4). The amusement, as we've seen, comes in the form of satirical sketches of the villagers while the instruction may be found in various practical tips like not wearing "silly thin shoes" (73) when navigating a swamp or not encumbering oneself with expensive furniture when moving into a log cabin. But while there is no mistaking the narrator's elitism in these and many other moments, the issue of the book's audience and its class affiliation is hardly as simple as it may at first appear. It probably was not with the "fashionable reader" (4) in mind, for example, that Kirkland decided silently to revise her property-holdings, reducing, as previously mentioned, her 1,300 acres in real life down to a mere 200. Nor can the presence of this same reader account for the peculiar defensiveness that overtakes the narrator when describing her fondness for flowers, an "enthusiastic love" that may, "to most readers, seem absolutely silly or affected" – indeed, something "of which I was vainglorious beyond all justification" (79). In this particular instance it's not the "fashionable reader" back east whom Kirkland has her eye on but the neighbor next door, perhaps the one who wants to know if Mary has "got 'them blossoms out of these here woods'" (79) or another who, "after putting [a hyacinth] to his undiscriminating nose, threw it on the ground with a 'pah!' as contemptuous as Hamlet's" (80). Although the string of apologetic phrases ("silly," "affected," "vainglorious") we find the author mouthing to herself are not directed to anyone in particular but form part of the general narration, the implied audience is clear enough. If, as we've seen, envy-avoidance is elsewhere presented as a matter of prudential calculation, as in the example of what to wear to a wedding, here it seems to have insinuated itself involuntarily into the mindset of Kirkland's narrator. In such instances, the judgment of the "sovereign people" momentarily shifts from being the object of ridicule to being silently internalized by the author herself.

In *Leaves of Grass* Whitman's "you, whoever you are" functions as a rhetorical placeholder meant to designate a generic second person. But the construct that Whitman takes for granted is what Kirkland cannot easily locate, so that the question of who will be reading *A New Home* keeps obtruding itself into the writing of *A New Home*. More than once the author wonders out loud how "such common-place people" as are portrayed between the covers of her book could possibly be described in terms "suitable to the delicate organization of 'ears polite'" (114–15) – an open question that manages to mock both parties in one stroke. Repeatedly she apologizes for the desultory, disorganized, and fragmented character of her narrative, going so far as to confess at one point that "if I thought I could do any better I would certainly go back and begin at the very beginning" (82). On the one hand, her discursiveness is likely to disappoint "the gentle reader" (115) who expects absorbing, well-crafted adventures of cougars and rattlesnakes, not "a meandering recital of common-place occurrences – mere gossip about every-day people, little enhanced in value by any fancy of ingenuity of the writer" (3). In what amounts to anxiety over frontier democracy's dreadful habit of "leveling downwards" (185), the worry motivating such disclaimers would seem to be that in treating mundane subjects the author will be dragged down with them: as she stands to, say, the malicious Mrs. Nippers, the town gossip, so does the refined reader stand to Kirkland, the purveyor of gossip about gossips. On the other hand, her "wandering wordiness" is just as likely to grate on the sensibilities of those closer to home. "I hope," she writes, making further apologies for "my rambling, gossiping style," that "my reader will not be disposed to respond in that terse and forceful style which is cultivated at Montacute" (82). Without a stable coordinate or reference point upon which to map experience, confidence in the existence of a common reader proves hard to come by. The trials of writing about the frontier do not seem in this respect all that different from living on the frontier, where any attempt to situate oneself within the range of what might be considered the typical or normal is endlessly contested. From this standpoint, the phrase "you, whoever you are" signifies genuine perplexity more than an imperturbable receptivity.

Kirkland and her family resided in Pinckney from 1836 to 1839, a period when "western fever" was at its height, attracting "thousands" to Michigan "each day" (24). No doubt the constant displacement of settlers caused by the boom and bust of land speculation, not to mention its destructive effect on any semblance of "home feeling" (22), only served to make any sense of a social whole or communal identity that much more vexed. Kirkland's misgivings over the episodic character of "these wandering sketches of mine," which depart "from all rule and precedent" (177), should be interpreted in terms of her consternation at this apparent withdrawal of some larger context that might rank and organize experience. Essentially a string of anecdotes, *A New Home* remains, we might say without prejudice, resolutely focused on the small picture. Important developments occurring during Kirkland's sojourn such as the admission of Michigan into the Union, the nearby construction of a major railroad line, the onset of a nationwide financial depression, and so forth go unmentioned. This is not because "History is not my forte," as the narrator puts it in another apologetic aside; if "this attempt to write one long coherent letter about Montacute" (177) falls short of success, that is because Montacute itself falls short of coherence, for it is unquestionably part of "the western country, where every element enters into the composition of that anomalous mass called society" (76). Overall the picture of the public that emerges from Kirkland's account is hopelessly divided: the "anomalous mass" is both ill-defined and oppressive, heterogeneous and monolithic. In a world where appreciating a woodland flower is enough to call down resentment on your head or where satirizing such irrationality is enough to call up the resentful feeling that you, too, may be deemed "decidedly low" by the "sophisticated reader" (4), the mere idea of extrapolating the common, the average, or the typical becomes a daunting task. It is not, in other words, the diversity of its inhabitants or the incidence of social mobility that makes the "anomalous mass called society" so anomalous in Montacute and elsewhere. It is, more primitively, the sheer obsession with comparative thinking that makes the mere concept of the mass look as though it were intrinsically objectionable.

Kirkland would probably object that the spin I am putting on her memoir is much too gloomy. Ultimately she sees herself as a mediator who hopes to promote better understanding between "the spoiled child of refined civilization" and "our unpolished neighbors." By reminding the more favored that it is only natural for the less favored to envy them, Kirkland, in drawing her text to a close, looks toward a brighter future. Were the more prosperous citizens to relent in their "pride and prejudice" the less prosperous would do the same. Ideally, this sort of mutual disarmament would result in a "leveling upwards [which] is much more congenial to 'human natur' than leveling downwards" (185). Tocqueville's judgment that "the charm of simple good manners" is the only effective response to the envious is seconded by Kirkland, who had earlier vowed to make her home a "silent example" of civility and now urges the prospective settlers among her readership to follow suit.[8] But the strain of inhabiting this middle ground is palpable, and Kirkland is too honest an observer to pretend otherwise. Her account ends with the narrator stranded between two worlds, no more identifying with the refined than with the unrefined:

> But I am aware that I have already been adventurous, far beyond the bounds of prudence. To hint that it may be better not to cultivate *too* far that haughty spirit of exclusiveness which is the glory of the fashionable world, is, I know, hazardous in the extreme. I have not so far forgotten the rule of the sublime *clique* as not to realize, that in acknowledging even a leaning toward the "vulgar" side, I place myself forever beyond its pale. But I am now a denizen of the wild woods – in my view, "no mean city" to own as one's home; and I feel no ambition to aid in the formation of a Montacute aristocracy, for which an ample field is now open, and all the proper materials are at hand. What lack we? Several of us have as many as three cows; some few, carpets and shanty-kitchens; and one or two, piano-fortes and silver tea-sets. I myself, as *dame de la seigneurie*, have had secret thoughts of an astral lamp! But even if I should go so far, I am resolved not to be either vain-glorious or over-bearing, although this kind of superiority forms the usual ground for exclusiveness. I shall visit my neighbours just as usual, and take care not to say a single word about dipped candles, if I can possibly help it. (186–87)

It's an exhausting business, this ducking and dodging of invidious comparison. Kirkland valiantly maintains a lighthearted tone, but it's obvious that her tacking back and forth between the vulgar and the haughty is likely to please neither. Not surprisingly, her fears about going beyond the bounds of prudence were well-founded; with the publication of her text, she incurred the wrath of her neighbors and was eventually compelled to leave the state. Mortified, Kirkland issued an apology, though could not resist complaining that, in the view of her hypersensitive audience, "every creation of my not very lively imagination instantly becomes a living, breathing, and very angry reality."[9] No reports survive of any attempts on the part of these more indignant readers to issue their own version of events, though it is interesting to speculate on what might result when a "lively imagination" is joined to a "very angry reality." If envy itself were allowed to speak, what would it say?

HAWTHORNE'S UNLOVELY TRUTH

Renouncing authorial privilege can take many forms. In Sigourney and Whitman we found a reader-oriented aesthetic that deprecates meaning as an individual possession while embracing the uses of indeterminacy. "No stander above men [or women]," the poet produces the illusion of equality by breaking the bounds of representation in the process of modeling a chain reaction of affect that proceeds from the reader within the text to the reader without. Literary texts that tell a story pose a different challenge. Unlike the lyric, narratives typically depend upon an asymmetry between author and reader in the simple sense that one knows more than the other. In *Problems of Dostoevsky's Poetics*, Bakhtin calls this superior knowledge "authorial surplus" and suggests that the "polyphonic author" is able to repudiate this surplus by treating his characters as independent agents "capable of standing alongside their creator, capable of not agreeing and even rebelling against him."[10] The lyric's endeavor to free the reader from the constraint of authorial imposition is here complemented by the novelist's endeavor to free his characters from the same thing, an endeavor which of course generates the further illusion that the "polyphonic" author, no more in charge than we, stands alongside his readers.

In the same way the narrator of *The House of the Seven Gables* often acts as though he's at the mercy of characters whose behavior is beyond his power to control. Why doesn't Colonel Pyncheon emerge from his study to greet his visitors as they arrive to celebrate the construction of his splendid new edifice? Why won't Hepzibah Pyncheon have done with her morning toilet and cross the threshold of our story? Why doesn't Judge Pyncheon get up from his chair? Has he forgotten that he has a busy day of appointments ahead of him? In expostulating with his characters as if they had a mind of their own – "pray, pray, Judge Pyncheon, look at your watch, now!" – the narrator makes a show of his own powerlessness while endowing the figures of his imagination with a strange autonomy. "Will she now issue forth over the threshold of our story? Not yet, by many moments ..."[11] It's as though the self-forgetfulness typically attributed to the reader, absorbed in the twists and turns of the plot and thus forgetting that it is indeed a fiction he or she is reading, had come to possess the narrator as well, who likewise appears to lose track of the difference between what is real and what is represented.

For Bakhtin, the novelist's sharing of authority with his characters is a crucial feature of the "dialogic form" – that "great dialogue ... in which characters and authors participate with equal rights."[12] But as readers of Hawthorne's novel will be quick to appreciate, this is hardly the effect produced by *The House of the Seven Gables*. For one thing, the apparent ceding of authorial control is restricted to one group of characters, the Pyncheons, who are consistently tied to aristocratic privilege and who are consistently addressed by the narrator in an arch, mockingly deferential manner that seems to parody the stance of a servant waiting in attendance upon his or her master. For another, the characters who act contrary to the apparent design of the narrator are either immobilized by anxiety (Hepzibah) or already dead (the Colonel and the Judge), and so hardly qualify for partnership in a dialogue, much less one characterized by "equal rights." But if the delimiting of the narrator's authority does not lead to the empowering of his characters, that would seem to be part of the point. Full of courtesy and regard, the narrator's professions of helplessness before his recalcitrant aristocrats simultaneously establish a bond with the reader (for we, too, are waiting in attendance) while suggesting that these figures are defectors from a dialogue they are unwilling or unable to engage ("Nay, then, we give thee up!" [200]). Given every opportunity to respond, the Colonel, the Lady, and the Judge are exposed as *in*capable of "standing alongside their creator"; they are, as Bakhtin might say, monologic figures in a dialogic world.

If this makes it sound as though the narrator has framed these characters – has in some sense set them up – that perhaps is in keeping with a book where the line between narrating and humiliating is not always easy to draw.[13] I am thinking not just of that masterpiece of hate, the novel's infamous, chapter-long taunting of the corpse of Judge Pyncheon, nor even of the arguably more over-the-top, satirical treatment of "poor Hepzibah," the "aristocratic hucksteress" (59) who is at one point shown scrambling on the floor of her shop in search of some errant marbles while the narrator invites us to join him in laughing at her. Although the plot concerns the ancestral crime of the Pyncheons against the Maules and how it is carried down through the generations, the narrator freely generalizes upon this theme, continually pointing up instances involving "the entanglement of something mean and trivial with whatever is noblest in joy and sorrow" (32). He is indeed inexhaustible on the topic. The original artist who drew the Colonel's portrait may have intended nothing but flattery, but with age "the unlovely truth of a human soul" cannot but peer through; regarding the Colonel's descendant, Jaffrey Pyncheon, the same "vast discrepancy" is marked by the contrast "between portraits intended for engraving, and the pencil-sketches that pass from hand to hand, behind the original's back" (351). Marveling at how it is that "so much of the mean and ludicrous should be hopelessly mixed up with the purest pathos [of] life" (32), the narrator forever keeps before us illustrations and emblems of how the high and noble are built upon the lowly and corrupt, like the poisoned spring that lies beneath the Pyncheon mansion. "Unlovely truth," in the novel's rendering, is anything but a loose expression: if the subjects portrayed in a daguerreotype look "unamiable," Holgrave explains to Phœbe, that is because the daguerreotype gets past "the merest surface" and "actually brings out the secret character with a truth that no painter would ever venture upon" (67). Given the trajectory of the plot, it seems safe to assume that the character is secret because it is shameful; it is the artist's distinctive task to bring this secret shame to light. In short, Hawthorne's novel views artistic "truth" and the revelation of "disagreeable traits" (67) as enjoying a privileged bond.

Of course, there's nothing necessarily malicious in the conception of art as uncovering buried truth. It's not as if, after all, the storyteller is another Matthew Maule, the disgruntled carpenter who, possessed by an "inveterate grudge" and various "hereditary resentments" (137) against the owners of the Seven Gables, gains control of Alice Pyncheon and drives her to an early grave by subjecting her to constant humiliation. But here we may be dealing with a difference in degree, not kind. Himself an occasional visitor to the House of the Seven Gables, the narrator is nothing if not accomplished in the art of gossip and innuendo, passing along village tales and retailing scandalous stories while coyly casting doubt on their credibility. As part of a choral "we," he is privy to an assortment of "chimney-corner traditions" (89, 141) and is not above insinuating some of his own (e.g., Colonel Pyncheon, a man of "great animal development" [88], was a philanderer). The discursive equivalent of those "pencil-sketches that pass from hand to hand, behind the original's back," gossip combines outward deference to figures of power and respectability with a relish for scandal that cuts them down to size. Like the "half-hidden sarcasm" (45) that accompanies Holgrave's exhortation to Hepzibah to break free of "the circle of gentility" by joining the ranks of laboring men and women, for some reason the use of rumor, hearsay, fable, confidential asides, "murmur[ings] under the narrator's breath" (88), and so forth dominate the telling of what A. N. Kaul terms "Hawthorne's parable of leveling democracy in America."[14]

Again, the association of gossip with an insubordinate or subversive rhetoric is doubtless relevant here, but it is important to add that whatever political edge is gained thereby is also somewhat dulled by being used so liberally. Gossip, that is to say, is not just used selectively against certain figures of privilege but is better understood, more loosely, as a kind of model for storytelling as such, governing the very rhythm and structure of narrative thought. Thus for example the same qualities that make Phoebe Pyncheon, resolutely grounded in "the Actual," a paragon of middle-class industry and good sense, also make "our little country-girl" (94), it is repeatedly hinted, insipid and docile; similarly, Clifford Pyncheon may harbor feelings for his cousin Phoebe "not less chaste than if she had been his daughter" but the narrator cannot forbear inserting the further observation that "the ripeness of her lips and the virginal development of her bosom" – indeed, "all her little, womanly ways, budding out of her like blossoms on a young fruit-tree" – causes "his very heart to tingle with keenest thrills of pleasure" (101). Even in the novel's climactic scene, where Holgrave declares his love for Phoebe, the remark is slipped in that under different circumstances the former might well have let the relationship die of its own accord (215). A seemingly gratuitous compulsion to set the ignoble beside the noble is additionally reflected in the novel's indiscriminate politicizing, where "aristocratic" roosters strut in the Pyncheon garden amid "plebian" (64, 66, 110) vegetables or where a little boy, eating a cookie in the shape of Jim Crow, is said to have "wrought an irreparable ruin [for] the structure of ancient aristocracy had been demolished by him" (39), as if the very theme of the book could not be introduced without being viewed as something of a joke. Now and then, it is true, narrative voice does speak with warmth and sincerity, as when it solicits sympathy for Hepzibah, but for the most part the unlovely truth is that it builds a rapport with the reader primarily through acts of shaming the high-born and deflating the beautiful.

This is not necessarily envy, but neither is it that far removed from it. To view the real thing, all we need to do is turn to Judge Pyncheon, whose mere appearance in Hawthorne's *House* excites such fierce contempt that we get indictments of his villainy to the exclusion of ever actually seeing it in action. The following extended conceit is typical not only for its indignation but for the confusion it seems to betray – a confusion intensified, in part, by the narrator's curious failure to prepare the ground with dramatic incidents that might provide a context for his assaults on the Judge's character. Likening the latter to "a sculptured and ornamented pile of ostentatious deeds," the narrator speculates on the existence of "some evil and unsightly thing" lurking under the "tall and stately edifice" of his public persona. To the narrator there is something oddly compelling about the analogy; he doesn't appear to want to let it go, even long after the point has been established. He continues:

Behold, therefore, a palace! Its splendid halls and suites of spacious apartments are floored with a mosaic-work of costly marble; its windows, the whole height of each room, admit the sunshine through the most transparent of plate-glass; its high cornices are gilded, and its ceilings gorgeously painted; and a lofty dome – through which, from the central pavement, you may gaze up to the sky, as with no obstructing medium between – surmounts the whole. With what fairer and nobler emblem could any man desire to shadow forth his character? Ah; but in some low and obscure nook – some narrow closet on the ground floor, shut, locked and bolted, and the key flung away – or beneath the marble pavement, in a stagnant water-puddle, with the richest pattern of mosaic-work above – may lie a corpse, half-decayed and still decaying, and diffusing its death-scent all through the palace! The inhabitant will not be conscious of it; for it has long been his daily breath! Neither will the visitors; for they smell only the rich odors which the master sedulously scatters through the palace, and the incense which they bring, and delight to burn before him! Now and then, perchance, comes in a seer, before whose sadly gifted eye the whole structure melts into thin air, leaving only the hidden nook, the bolted closet, with the cobwebs festooned over its forgotten door; or the deadly hole under the pavement, and the decaying corpse within. (162–63)

It's not the corpse alone that matters but the presence of the corpse in a palace; it's not what the Judge has done that stands out but the fact that it is a Judge who has done it. Here, as in the book as a whole, envy muddles the moral message. Wrongdoing is not wrong so much as it's *embarrassing* – decaying bodies give off a foul smell. With due allowance for the influence of gothic convention, the sheer relishing of the contrast between the majestic and the mean – evident enough in the tone of gleeful exposure – is matched only by the lovingly detailed description of the palace itself, gorgeous ceilings and all. What was Hawthorne thinking?

According to one school of thought, he was thinking that it would be nice to write a commercially successful work of fiction for a change, one that would cater to popular taste and help dispel the author's reputation as a producer of gloomy, morbid fiction. Alluding to this motive and applying it to the transparently contrived happy ending of the novel, where the newly-weds Holgrave and Phoebe move into the Judge's estate, accompanied by Hepzibah, Clifford and "a couple of hundred thousand" (225), Michael Gilmore discerns a resemblance between Hawthorne and the villain of his story in that both put on a sunny mask to please public opinion.[15] But perhaps the question most worth asking is not whether Hawthorne is as much of a hypocrite as the Judge but why he thinks the Judge is a hypocrite in the first place. This seems like a strange question, if only because the narrator, with his allusions to rich odors masking the scent of corruption, is constantly affirming otherwise. As I've suggested, though, the more we ponder the terms of reproach directed against the Judge, the more difficult it becomes to make sense of them. This is not because the Judge's character is spotless but because it is irrelevant. There's nothing personal, so to speak, about his hypocrisy, which is one reason why the narrator has trouble depicting it. As Uncle Venner confides to Hepzibah at one point, "old gentlemen" in the time "before the revolution" may have put on "grand airs," but "nowadays ... [anyone who] feels himself superior to the common folk ... only stoops so much the lower to them" (47). Later in the story Hawthorne enlarges upon this insight in the course of deriding, once again, the Judge's hypocrisy:

With a bow to Hepzibah, and a degree of paternal benevolence in his parting nod to Phoebe, the Judge left the shop, and went smiling along the street. As is customary with the rich, when they aim at the honors of a republic, he apologized, as it were, to the people, for his wealth, prosperity, and elevated station, by a free and hearty manner toward those who knew him; putting off more of his dignity, in due proportion with the humbleness of the man whom he saluted, and thereby proving a haughty consciousness of his advantages, as irrefragably as if he had marched forth, preceded by a troop of lackeys to clear the way. On this particular forenoon, so excessive was the warmth of Judge Pyncheon's kindly aspect, that (such, at least, was the rumor about town) an extra passage of water-carts was found essential, in order to lay the dust occasioned by so much extra sunshine! (94)

The hypocrisy presented here is plainly a by-product of the Judge's social standing. Were he impoverished and of humble station, there would be nothing to apologize for and nothing to dissimulate – he wouldn't need to pass himself off as one of "the people" because he would be one of the people. But since he's not and since walking around town preceded by a troop of lackeys is unacceptable, the Judge needs to make a show of his humility. And if the narrator's complaint is that in doing so the Judge overplays his hand, becoming more haughty as he becomes more humble, we can also see that his insistence on viewing the Judge as a hypocrite is in reality nothing more than a stalking horse for what really aggravates him, which is of course the Judge's failure to apologize sincerely for his "elevated station," his failure, to recall Tocqueville's phrasing, to sacrifice his pride.

Thus the narrator finds himself in the awkward position of believing the Judge is damnable and of telling us that he is damnable but not quite being able to put his finger on what makes him damnable. One thing the narrator does know: bad things happen to bad people – "perpetual remorse of conscience, a constantly defeated hope, strife among kindred, various misery, a strange form of death" (132) – such are the calamities visited upon the Pyncheon line. But if any of this, except for the manner of his death, applies to the Judge, we don't see it; in fact, at the very end of the book we are told that the Judge found it easy to "dispose of" any guilt he might have felt about his Uncle's murder (220)! Like the feeble joke about hosing down the streets of the town once the Judge has passed through, the narrator's pat moralizing only draws attention to the impotence of his spite. For it seems that what infuriates the narrator isn't finally what the Judge has done or what he owns but more primitively the kind of person he is – a man of wealth who makes others feel inferior and gets away with it. (He's also a murderer, though again this doesn't explain why Hawthorne should want to *devalue* the Judge, as opposed to simply condemning him.) In his treatise on *ressentiment*, Max Scheler speaks of "existential envy, which is directed against another's person's very nature," indeed whose "very existence is felt to be a 'pressure,' a 'reproach,' and an unbearable humiliation."[16] In hindsight it seems obvious that the narrator's exhilaration in jeering at the dead Judge stems directly from the lifting of this intolerable presence, what the narrator calls "a defunct nightmare" (178). Imagining himself as a mouthpiece for "The Avenger," the narrator's gloating over the helplessness of the immobile form before him (e.g., "Canst thou not brush the fly away ... art thou too weak that wast so powerful? Not brush away a fly!" [200]) suggests the jubilant relief of the weak and humiliated who have found in the death of a dreaded nemesis not simply justice but satisfaction.

One hesitates to call the narrative voice of *The House of the Seven Gables* "unreliable," just as one hesitates to assume that it is a faithful reflection of Hawthorne's state of mind. The truth probably lies somewhere in the middle, all the more so given the well known preference of his fiction to amplify and exaggerate psychological distress rather than run away from it. With his next book, *The Blithedale Romance*, Hawthorne again turns to an enfeebled, resentful narrator who compulsively moralizes upon the narcissism and sexual bravura of another powerful male, Hollingsworth, only this time Hawthorne does enlarge the distance between himself and his storyteller by giving the latter the name of Coverdale and a limited dramatic role. In any event, the significance of envy in *The House of the Seven Gables* goes well beyond a grudge between author and character. For if the spectacle of the Judge playing at the game of equality without really meaning it draws the narrator's ire, readers of the novel, as I mentioned, have likewise been perplexed by the appearance of Hawthorne doing the same thing, most notably by having Holgrave, at the very end of the story, conveniently discard his radical views on property and marry into it himself. Indeed, the classic scenario of the envious using calls for social justice as a cover for personal advantage comes suspiciously close to describing Hawthorne's hero, whose concealed identity as a Maule encourages us to regard him as a figure of working-class dissent while his eventual enjoyment of the Judge's ill-gotten wealth strongly implies the consummation of personal revenge. Where do we draw the line between justice and mere resentment? In leaving this question hanging at the end of the story, Hawthorne brings a new level of seriousness to his treatment of this theme, suggesting that envy lies at the very foundation of his "parable." Having noted some of the ways in which the narrator indulges in this particular vice, I want now to turn to a consideration of how he also attempts to analyze and diagnose it.

We can begin by noting that, like Tocqueville, Hawthorne views envy primarily as a historical phenomenon. Chapter One, "The Old Pyncheon Family," contains a passage recounting the "ancient prejudices ... of the ante-revolutionary days, when the aristocracy could venture to be proud and the low were content to be abased" (20). In fact "there is something so massive, stable, and almost irresistibly imposing, in the exterior present-ment of established rank and great possessions" that "few poor and humble men have moral force enough to question it" (20). Because they know their place, the poor and the humble, in the thrall of "ancient prejudices," are beyond the reach of comparative thinking. A glimpse of their contented subservience is provided in the novel's opening scene, where "the trades-man, with his plodding air, or the laborer in his leather jerkin," each of whom may have had a hand in constructing Colonel Pyncheon's "stately mansion," are described as "stealing awe-stricken into the house which [they] had perhaps helped to build" (11). For their descendants, on the other hand, the situation is reversed, for "in this republican country, amid the fluctuating waves of our social life, someone is always at the drowning point" (29). With "the exterior presentment of established rank" made a relic of the past, no one, it appears, is immune from the vicissitudes of comparative thinking. Thus no sooner does Hepzibah, in completing her transformation from "patrician lady" to "plebian woman" (29), assume her place behind the counter of her cent-shop than she acquires "a sentiment of virulence ... towards the idle aristocracy to which it had so recently been her pride to belong" (41). Consequently, when she glimpses, on her first day of work, a specimen of this "aristocracy" sauntering down the street ("a lady, in a delicate and costly summer garb, with a floating veil and gracefully swaying gown" [41]), Hepzibah reacts with disgust, "giving vent to that feeling of hostility, which is the only real abasement of the poor, in the presence of the rich" (42). This ironically repeats the immediately preceding scene when a "vulgar creature" (41) is described visiting the cent-shop, not to do business but to gape at the "mildewed piece of aristocracy" (41) behind the counter. Though passed over in critical accounts of the novel, the general trajectory here is clear enough. If "ancient prejudices" serve to abase the poor and humble by making them mindlessly contented, the modern version does the same thing by making them mindlessly resentful.

There is, it is true, an important exception to this general transformation. Like the laborers who steal awestruck into the house they helped build, Phoebe, a throwback of sorts, is consistently portrayed as having difficulty seeing through "the exterior presentment" of authority. Doubts as to "whether judges, clergymen, and other characters of that eminent stamp and respectability, could really, in any single instance, be otherwise than just and upright men" produce a "fearful and startling effect" (94) on her mind; to such a "trim, orderly, and limit-loving" sensibility, the mere chance that "rank, dignity, and station" are not in themselves worthy of "human reverence" cannot be entertained without her world "tumbl[ing] headlong into chaos" (95). In short, Phoebe's nature is organized around a wish to "keep the universe in its old place": if the narrator looks at the Judge and can only see corpses under the pavement, she looks at the Judge and is drawn to "smother" any such intuition. To her is denied the "stern enjoyment" – the phrase is telling – that comes with the discovery that "a high man is as likely to grasp his share of [evil] as a low one" (95). It is Phoebe's utter freedom from emulous striving – "the fact of her having found a place for herself" (98) – that defines her "perfect health" (101), a phrase that only the inattentive can take at face value. Many commentators have pointed out how her "sweet breath and happy thoughts" (54) serve to dispel the gloom of the past while purifying the practices of the capitalist present, but her imperviousness to envy also renders "the unsuspecting girl" (210), with her "sweet and order-loving character" and "horror" of being "at issue with society" (215), a frequent target of the narrator's condescending interjections, as if her very envylessness were only another spur to his own envy.[17]

Be that as it may, if succumbing to envy is the only real abasement of the poor, it would seem that being insusceptible to it is not that much of an improvement so far as the novel is concerned. Between the two extremes is placed Holgrave, whose "reverence for another's individuality" (151) is linked to his ability to reverence his own. However rootless and impermanent his existence may seem, "putting off one exterior, and snatching up another, to be soon shifted for a third," the daguerreotypist "had never violated the innermost man" (126). It is "his integrity to whatever law he acknowledged" that sets him apart. Being a law unto himself, he repudiates blind acceptance of social authority; adhering to this law with integrity, he evades a cynical resentment of it. In Holgrave Hawthorne constructs an ideal type who, at once independent and intact, has no place and yet always knows his place. Because "he had never lost his identity" (126), he has no reason to look for it in others – a formula for neutralizing envy that, as readers of the novel will recall, is exemplified in Holgrave's refusal to acquire "empire" over Phoebe Pyncheon's spirit when she falls into a trance while listening to a story involving another Maule who does usurp the identity of another Pyncheon in order to "wreak a low, ungenerous scorn upon her" (149). "Let us allow him integrity," the narrator comments, in resisting the temptations of resentment and forbearing to add "one link more" (151) that would have rendered his control over another's individuality complete.

"There is a time in every man's education," Emerson writes in "Self-Reliance," "when he arrives at the conclusion that envy is ignorance [and] that imitation is suicide."[18] Emerson's essay is frequently cited as a key influence on Hawthorne's portrayal of Holgrave, particularly with regard to the latter's contempt for tradition, family ties, inherited wealth, and social institutions. But the affinity goes deeper. Emerson's understanding of self-reliance is grounded in his sense of character as an entity that must be understood as a whole and not a part. Said to resemble "an acrostic or Alexandrian stanza; – read it forward, backward, or across, it spells the same thing," Emersonian character is "self-dependent and self-derived." In it is revealed a unity such that "it will be found symmetrical, though I mean it not, and see it not." That is why "the objection to conforming to usages that have become dead to you is, that it scatters your force." Conformism disunites and disperses. It has no center. Integrity, not nonconformity, is its true antithesis. Hope, fear, pity, gratitude, discontent, self-division – anything that "supposes dualism and not unity in nature and conscious-ness" are unworthy of the self-reliant.[19] No more reducible to one's acts than one's beliefs, self-reliance is what happens when the self is given over entirely to "the law of [its] being," obeys "what is after [its] constitution," and so "live[s] wholly from within." Whatever suggests a fall from this intactness or indivisibility of character excites Emerson's mistrust; it is in this vein, for example, that he speaks disdainfully of the philanthropist and of the popular esteem for "a man *and* his virtues." A selective application of the self's energies, "put on and off as the wind blows and a newspaper directs," is contrary to the element of disinterestedness and impersonality that distinguishes the self-reliant individual, whose conduct engages "the whole act of the man."[20]

 Why this conception of character as a unitary, unvarying force should receive so much emphasis is explained in the first paragraph of the essay. There Emerson alludes to a certain "admonition" heard by the soul when confronted by "great works of art"; he also speaks of being "forced to take with shame our own opinion from another" should we discover that "a stranger" has articulated "with masterly good sense what we have thought and felt all the time." In cherishing the greatness of others, Emerson explains in this first paragraph, we are in reality cherishing ourselves, for "in every work of genius we recognize our own rejected thoughts: they come back to us with a certain alienated majesty."[21] The inspiration we take from "every work of genius" is made inseparable from the recognition that something has been taken from us, or, more exactly, that we have allowed something to be taken from us. Owing to the radical equality of all souls, greatness is both an inspiration and an accusation: those are not simply Plato's thoughts but our own, not a stranger's opinion but precisely what we've been thinking and feeling all the time. In the manner of Hawthorne we might say that a psychology of envy lurks at the very foundations of Emersonian self-reliance; indeed we might go further and say that it is something that self-reliance depends upon and invites. From this standpoint, the essay's subsequent valorizing of integrity as an indispensable feature of achieved self-reliance makes sense, for out of the vicissitudes of comparative thinking emerges a figure who experiences value prior to or independently of the values of others.

Moreover, Emerson supplements this image of a supremely integrated self with a shadow public that goes by names such as "the Universal Mind," the "Over-soul," or "the aboriginal Self." As we shall see in more detail in the next chapter, these guardians of the whole project and protect an imagined totality that, in symbolizing equality, hovers above and between individuals. Because the "Universal Mind" is not a real mind and because the "Over-soul" is not anybody's soul in particular, these abstractions serve as a reference point for a world of equals, a collective body or central power that stands between the self and other. They call to mind Tocqueville's description of the sovereign, who, "being of necessity and incontestably above all the citizens, does not excite their envy [for] each thinks that he is depriving his equals of all those prerogatives which he concedes to the state" (673). In Hawthorne, on the other hand, the availability of such abstractions of the whole is fleeting at best; observing a political procession as it marches through town, for example, Clifford is moved by a vision of "one broad mass of existence – one great life – one collected body of mankind, with a vast, homogeneous spirit animating it" (118). A moment of true democratic sublimity, the scene imagines "an impressible person standing alone over the brink" of the mass procession, no longer beholding "the tedious common-place of each man's visage," but finding in the "depths" of the "aggregate" a "kindred depth" within the observer. In context, though, Clifford's urge to leap into this "mighty river of life" is ultimately portrayed as a desperate attempt on the part of "a lonely being, estranged from his race … to renew the broken links of brotherhood with his kind" (119), so that the pathos of the one overshadows the glorious experience of "contiguity" and its "vast, homogeneous spirit."

Both Kirkland's *A New Home* and Hawthorne's *House* describe worlds that expressly ask to be taken as microcosms of larger social developments even as they cast about for ways of adequately conceptualizing that "anomalous mass called society." As we have seen, Kirkland invites us to see the frontier democracy treated in her pages as typical of frontier democracy more generally even as it is made clear that an essential feature of frontier democracy is that nobody's experience may be recognized as typical or representative. Hawthorne in turn organizes his novel around the grand, Tocquevillean theme of aristocracy's displacement by the forces of democracy even as he leaves us guessing about the exact status of the new social order that confronts us in the book's final scene, when Holgrave and Phoebe take possession of the Judge's country estate. Plainly meant to turn a new page, the pairing of the self-reliant man with the envyless woman not only settles an old score between the Maules and the Pyncheons but ushers in a new era of middle-class domesticity. For a majority of the book's interpreters this has indeed been its agenda all along. Thus T. Walter Herbert describes the fairy-tale ending as affirming "a domain mythically separated from the conflicts of public life [in which] womanly possession and subordination are asserted as the ground on which manly virtue is established." On this view, there is no mystery about locating a social whole inasmuch as the sheer wishfulness of the final pages only serves to betray, in Herbert's words, "the exploitation and oppression of the emerging middle-class order [which] are made to vanish into the intense purity of Phoebe, but remain there, hidden."[22]

True to the spirit of this perverse book, however, Hawthorne beats his critics to the punch. In the manner of somebody giving us what he thinks we want but spoiling it all the same, Hawthorne discredits with one hand what he proffers with the other. Nothing in the story, for example, requires "the wild reformer" (220) Holgrave to accept the Judge's money, much less to make a point of telling us that he intends to rebuild the Judge's estate in stone. Nothing requires the narrator to continue to belittle "our little village-maiden" (220) even if (or especially because) "little Phoebe" (221) is supposedly the linchpin on which our acceptance of domestic ideology turns. Nothing in the story requires that exposing the Judge's perfidy at last and thereby exonerating Clifford should be achieved through the services of a mesmerist hired by Holgrave (219). Too furtive to cohere as a meaningful counterplot, such asides are just frequent enough to serve as an ongoing irritant. "Life is made up of marble and mud," Hawthorne had earlier remarked, and in the gratuitous complications of the ending it is not unreasonable to suppose he is simply being faithful to the spirit of this adage. It's not the comforts of "poetic insight," endowed with the power to coax "majesty and beauty" from the "sordid" (34), but on the contrary a wish to reverse this process that informs the ending, which is not wishful so much as cynical. If this unlovely truth seems a rather harsh judgment to be leveled against an acclaimed classic of the American Renaissance, it at least has the virtue of making the conclusion consistent with the rest of the book, not to mention bringing to light a crucial source of its dramatic tensions and energy.

THE CHARM OF ENVY IN *OUR NIG*

Like Kirkland and Hawthorne, Harriet Wilson begins *Our Nig* by attempting to position her work in relation to a receptive public. For reasons the Preface makes clear, this is no easy task. In documenting the abuse and exploitation suffered by a nominally free black in a nominally free state, Wilson knows that she is echoing a story told many times in pro-slavery literature, where sadistic capitalists prey upon defenseless workers, especially those in domestic service. (Indeed, *Our Nig*'s portrayal of the vicious Mrs. Bellmont calls to mind similar household tyrants depicted in the anti-*Tom* parodies discussed in Chapter Two; even the title, with its jaunty familiarity, makes the novel sound as though it were another contribution along these lines). Wilson is careful to disclaim any wish to "palliate slavery at the South, by disclosures of its appurtenances North," adding that "my mistress was wholly imbued with *southern* principles."²³ But this last observation, as the reader of *Our Nig* will go on to discover, is a distortion. There is nothing regional, much less anomalous, about the bigotry of the white mistress, who encounters no serious resistance by any of the other Northerners in the story. Wilson, we might say, tells a small lie so that a greater one might be exposed; she is especially mindful of not antagonizing "our good anti-slavery friends at home" so that her story might be well-received. Despite this show of prudence, however, in the very next sentence Wilson does not hesitate to state explicitly that her lot as an African-American woman of the North was "unfavorable in comparison with treatment of legal bondmen" – precisely the sore point for "our good anti-slavery friends" that needed to be suppressed (3). In a mere nine sentences, that is to say, Wilson's Preface winds a coiled spring of enforced defensiveness. The combination of deference and defiance may be further inferred in the author's frank declaration that she's written the book to raise money even as the book itself ends on a bleak, decidedly non-uplifting note. Or more immediately we encounter the formulaic apology to "the refined and the cultivated" for "these crude narrations," behind which stands a pride that shrugs off such manifest "defects [as being] so apparent that it requires no skillful hand to expose them" (3).

Telling the truth to people who may not necessarily want to hear it is a well-known source of tension in black women's autobiographical writing of this period. As William Andrews demonstrated some time ago in his now classic study, *To Tell A Free Story*, slave narratives are often drawn to thematize such a tension, so that in a text such as Harriet Jacobs's *Incidents in the Life of a Slave Girl* issues such as shame, secrecy, and disclosure do not simply constitute a burden for the author but become a matter for reflection as she interrogates the politics of confidence both within and outside her text.[24] But while it is frequently compared to a slave narrative, the questions engaged by *Our Nig* are set up rather differently. The note of aggravated pride suggested in the Preface becomes still more pronounced in the novel's opening sentences, where the protagonist's mother, Mag Smith, is introduced as an orphan growing up "unprotected, uncherished, uncared for" (5). With laconic efficiency, Wilson describes Mag's encounter with an unnamed "charmer" and her ensuing seduction and betrayal. Upon first hearing "the music of love," the victim finds that

it whispered of an elevation before unaspired to; of ease and plenty her simple heart had never dreamed of as hers. She knew the voice of her charmer, so ravishing, sounded far above her. It seemed like an angel's, alluring her upward and onward. She thought she could ascend to him and be an equal. She surrendered to him a priceless gem, which he proudly garnered as a trophy, with those of other victims, and left her to her fate. The world seemed full of hateful deceivers and crushing arrogance. Conscious that the great bond of union to her former companions was severed, that the disdain of others would be insupportable, she determined to leave the few friends she possessed, and seek asylum among strangers. Her offspring came unwelcomed, and before its nativity numbered weeks, it passed from earth, ascending to a purer and better life.

"God be thanked," ejaculated Mag, as she saw its breathing cease; "no one can taunt *her* with my ruin." (6, original emphasis)

The mother's relief at the death of her infant has been compared to similar moments in slave narratives, such as when Jacobs, while musing over her child, "sometimes … wished that he might die in infancy."[25] But aside from the fact that the mother in this particular case is no slave and her child is not born into slavery, the most obvious difference is that Mag is relieved by the thought that her child will be spared, not the horrors of bondage, but the shame of her mother's embarrassment. That the mother should actually envy her own child's death takes the measure of her pride and humiliation. For Wilson supplements the familiar story of youthful seduction with the stirring of a new and sudden hunger for "elevation"; in the attention of her seducer, Mag envisions a step up the social ladder that does not simply promise "ease and plenty" but a validation of her worth as an equal. This is why the betrayal of her trust is experienced as a form of taunting, the faithless lover "proudly" claiming her virtue "as a trophy," the "world" not just disapproving but filled, in its "disdain," with a "crushing arrogance."

In documenting Mag's subsequent decline, Wilson's narrator describes the terrible slide from the experience of a legitimate grievance to the creation of an aggrieved personality. Not just resenting but feeding off "a feeling of degradation oppressing her" (7), it's made clear that Mag both suffers from and identifies with the role of outcast. "She vowed to ask no favors of familiar faces; to die neglected and forgotten," we are told at one point; "morose and revengeful, refusing all offers of a better home," she is described as "hugging her wrongs, but making no effort to escape" (8). Mag's paradox is in effect to have so completely internalized social norms as to turn them inside out. She only transgresses against these norms because she has allowed herself to become so utterly possessed by them that rage and shame are the only friends she will tolerate. Illustrating Kierkegaard's perception that envy is "the negative acknowledgement of excellence," both the rage and the shame pay tribute to her initial hope for acceptance, "alluring her onward and upward," by making a mockery of it.[26] Thus she methodically strips herself of all pretension to respectability. In desperate straits, she accedes to the approaches of a "kind-hearted African," Jim, and agrees to marry him; upon his death, she takes "another step down the ladder of infamy" (13) by living with his business partner and fellow African-American, Seth. From Mag's point of view, neither relationship has much to do with affection; in the absence of any further insight, we are left to infer her decision to spurn even marriage with Seth derives equally from defiance and self-abasement.

Mag Smith's significance to the story is to establish what it means to be taken down by a sense of *undeserved inferiority*. Interestingly, her only respite is her marriage to Jim, which is shown in a positive light, even though "she cared for him only as a means to subserve her own comfort" (15). When he dies of consumption, the feeling of "cold desolation" (16) returns while the contempt of the surrounding white community deepens. Notably, her two children provide no comfort. Although the narrator characterizes her as lapsing away into dull "insensibility," her final act in the novel before she vanishes from sight suggests something more. For in abandoning her eldest child, the six-year-old Frado, on the doorstep of the neighborhood sadist, a "she-devil" by the name of Mrs. Bellmont for whom Mag has worked in the past (and "she-devil" is Mag's own name for her), the mother not only ensures that she will continue to be taunted for her wrongs, but knowingly commits what can only be called an act of sadism of her own. Outraged at the judgment of "a sneering world" (7) that she cannot let go, Mag not only exemplifies the pathos of enforced humiliation but leaves her daughter in an environment where the same fate is likely to overtake her as well.

The affinity between the two white women does not stop here, however. Overcome by self-pity, rage, and shame; becoming increasingly irritable;

"yielding to fits of desperation, bursts of anger, and uttering curses too fearful to repeat" (16); and referring to her own children as "black devils" (16), Mag foreshadows a number of the features that make up Mrs. Bellmont's "vixen nature" (41). The latter's rage is obvious enough in the incessant scolding, kicking, whipping, beating, and general maltreatment Frado suffers at the hands of her mistress. (The narrative also contains hints that the two sons, James and Jack, may have been abused by their mother in childhood as well.)[27] Her shame is only a little less obvious, but equally prevalent. Without minimizing the complicity the other members of the Bellmont family must bear in permitting Frado's abuse to continue, they are clearly disturbed and frightened by the mother's temper, "a whirlwind charged with fire, daggers and spikes" (24–25). For the most part, the abuse occurs behind closed doors, out of earshot, and with threats of reprisal if exposed. Even as Mrs. Bellmont declares openly to her husband "I'll beat the money out of her, if I can't get her worth any other way" (90), it's not as though the beatings themselves are a public demonstration of power and intimidation in the way that the whippings and physical torture displayed in the slave narrative are expressly meant to be. Upon learning that Frado has attended church and has been invited to relate her experiences, Mrs. Bellmont's first thought is to wonder whether her victim has betrayed her. The next morning she threatens to whip Frado to death if she ever goes back (103–04).

The mother's sadism has attracted a variety of interpretations, some focusing on its role in facilitating the exploitation of Frado's labor and others on its role in enforcing racial distinctions. For Xiomara Santamarina, for example, the relentless mental and physical abuse serves to mask the ongoing economic benefits reaped by the Bellmont family in having an unpaid servant do virtually all the work inside and outside the home. It is, in other words, Frado's productivity that motivates the abuse. For Robert Reid-Pharr, on the other hand, it is Frado's status as a mulatto and her threat to racial purity that accounts for the fury of Mrs. Bellmont, who "trains up" Frado to be "our nig" by cutting her locks, dressing her in coarse cloth, and exposing her to the sun in order to darken her skin.[28] My description of these different points of emphasis should not obscure the extent to which they overlap, for as both these and other critics note, the complicity between racial oppression and class oppression is precisely one of the distinctive features of Wilson's text. At the same time, the very readiness of the text to confirm such hypotheses, with Mrs. Bellmont speaking openly of her intent to beat the money out of the hired help or ordering Frado outdoors to darken her skin lest she appear too white, suggests that what may seem like causes of behavior are in reality better understood as pretexts for something else.

For Mrs. Bellmont is, to put it mildly, a hard case. What else can be said of someone who, while entertaining guests, likes nothing so much as to dart into the kitchen from time to time, administer "a few sudden blows," and "then return to the sitting room, with *such* a satisfied expression, congratulating herself on her house-keeping qualities" (66; original emphasis)? With the exception of her daughter, Mary, who dies in her teens, she is not on good terms with her children. More feared than loved, she is indeed something of an outcast in her own home. She alienates her eldest daughter, Jane, in meddling with her choice of a husband and deceives a daughter-in-law in attempting to destroy, for no apparent reason, her marriage; her eldest son does not even call for her on his death-bed (he calls for Frado instead) while another looks on with delight when his mother's authority is ridiculed by Frado in front of the rest of the family. Because her husband and his sister jointly own the house and surrounding farm, Mrs. Bellmont has no economic standing, a source of further "alienation" and resentment (22, 45). On the other hand, so far as she is concerned, Frado's "time and person belonged solely to her" (41). Not surprisingly, Frado's very helplessness and vulnerability only seem to fuel Mrs. Bellmont's sadism until it becomes an overpowering addiction. A dreadful intimacy develops between the child and her persecutor, with the latter described at one point as "smother[ing] her resentment until a convenient opportunity offered," savagely beating the unloved girl behind closed doors, and threatening to " 'cut her tongue out' " (72) should Frado tell Mrs. Bellmont's son James. The threat is not only an admission that the violence is excessive (though of course this is small consolation to the victim) but ties the white woman to the black child through the mutual experience of humiliation and lost respectability.

" 'You have not treated her, mother, so as to gain her love,' " says her son, James, " 'she is only exhibiting your remissness in this matter' " (72). James is pointing out that his mother must share in the responsibility for Frado's unruly behavior, but the possibility that Frado serves to exhibit the mother's own "remissness" in a deeper sense becomes unmistakable as the novel unfolds. Wilson lays the ground for such an interpretation by telling us early on "no matter what occurred to ruffle [Mrs. Bellmont], or from what source provocation came, real or fancied, a few blows on Nig seemed to relieve her of a portion of her ill-will" (41). Needless to say, it is a short step from taking it out on Nig to shore up one's self-respect to seeing in Nig the embodiment of everything that is weak and shameful – even in oneself. The sense of a disavowed identification seems indeed palpable in the numerous scenes of violence in the novel, as in the following vignette, which emerges in the context of Frado's first serious bout of poor health owing to her overworked condition. Here the momentary uncertainty occasioned by the abrupt shifting of pronoun references seems to denote the virtual introjection of Frado, "the black devil" (16) who must be cast out from the white "she-devil" (18):

> But it was increasing upon [Frado] that she could no longer hide her indisposition. Her mistress entered one day, and finding her seated, commanded her to go to work. "I am sick," replied Frado, rising and walking slowly to her unfinished task, "and cannot stand long, I feel so bad."
>
> Angry that she should venture a reply to her command, she suddenly inflicted a blow which lay the tottering girl prostrate on the floor. Excited by so much indulgence of a dangerous passion, she seemed left to unrestrained malice; and snatching a towel, stuffed the mouth of the sufferer, and beat her cruelly. (82)

To stuff the mouth of the sufferer (neither the first nor the last time this method is followed) is of course to turn her into a thing, a mere object writhing on the floor. By stripping her of all dignity, Mrs. Bellmont exults in the supremacy of her power and in the abasement of her victim. It seems wrong to say that she treats Frado as an inferior. What she does – what she above all desires – is to show Frado what it feels like to be made to feel inferior. In this way Mrs. Bellmont, said to be "so ugly" (18) the help can't abide her presence, takes "a beautiful mulatto, with long, curly black hair, and handsome, roguish eyes, sparkling with an exuberance of spirit almost beyond restraint" (17) and leaves her "all broken down" (120), not just ruined in health but convinced that owing to her "ugly," "black" features "no one would love her" (108).

Thanks to the investigations of Barbara White we now know that Mrs. Bellmont was Rebecca Hutchinson in real life, a direct descendant of Anne Hutchinson, of all people.[29] White's speculation on the possible history of child abuse in the family, along with its apparent decline in prestige, confirms what any reader of *Our Nig* will already suspect; but the further point here is to note how Wilson, in transmuting lived experience into fiction, uses Mrs. Bellmont's sadism to extend the theme of enforced inferiority sounded at the outset of the novel. For just as Mag Smith regards her deceased daughter as the literal embodiment of her disgrace, Mrs. Bellmont would beat the blackness out of herself by beating it into Nig in a ritual of compulsive rage that both victim and victimizer are helpless to stop. Hardly reducible to a personal infirmity, the theme of enforced inferiority spreads into widening circles of implication such that, once Frado gets free of the Bellmont household, she soon encounters fresh evidence of the same pathology in the politics of the anti-slavery protest, where "illiterate harangues" are delivered by fugitive slaves to "hungry abolitionists" (128). To the degree that white Northerners are most receptive to black Americans who make a display of their own abjection, Frado finds that the lecture platform has become a minstrel show. A continuation of Mrs. Bellmont's methods by other means, it, too, stuffs a towel in the mouth of the sufferer. Lest this seem an overstatement Wilson is careful to point out the purely nominal character of Frado's freedom in the novel's concluding pages, where she is "watched by kidnappers [and] maltreated by professed abolitionists, who didn't want slaves at the South, nor niggers in their own houses, North" (129).

"Equality is normally the language of the underdog," notes the historian J. R. Pole, "and habitually loses some of its magnetism on the attainment of a sufficient degree of success."[30] Without necessarily intending to, Pole's characterization comes close to collapsing equality into envy, making the former indistinguishable from the latter. In the history of conservative political thought, this connection is of course made much more openly, while Freud goes still further in speculating that envy lay at the foundation of all modes of social organization, egalitarian and otherwise. But if the general idea here is that a craving for social equality is nothing but the desire of the "underdog" to get even, the texts we've been considering betray a different emphasis. In terms of social status, power, and education, Mrs. Bellmont is anything but an "underdog," but that doesn't prevent her from embracing the role, loudly complaining, for example, once it's revealed that Frado has attended church, that "we should soon have her in the parlor, as smart as our own girls" (89). And just as Kirkland makes it clear that resentments on the frontier intensify precisely as differences in the ownership of resources become more and more insignificant, we have also seen how, in Hawthorne's novel, it is possible for an author actually to envy one of his characters – a feat of literary leveling that not even Bakhtin could have imagined. In short, the classic stand-off of the haves and the have-nots is superseded by the sense that envy has become an all-purpose signifier of discontent, attaching itself to those in relatively powerful and privileged positions no less readily than to the dispossessed and oppressed.

In a surprisingly tender passage, Tocqueville speaks of how equality "every day gives every man a multitude of little delights. The charms of equality are felt every hour and are within everyone's reach; the noblest hearts are not insensitive to them and the commonest souls delight in them." The charm of equality is to de-centralize and diffuse social esteem, placing it within the reach of a broad range of sensibilities and rendering it a familiar, even homely presence. At the same time, such a development makes ideas about what counts as a "sufficient degree of success" (to recall Pole's phrasing) somewhat more variable and therefore more ambiguous and more abstract than they might otherwise seem in a culture where honor and rank are more centrally monitored and distributed. As always in Tocqueville, the internalization of a social norm implies a process of abstraction. Judging from their tendentious appeals to fairness (think, for example, of Mag Smith's self-pity or Hawthorne's struggle to explain what makes the Judge reprehensible), the envious have trouble getting past the discrepancy between what they feel is owed to them and what they get. The nature of their grievance, that is to say, is neither private nor public but arises in the failure of the two realms to agree. The envious are at the mercy of the charms of equality, the promised harmony of private and public conceptions of worth that lie behind the homely feeling of sweet consolation and perpetual delight made available by the democratizing of esteem.

PART III

Equal but separate

I am myself; you are yourself; we are two distinct persons, equal persons. What you are, I am. You are a man, and so am I. I am not by nature bond to you, or you to me. Nature does not make your existence depend upon me, or mine upon yours. I cannot walk upon your legs, or you upon mine. I cannot breathe for you, or you for me; I must breathe for myself, and you for yourself.

Frederick Douglass, "Letter to His Old Master"[1]

Old Tiff is the name Harriet Beecher Stowe gives to the loyal slave of a destitute and dying woman and her three children in *Dred: A Tale of the Great Dismal Swamp* (1856). The name Old Tiff gives himself, on the other hand, is somewhat different. "I's Tiff Peyton, I is," he explains, "raised on de great Peyton place."[2] "One of the most celebrated families in Virginia" (89), the Peytons, it is true, have fallen on hard times, the plantation now "worn-out and broken-down" and the daughter, Tiff's current mistress, disgraced and exiled for marrying a man below her station. Nevertheless, Old Tiff's devotion to the Peyton's "ancestral greatness" (89), which is forever on his mind, remains unshaken. So complete is his loyalty that Old Tiff, "though crooked and black, never seemed to cherish the slightest doubt that the whole force of Peyton blood coursed through his veins and that Peyton honor was intrusted to his keeping" (90). Nothing in the novel suggests that there is any basis for this belief about his ancestry; rather, we are encouraged to regard Tiff's insistence that he's been "fetched up in the very fustest families of Old Virginny" as "an aristocratic weakness" (91), like his habit of wearing spectacles made of plain glass over his perfectly healthy eyes. Harry Gordon, another slave who actually does have the blood of his master coursing through his veins, puts it best when he says simply of Old Tiff "he just identifies himself with his mistress and her children" (109).

In most abolitionist writing of the period, the identification of the slave with the master is sure to be featured as one of slavery's pathologies. "They seemed to think that the greatness of their masters was transferable to themselves,"[3] writes Frederick Douglass of the quarreling among slaves from adjoining estates as to who had the better master, a quarrel repeated in the verbal duel between Old Tiff of the Peytons and Old Hundred of the Gordons. But whereas for someone like Douglass the respect paid to the master is directly proportional to the self-respect denied the slave, Stowe goes out of her way to pre-empt any such inference, stating explicitly that Old Tiff "was on the happiest terms of fellowship with himself, he *liked* himself, he believed in himself" (91; original emphasis). Instead of turning to the greatness of the master to prop up an injured pride, Tiff Peyton props up the failing family "honor" so that when Susan Peyton dies he drives away her shiftless, alcoholic husband and takes it upon himself to raise the children, seeing to it that they speak, dress, and act in accordance with the genteel standards of "old Virginny" (548). Perhaps we should say that Tiff doesn't need the prestige of the master to feel better about himself because he doesn't retain a sense of self to begin with – doesn't retain, that is to say, a sense of himself as a separate entity distinct from the interests and identity of those he serves. "He don't seem to have a root of his own," remarks one character, marveling at the utter selflessness of Tiff's devotion, "he seems to grow out of something else" (285).

The devoted slave is of course a stock character in the fiction of the time and in this case is no doubt intended by Stowe to serve as a comic foil to the bitter fulminations of Dred, the novel's designated "herald of wrath and woe" (210). All the same, the syndrome exemplified by Old Tiff is not really all that unique. For example, John Gordon, uncle of the book's heroine, Nina Gordon, and owner of a large plantation, believes "in the equality of *gentlemen* and the equal rights of well-bred people" (289; original emphasis) while at the same time he shows no hesitation in attending a camp meeting and praying beside poor whites and slaves. Uncle John is not especially well disposed toward either group: regarding the whites, he's in favor of getting together "hunting parties" to "exterminate" (190) the "poor, miserable trash" (191) who squat on his land; as for the slaves, he is forever complaining that, given all the trouble they cause, he works for them and not the other way around. Oddly enough, though, this disdain doesn't preclude a certain familiarity with both of them. Whether it's rubbing shoulders with "that rabble," as his wife reprovingly exclaims, of "such very common people" (281) or playing the part of tyrannous master (we first meet him as he's about to whip one of the servants, only to stumble and fall) when neither he nor his slaves take the role seriously, Uncle John is remarkably cavalier about maintaining his distinction as one of the "well-bred." That's not to say that the master identifies with the slave in the same way the slave identifies with the master – it's not as if Uncle John walks around thinking that he has Negro blood in his veins. Still, a certain resemblance does come into play. If Old Tiff provides comic relief for Stowe's tragic story by virtue of his aristocratic pretensions, Uncle John, teased at one point as "the greatest democrat that ever walked" (289), provides something of the same thing in his unseemly interactions with his inferiors.

By definition equality of conditions does not think in terms of superiors and inferiors but arranges people in lateral relationships. They exist side by side. As we saw in the last two chapters, this invests the social whole with a special immediacy, facilitating an instant identification between the many and the one. From this it would seem to follow that the essence of inequality of conditions is to divide and insulate. This is certainly Stowe's understanding. "It is the aristocratic nature of society at the South," the narrator remarks halfway through the novel, that "so completely segregates people of a certain position in life from any acquaintance with the movements of human nature in circles below them" (280). Thus for someone like Nina Gordon "the horrors and sorrows of the slave-coffle were a sealed book," while those who might be aware of such "fearful things … took very good care to keep out of their way" (280). The general idea here is not difficult to grasp. Inequality encourages superiors to view the suffering of inferiors as inconsequential since they are, after all, inferiors. It circumscribes or denies the extension of sympathetic identification with the disenfranchised and the oppressed that a genuine spirit of equality is thought to promote.[4]

The interest of figures like Old Tiff or Uncle John is to introduce a crucial qualification to this familiar contrast. In Old Tiff we have a character who has taken identification with the other about as far as it can go; by the time he takes unofficial custody of the Peyton children, it is remarked that "he verily thinks they belong to him" (285), an impression that is confirmed by the end of the book when Old Tiff (also called "Uncle") sends the son off to school and the daughter off to marriage. But of course this sort of identification exists because of and not despite Tiff's position as servant. In the same way, Uncle John "isn't afraid to kneel at the altar with Bill Dakin, or Jim Sykes, because he's so sure that his position can't be compromised" (290). The two individuals mentioned happen to be a slave catcher and slave-trader, just the sort of "miserable whites" that Uncle John would "kick off my doorstep" (289). But aristocratic pride, by keeping racial and class barriers firmly in place, may therefore make it easier for those barriers to be crossed. As Nina explains, if Uncle John doesn't mind fraterniz- ing with people he otherwise despises, "it's only because he's so immeasurably certain of his superior position" (289–90) – just as Old Tiff doesn't mind fancying himself a member of the family he should otherwise resent because he is so immeasurably sure of his inferior position. In such cases, the very extremity of social distance has the paradoxical effect of facilitating a surprising degree of familiar- ity or even a blurring of identities.

Hegel's parable of the lord and the bondsman, with its talk of one consciousness alienated in the breast of another, makes the same point even more vividly. The pathology of inequality is that it renders interpersonal boundaries too fluid, too susceptible to dissolution, not unlike the example of the slaves mentioned by Douglass who can't keep their identities separate from their masters'. This would seem to imply that the health of equality must in some sense involve enforcing those boundaries and maintaining that separateness. The tendency to posit a strong connection between sympathetic identi- fication and equality is not wrong but the countervailing impulse is no less important. If I am just as good as you and you are just as good as me then we each need to go our separate ways. Having lost himself in the borrowed grandeur of the Peytons, Old Tiff cannot go his separate way. He has abandoned himself, as it were. If a kind of inattentiveness or self-forgetfulness marks extreme inequality, one might anticipate a no less pronounced vigilance or even territoriality about boundaries, personal and otherwise, as a hallmark of egalitarian culture.

The next two chapters examine different manifestations of this urge toward self-differentiation. As Tocqueville saw, the paradox whereby extreme social distance can sometimes facilitate an identification between master and servant, as we have seen in the individual cases of Uncle John and Old Tiff, has its counterpart in the paradox whereby those who are equals in spirit must maintain distance if they are to maintain their standing as equals. The writings of Emerson, Fuller, and, to a lesser extent, Thoreau do not reflect the second half of this statement so much as codify and endlessly comment upon its complications. In particular, with transcendental-ist conceptions of friendship, identification with the other is both inescapable (since we are all spiritual equals we are all one) and abhorrent (since, being all spiritually one, we must each be individ-uals). The result is a baffling combination of lofty idealization and cynical deflation whose convolutions many interpreters have errone-ously ascribed to an "apolitical" or "asocial" bias in transcendental thought. The final chapter analyzes the impact of notions such as self-reliance and self-realization on work, notions which, of course, were first popularized by figures like Emerson and Fuller. Here my interest is in the same dialectic of identification and counter-identification we find governing definitions of friendship, for at the same time that work becomes increasingly extolled through the first part of the century as a mark of equality that levels distinctions between individ-uals, it is increasingly taken to be an activity that should never define who or what the worker is. Various sites and texts, from Fourier's phalanstery to a memoir by a Lowell "factory girl" or a novel by Louisa May Alcott, furnish illustrations of what occurs when the logic of equal but separate enters the workplace.

CHAPTER FIVE

Transcending friendships

Ralph Waldo Emerson is American culture's evangelist of equality. Finding established religion corrupt, he saw in supposedly secular developments such as egalitarianism and a newfound demand for inner worth a more authentically religious impulse. The good news he brings is that a permanent inequality of the spirit is an impossibility, that, somewhat in the manner of contemporaries like Douglass or Walker, equality is a reality whose denial leads to error and mystification. In his writings the mere invocation of equality is a source of wonder. What the genius of Plato may have thought or the legendary saint may have felt is really of secondary consequence for the reader who can see that "what Plato has thought, he may think; what a saint has felt, he may feel."[1] Conveyed with all the fervor of a conversion experience, such epiphanies appear repeatedly in *Essays: First Series* (1841), arguably Emerson's major work, the volume whose themes would set the pattern for the rest of his writing career. If Emerson can be said to have invented a religion of democracy, then its central tenet and inspiration is the summoning of an equality in the form of a radical likeness connecting each to all.

But if equality is a source of inspiration, what exactly does it inspire? For Emerson, as for almost everybody then and since, the answer is obvious: it inspires self-reliance. If I can think what Plato thought then there's no reason why I should defer to Plato's opinion. I need to venture forth and create my own. To be equal is to want to be autonomous. The more I am persuaded that I'm just like everybody else, the more I will be inclined to covet my own distinctiveness – that is equality's mandate, so to speak. The experience of relatedness and the urge toward separateness go together.

From this perspective, equality does not eliminate so much as it reframes and relocates social distinction. As much as it abolishes caste and the traditions of rank (or at least appears to do so), it places a special emphasis on the need to stand apart. Indeed, in certain circumstances failure to respect this demand may have genuinely shameful consequences, as we noted in the previous chapter. Thus one of the worst things an equal can do is to think and act like another equal. When that happens we find ourselves in the sorry fix of being "forced to take with shame our own opinion from another" (259). Precisely because we are all the same, we must be different: in making sense of this general principle, we don't need to postulate the corrupting influence of elitism or an invidious desire to stand above the crowd. A commitment to egalitarian norms will suffice. Thus, to pursue the example of taking our own beliefs from another, if I find myself mouthing opinions of those who are close to me (my neighbor, say), then I am in trouble; whereas if I find myself capable of thinking the thoughts of those who are remote from me (Plato or a saint, for example), then I am inspired. Egalitarian norms, like any norm, are expressly hierarchical in that they have their own distinctive rankings and orders of preference, enforcing some behaviors and disallowing others.

A common procedure in critical discussions of *Essays: First Series* has been to pit self-reliance *against* equality, as when critics contend that it is Emerson's individualism that is responsible for his ambivalence – for some, even indifference – to social reform.[2] But taking seriously the idea that Emerson "was the natural product of a society in which it was held that every one was equal to every one else,"[3] as Henry James once put it, casts this hackneyed opposition in a new light. Essays such as "Friendship" and "Love" are nothing if not ambitious in dramatically revising standard conceptions of these topics in order to make them conform to a new politics of equality. At the same time, the dialectic of an all-embracing relatedness and the imperative to stand apart introduces complications that may also be found in Emerson's views on self-reliance and political activism more generally. In Margaret Fuller's case these complications are no less apparent, as can be seen in *Woman in the Nineteenth Century*, where affirmations of an absolute sameness between women and men curiously alternate with affirmations of an insurmountable and essential difference.

EMERSON'S STRANGE EQUALITY

Even by Emerson's standards, the essay on "Friendship" is riddled with contradiction and paradox. A "beautiful enemy" (351), the friend is both ally and antagonist; a virtual mirror or "semblance of my being" (348), the friend must be something more than a mere echo; "so real and equal" that we cannot doubt his existence, the friend is a product of fear and fantasy" (347). We need friends to alleviate solitude; we need friends to enrich solitude. Complete sincerity is a hallmark of friendship; complete sincerity is impossible once a second party appears. And so on. The general idea that "a friend is a sort of paradox in nature" (348) is, to be sure, a common theme in the literature on the topic, but in reworking his sources Emerson shows little hesitation in allowing the paradoxes to proliferate. Exhausting to read, the essay must have been exhausting to write; the internal corrections and increasingly fussy discriminations on what may or may not count as "true relations" verge on the pedantic. By the end of the performance, even the essayist confesses his weariness, acknowledging that "it would indeed give me a certain household joy to quit this lofty seeking, this spiritual astronomy, or search of stars, and come down to warm sympathies with you" (353–54). But of course, as the contrast here between the skyward and earthbound suggests, the transcendentalist can't contemplate the domestic alternative without condescending to it. For better or worse, he is bent on pursuing a "higher" (352) treatment.

Many have seen in this rather austere outlook evidence of personal limitation. Emerson, we are told, was a cold fish. The first to raise this criticism was Emerson himself, who self-consciously tries to parry "the imputation of unnecessary hardness and stoicism" (327) in his thinking about love in the essay of that name, an essay that directly precedes the one on friendship. Oddly enough, however, both essays begin by evoking a world suffused by a boundless, ever-expanding affection. The first two sentences in "Love" are not lacking in ardor: "Every promise of the soul has innumerable fulfillments, each of its joys ripens into a new want. Nature, uncontainable, flowing, forelooking, in the first sentiment of kindness anticipates already a benevolence which shall lose all particular regards in its general light" (327). "Friendship" likewise pays tribute to a universal bliss: "We have a great deal more kindness than is ever spoken. Maugre all the selfishness that chills like east winds the world, the whole human family is bathed with an element of love like a fine ether" (341). Henry James may have been right to complain of Emerson's disembodied spirituality, but he was wrong to equate this with passionlessness.[4] Distance here is conducive to passion, not opposed to it. Coldness becomes a kind of warmth.

Rather than a passing idiosyncrasy, this paradox is in fact the source for most of the other paradoxes in the essay, informing virtually everything Emerson has to say about friendship. Its importance is made clear from the outset, where we are presented with a little narrative, a parable of sorts, worth quoting in its entirety.

A commended stranger is expected and announced, and an uneasiness betwixt pleasure and pain invades all the hearts of the household. His arrival almost brings fear to the good hearts that would welcome him. The house is dusted, all things fly into their places, the old coat is exchanged for the new, and they must get up a dinner if they can. Of a commended stranger, only the good report is told by others, only the good and new is heard by us. He stands to us for humanity. He is what we wish. Having imagined and invested him, we ask how we should stand related in conversation and action with such a man, and are uneasy with fear. The same idea exalts conversation with him. We talk better than we are wont. We have the nimblest fancy, a richer memory, and our dumb devil has taken leave for the time. For long hours we can continue a series of sincere, graceful, rich communications, drawn from the oldest, secretest experience, so that they who sit by, of our own kinsfolk and acquaintance, shall feel a lively surprise at our unusual powers. But as soon as the stranger intrudes his partialities, his definitions, his defects, into the conversation, it is all over. He has heard the first, the last and the best he will ever hear from us. He is no stranger now. Vulgarity, ignorance, misapprehension, are old acquaintances. (341–42)

We see the basic paradox: the only kind of friend worth having is one who remains a stranger. And of course what makes the stranger a stranger has nothing to do with the fact that "we" have little to go on concerning "him" beyond a "good report." The crucial thing is that the stranger is not a person at all but many persons in one: "He stands to us for humanity." Further, it is presumably because he does so that we are inspired by a sense of "unusual powers." Projecting a sameness or commonality that is evoked with all the commingling of anxiety and delight one would expect from a sublime encounter, the stranger is Emerson's harbinger of democracy. Like Whitman's Answerer, he gives the "sign" of an unsuspected connectedness. Somehow the sublimity of the stranger and the expectations that accompany his appearance are bound up with the sublimity of experiencing equality itself.

So conceived, friendship emerges as a thoroughly politicized concept from the outset, with the interest and excitement of personal relations defined in terms of democratic relations. In itself this is not particularly surprising. The notion that the relationship between friends may serve as a model for the relationship between citizens is a familiar theme from Aristotle onward. But what is noteworthy in this case is the suggestion that democratic relations require us to treat personal relations impersonally; after all, once the stranger stops being a stranger, "it is all over." According to the essay's paradoxical code, to be a friend and nothing more is to be a mere individual and, as always in Emerson, to be a mere individual is at bottom to be partial, constricted, needy, other-directed and incomplete. Alternatively, to surrender individuality to a higher power is to be disinterested, enlarged, impervious, and complete. The friend is a door that may open out in either direction, which is one reason why the sensation he inspires is "betwixt pleasure and pain." So long as "the Deity in me" acquaints itself with the Deity in my friend, then together they can surmount "the thick walls of character, relation, age, sex, circumstance," confident in the knowledge that their union "now makes many one" (343). Both interpersonally and intrapersonally, then, strangeness is a vital feature of friendship. It's not just that the friend needs to be a stranger to me; I need to be a stranger to myself. And this seems to make perfect sense. If each stands to the other "for humanity," then neither can stand before the other as an individual. As Emerson explains, "the soul does not respect men as it respects itself" (344).

Friendship's primary virtue is thus to educate, in the root sense of educing or drawing forth latent, universal powers. It pulls you out of "the infinite remoteness" that prevails between individuals (indeed, that is the condition of individuality itself) and unveils the representative soul dormant within. "Let us feel, if we will, the absolute insulation of man," Emerson remarks, "we are sure that we have all in us" (353). Let us, that is to say, insist as much as we please on our separateness. The truth is that beneath the superficial divisions subsists an underlying commonality. And since, as we have seen, true friendship consists in the uncovering of this commonality, friendship and inequality are incompatible. In fact, even the suggestion of inequality in one relationship, we are told, spoils all the rest (345). As for the acquaintance who fails to keep pace, there is no cause for concern: "if he is unequal, he will presently pass away" (354). In coaxing from us a recognition of a hidden sameness, the strangeness of the friend and the transcendence of equality converge on the same point in lifting us beyond mere personhood.

It's only fair to add, though, that the very logic that allows us to triumph over self-enclosure also insists upon it. As Emerson says, "there must be very two, before there can be very one" (350). His assurance that an "absolute insulation" separates us in appearance only, that a universal Allness is sure to prevail, may be turned around. Let us insist, if we like, on a universal Allness that equalizes everyone; we must be sure to maintain a proper distance lest that Allness be corrupted. A basic polarity becomes apparent as the essay develops. The democratic self is to be receptive, expansive, and ready to yield itself up to a sublime equality that links one soul to another; the democratic self is to be vigilant, territorial, and ready to repel any false pretender that stands in the way of "my mighty gods" (354). With a rigor as exacting and as intricate as any code of manners from the Old World, Emerson outlines the proper boundaries of interpersonal conduct.

Let me be alone to the end of the world, rather than that my friend should overstep, by a word or a look, his real sympathy. (350)

I cannot choose but rely on my own poverty more than on your wealth. I cannot make your consciousness tantamount to mine. Only the star dazzles; the planet has a faint, moon-like ray. (344)

It makes no difference how many friends I have, and what content I can find in conversing with each, if there be one to whom I am not equal. If I have shrunk unequal from one contest, the joy I find in all the rest becomes mean and cowardly. I should hate myself, if then I made my other friends my asylum. (345)

We must have society on our own terms, and admit and exclude it on the slightest cause. I cannot afford to speak much with my friend. If he is great, he makes me so great that I cannot descend to converse ... though I prize my friends, I cannot afford to talk with them and study their visions lest I lose my own ... (353)

So I will owe to my friends this evanescent intercourse. I will receive from them, not what they have but what they are. They should give me that which properly they cannot give, but which emanates from them. But they shall not hold me by any relations less subtle and pure. We will meet as though we met not, and part as though we parted not. (354)

The "thick walls of individual character" (343) protect as much as they impede. The self, open to the "divine affinity" of a radical oneness, must also be dug in and well-defended. Even the experience of empathy in the everyday sense of putting oneself in the place of another becomes an adventure fraught with peril. It is acceptable for the stranger to dazzle as long as the simple friend casts a pallid, borrowed light.

So even as Emerson insists that friendship and equality go together we see that intimacy and equality cannot. In "Love" he takes the most personal of topics and enjoins us to treat it impersonally. He extols "a love which knows not sex, nor person, nor partiality" (337). The ideal relationship is, astonishingly, one where the lovers "should represent the human race to each other" (336), just as the ideal friendship is one where "each [friend] stands for the whole world" (352). The key thing is not to relate to another so much as to relate, as it were, to relatedness itself – not to Henry and Walt and Margaret and Ellen but to "the deep identity which beneath [their] disparities unites them" (350).[5] Accomplices in crime, Emerson notes at one point, may speak to one another on "even terms," but the same cannot be said of "those whom we admire and love" – at least not "at first" (351). Even the experience of crime produces what intimacy, left to itself, has difficulty reaching, namely, that "higher platform" where similarity may be discerned and souls may meet.

Because the close must be made far and the far must be made close, an air of unreality can threaten to overtake "Friendship." Equilibrium between the two extremes is difficult to sustain, all the more so once we see that there is no telling when the mere friend may betray a redemptive strangeness or when that strangeness fades away and leaves us once again to confront our "counterpart … a sort of beautiful enemy" (351). This reversibility, masterfully rendered by Emerson's edgy, angular prose, can make a mess of personal relations.

I must feel pride in my friend's accomplishments as if they were mine, – and a property in his virtues. I feel as warmly when he is praised, as the lover when he hears applause of his engaged maiden. We over-estimate the conscience of our friend. His goodness seems better than our goodness, his nature finer, his temptations less. Every thing that is his, – his name, his form, his dress, books, and instruments, – fancy enhances. Our own thought sounds new and larger from his mouth. (343)

Pride in the friend's accomplishments slides off into idolatry of the friend's accomplishments. Like a train helplessly riding off the rails, identification with the other can barely get going before it flips over into a form of servitude. Then again, at the other end of the spectrum, if we proudly refuse to submit to any such servitude, we may nevertheless find that this only deepens a sense of intimate connection we had thought we were renouncing:

A man who stands united with his thought conceives magnificently of himself. He is conscious of a universal success, even though bought by uniform particular failures. No advantages, no powers, no gold or force, can be any match for him. I cannot choose but rely on my poverty more than on your wealth. I cannot make your consciousness tantamount to mine. Only the star dazzles; the planet has a faint, moon-like ray. (344)

Here it's as if the mere recital of the other's assets triggers the need for a countering response, with the unnamed "he" magically and without warning turning into a "you" addressed by an "I." So even as the passage insists on maintaining a distance between self and other, the unexpected turn to the second person belies that message. More perversely still, since the "universal success" of the one plainly consists in transcending worldly powers and possessions ("no gold or force, can be any match for him"), the determination of the other to cling to "my poverty" would appear to replicate more than repudiate the terms on which "your wealth" is acquired. Altogether, then, the effect is to create an impression of interchangeable selves even in the effort to insist on their separateness. "Friendship,"

Emerson notes later on, "requires that rare mean betwixt likeness and unlikeness" (350). To the extent that an underlying likeness drives the need for unlikeness, the prospects for a companionship "so real and equal" (347) that it can't be doubted appear inherently unstable.

No wonder Emerson finds in friendship "a perpetual disappointment" (345). Where an innate equality is thought to lurk in every breast, the either–or of dominance and submission is likely to haunt the interpretation of every relationship. "Individuals, like nations," Thoreau explains in *Walden*, "must have suitable broad and natural boundaries, even a considerable neutral ground, between them."[6] Without sufficient distance, the exchange of ideas may become lethal: "the bullet of your thought must have overcome its lateral and ricochet motion and fallen into its last and steady course before it reaches the ear of the hearer, else it may plough out again through the side of his head" (94). In one ear and out the other is presumably the idiomatic expression Thoreau is playing off of here, the main idea being that, without due reflection, thoughts will scatter and elude the listener's understanding. As with "Friendship," however, the terms in which the point is made work against the ostensible message. Although Thoreau is describing the optimal conditions for conversation, the gruesome brutality of his metaphor overwhelms the apparent intent. The image of a bullet lodging in the ear, much less passing through the other side of the head, makes the line between taking in someone's meaning and being taken out by it rather uncertain. Thus, when Thoreau wonders "what sort of space is that which separates a man from his fellows and makes him solitary" (89), the force of the question is not to ask how solitude may be overcome but how it might be achieved. "If we speak reservedly and thoughtfully," he writes in the chapter entitled "Visitors," which immediately succeeds "Solitude," "we want to be farther apart." In order "to enjoy the most intimate society," "we must not only be silent, but commonly so far apart that we cannot possibly hear each other's voice in any case" (95). Ultimately we are left with the picture of the author and his visitors, shoving their chairs back "until they touched the wall in opposite corners, and then commonly there was not room enough" (95).

"There can never be deep peace between two spirits," Emerson declares, "never mutual respect, until, in their dialogue, each stands for the whole world" (352). But if this is true, so is the reverse; "deep peace" and ongoing strife are two sides of the same coin. For where each stands to each as a representative soul, undue attention to the other is at best superfluous and at worst self-destructive. Why else should we fear that, in studying the "visions" of our friend, we risk losing our own? For Emerson, as we have seen, the solution is to recast sharing between friends as a purely impersonal transaction between strangers. This is why "the only joy I have in his being mine, is that the *not mine* is *mine*" (350, original emphasis). And, of course, to the extent that it is conceivable that the friend become stranger may convert what is mine into *the* not mine, I (or rather the stranger within) return the favor. Characteristically, Thoreau's sense that we need to be so far apart that "we cannot possibly hear each other's voice in any case" makes a version of the same point by way of a pun – with sufficient distance, the voice will have no case, no definite pronoun that may be assigned to it. Inevitably, this dismantling of mere personhood extends to the author himself, who finds that "however intense my experience, I am conscious of the presence and the criticism of a part of me, which, as it were, is not a part of me"; this, too, is a manifestation of the stranger within or what Thoreau calls a "spectator," who likewise cannot be heard in any case since, in "sharing no experience but taking note of it … [it] is no more I than it is you" (91). To be authentic, democratic friendship requires a ruthless process of abstraction. Thoreau's concluding remark that "this doubleness may easily make us poor neighbors and friends sometimes" (91) is as ironic as it is true.

Here we find the true rationale behind transcendentalism's famous mistrust of social reform or indeed any kind of collective action. As Emerson writes in "Friendship," "almost all people descend to meet. All association must be a compromise" (345), scruples that he expresses at greater length in "New England Reformers," where we are told that "each man, if he attempts to join himself to others, is on all sides cramped and diminished … ; and the stricter the union, the smaller and the more pitiful he is" (599). If joining up means selling out for the transcendentalist, that is because the preferred mode of activism consists of a silent meeting of the minds ("this union must be inward, and not one of covenants" [599]) that respects the strict separation of each. Again, association among the like-minded and equal is apt to result in compromise, while action performed at a distance and under the auspices of a higher "union" of souls, equal but separate, is the more efficacious way of combating social injustice. It's not that the various platforms of social reform should not be taken seriously, but they are doomed to fail, according to Emerson, until the reformer can lift us up to "some higher platform" that enables us to glimpse "the secret soul" that allows for a "perfect union" (604, 599). Without the guidance of a primal, innate equality, "the first and last reality" that "works over our heads and under our feet" (607), the pursuit of worldly reforms is pointless.

Although Emerson's scruples regarding social activism are routinely taken to betray his political conservatism, once applied to a different context these same scruples can create a very different impression. For example, in "Love" he offers a rather devastating portrayal of matrimony: like the true reformer who must stand apart in order to be effective, the partners to a "real marriage," in coming to see that the passion that originally brought them together is sure to wither and die, will accordingly go their own way, each "lending a cheerful, disengaged furtherance" (336) to the other's aspirations. Properly understood, "our affections are but tents of a night," and where the passions are understood to be nomadic at heart, marriage will seem like a prison. Thus peering through the relentlessly sunny prose is, at the very end of the essay, a rather grim snapshot of "two persons, a man and a woman ... shut up in one house to spend in the nuptial society forty or fifty years" (337). Like the temperance convention or the anti-slavery rally, the domestic circle is more of a trap or an encumbrance than a worthy site of sociability – something "the progress of the soul," like it or not, is destined to overrun, just as it is destined to overrun pretty much all sites of repose. Entirely contrary to the pieties of the time, the moral of "Love" is that the only kind of love worth cherishing is "that which you know not in yourself, and can never know" (333). To fix its special "radiance" to a specific person, site, or sexuality is to extinguish it.

All the same, these appeals to a higher platform or to the progress of the soul cannot avoid some obvious questions: does the transcendentalist define friendship and love in such rarefied terms as to render equality an unreal, otherworldly concept? Does the correlation he draws between strangeness and equality only serve to put equality out of reach, especially when attempting to effect social reform? Even Emerson, while maintaining that "it is foolish to be afraid of making our ties too spiritual" (353), concedes that "the higher the style we demand of friendship, of course the less easy to establish it with flesh and blood" (352). Moreover, it seems telling that with the final paragraph of "Friendship" it is the concept of friendship that gets enshrined while "the crude and cold companion" is unceremoniously shunted aside. Driving its premises to their utmost conclusion, the essay ends by paying tribute to a "true love" that does not merely "transcend the unworthy object" but, in leaving behind persons altogether, "dwells and broods on the eternal . . . feels rid of so much earth and feels its independency the surer" (354). The essay ends, that is to say, by spiritualizing friendship to such an extreme that, as "the poor interposed mask crumbles," companionship is purged of companions. Deifying the "unworthy object," friendship deifies itself, and in so doing affirms an equality that would appear to be out of this world.

And yet to say that an essay like "Friendship" embraces equality in order to render it more remote misses the point. Far from backing off from a commitment to equality, the essay is an exceptionally rigorous, even fanatical attempt to apply its logic to the realm of personal relations. Indeed the very purity of its commitment is what makes its findings appear perverse or unacceptable. Like the truths brought back from Plato's cave that are too dazzling for mere mortals to comprehend, the truths expounded in "Friendship" are embraced with too much clarity and fixity of purpose for us to assimilate. Emerson, in other words, was not just ahead of his time, but remains ahead of ours. Treating authors as if they transcended the limits of their own time (much less our own) is, I realize, out of fashion; we academic critics aren't supposed to talk that way anymore. But the transcendence I have in mind comes about not because Emerson surpasses his culture but because he happens to be more single-minded than most in prosecuting its most defining ideal. Those who find it useful to judge the writings of someone from the past as "ahistorical" or "apolitical" are generally moved to do so because those writings are thought to betray values that are either too "individualistic" or too "universalizing." As we have begun to see, though, the temptation to treat these two characteristics, both especially prominent in Emerson, as evidence of escapism is a mistake. To see this more fully we need a better understanding of how the individual and the universal are tied together in his essays and how the logic of equality sheds light on their interaction.

QUESTIONING AUTHORITY

In transcendentalist accounts of friendship, it's the thought that counts. "[B]ig thoughts in big words" (94), Thoreau's epithet for the conversations at Walden Pond, equally applies to the sessions presided over by Bronson Alcott or Margaret Fuller. The impossibly high-toned intellectuality of transcendentalist talk – what Perry Miller once called its "somewhat ludicrous cerebral frenzy" – has been an easy target of ridicule, but its excesses amount to something more than a cultural pose.[7] Inasmuch as the purpose of "friends [is to] encourage mental self-reliance in each other,"[8] as George Kateb puts it, there is an obvious and indispensable connection to be drawn between friendship and thought. Pressing beyond the Aristotelean notion that the friend is a second self, transcendentalist rhetoric engages in what might be called a process of personification in reverse: rather than ideas dressed up as human beings, we get human beings defined as ideas. Emerson's sense of the friend as "a picture and effigy [of my soul]" (344), like Fuller's sense of "the daughters and the sons of time [as] the twin exponents of a divine thought," testifies to the pervasive bond between subjectivity and idealism. It goes without saying that "thought" in this context has nothing to do with propositional content. Just because Thoreau confidently affirms that "the value of a man is not in his skin, that we may touch him" (92) doesn't mean that he thinks that the value of the man is in his ideas, that we may learn from him. As we have seen, Emerson wants his friends "to give me that which properly they cannot give" (354); what he wants, that is to say, is not *their* thought but "thought," with "thought" understood not as a claim or assertion but as a token of relatedness.

Admittedly all this talk about the abstraction of thought doesn't seem to have much to do with self-reliance, the concept with which Emerson is most often associated. Indeed with this concept we appear to encounter the opposite viewpoint in that self-reliance presumably urges us to trust our own thoughts and to take possession of our own beliefs. In the two texts leading off *Essays: First Series*, "History" and "Self-Reliance," Emerson outlines what Richard Poirier has termed "the work of knowing" – the idea that knowledge is most authentic when we have "verified it for ourselves," when abstract truths and formal rules are set aside so that as interpreters we might "do the work itself."[9] In noticing the distance between this more pragmatically-minded Emerson and the celebrant of an abstract "thought" or timeless "soul," most readers are likely to take the inconsistency in their stride, noting that Emerson, after all, prides himself on just this quality. Here I want to pursue the suggestion that not only is there a necessary link between these two sides of Emerson but that they are connected by the logic of same-and-therefore-different we've been tracing elsewhere in his prose.

In the course of the first volume of *Democracy in America* (1835) Tocqueville remarks, almost in passing, that for Americans it is often the case that having an opinion is less important than making sure that the opinion, whatever it may be, is *theirs*.[10] In the same way we can see that when Emerson tells us that he cannot study the "visions" of his friend lest he lose his own, the overriding concern is not over what those visions signify but whose they are. Nor, for that matter, does "Self-Reliance," when urging us to speak out lest "we shall be forced to take with shame our own opinion from another" (259), bother to raise the question whether the opinion is worth having. For that's clearly beside the point, just as it's beside the point whether one agrees or disagrees with the "foolish philanthropist" berated in the same essay, whose meekness and handwringing are further signs that "we are become timorous and desponding whimperers" (274). Even in his subsequent embrace of John Brown, hailed as "the rarest of heroes, a pure idealist," the same outlook holds. What sets Brown apart are not his ideals – desponding whimperers want to end slavery, too – but the purity with which they are held, a purity that even Southern politicians cannot but help admire.[11] More than anything else, what moves Emerson in his speeches on Brown's behalf is the sheer charisma of the latter's "romantic character" and how it puts a stamp of authenticity on his actions that makes the actual content of what he believed less interesting than the commanding manner in which he held those beliefs. Imitating the talents of others, Emerson tells us in "Self-Reliance," gives us "only an extemporaneous, half possession" (276) while the achievement of figures like Brown is bound up with his self-possession, in the many different senses of that term.[12]

The notion that democratic subjects cherish their opinions because they are indeed theirs struck Tocqueville so forcibly that in the second volume of *Democracy* (1840) he returns to the theme and makes it the point of departure for its opening chapters. To the extent that "they recognize no signs of incontestable greatness or superiority in any of their fellows, [Americans] are continually brought back to their own judgment as the most apparent and accessible test of truth" (430). A general expectation that people judge things for themselves – that "they seek by themselves and in themselves for the only reason for things" (430) – marks the transition from dependence on external forms of authority to an internal process of verification. In "History" Emerson echoes the same point in a ringing declaration: "Every mind must know the whole lesson for itself, – must go over the whole ground. What it does not see, what it does not live, it will not know" (240). As readers of the essay know, its main message is to suggest that by working through the ideas of other people, as opposed to passively ingesting them, we in some sense take possession of them. In effect, then, Tocqueville's account simply spells out what is continuously implied in Emerson's essays, namely, that democratic culture creates a powerful predisposition for its members to establish a proprietary relationship to their beliefs. Like the friend who might turn into an enemy, beliefs must be made yours if they are not to tyrannize over you.

Emerson presents self-reliance in the essay of that name as an arduous, demanding ideal, in principle available to all but in reality too often worn down by social conformism and groupthink. Tocqueville, on the other hand, assumes that the fundamental precepts of intellectual independence have become so fully (and unconsciously) absorbed by the people of the United States that it serves as an overriding national dogma – "a philosophical method shared by all" (429). In fact the central question posed by the opening chapters of his second volume is to ask what happens when an entire citizenry takes it for granted that self-reliance is not just desirable but the only acceptable method for ascertaining the truth. The brief answer is that it places this citizenry in an impossible position. For if it's impermissible to rely upon the judgment of your peers in forming your beliefs – for that violates the spirit of "independence of mind" that is now felt to be a cultural imperative – it's nevertheless untenable, Tocqueville points out, to rely exclusively upon your own – for nobody can "do the work itself" in verifying *all* one's opinions and beliefs. So the question is not whether democratic subjects can transcend the need to take things on faith – they cannot – but where that faith shall be placed. If one's immediate peers are ruled out, the next most likely candidate would appear to be a group of one's peers, the larger the better. "In times of equality men being so like each other, have no confidence in others, but this same likeness leads them to place almost unlimited confidence in the judgment of the public" (435). Scorning to rely upon the opinions of fellow individuals but not knowing where else to turn, the American turns with relief to public opinion for guidance. Making a priority of intellectual independence does not solve the problem of conformism and groupthink. It causes it.

Thus, while a contemporary like John Stuart Mill might recommend "the more and more pronounced individuality of those who stand on the higher eminences of thought" as "the counterpoise and corrective" to the "opinions of merely average men [who] are everywhere becoming the dominant power,"[13] what looks like a solution to the author of *On Liberty* is for Tocqueville just another repetition of the problem. To the degree that the ban on identifying with other individuals creates the impetus for identifying with the mass, the pursuit of "more and more pronounced individuality" is obviously doomed to be self-defeating.[14] Obviously, too, Emerson, like Mill, lays great stress on "independence of action and disregard of custom" in his thinking, though it is also true, as many of Emerson's readers have complained, that he tends to pair these appeals to intellectual independence with panegyrics to the Universal Mind, Oversoul, and aboriginal Self, each denoting an abstract commonality that commands and guides the self-reliant individual. The interest of Tocqueville's perspective is of course to suggest that this connection is less a regrettable lapse than a natural development. Thus if the main thrust of "History" is, as noted previously, that each interpreter is to "do the work itself" of re-experiencing the past and "verifying" it for him or herself, the first sentence of that essay also states categorically: "there is one mind common to all individual men" (237). The minds of the many are said to be incarnations of this one mind, "the only and sovereign agent" (237); to submit your agency to this greater agent is to "accept the place that divine providence has found for you" ("Self-Reliance," 260). True to Tocqueville's script, the drive for intellectual empowerment somehow leads to the ventriloquizing of subjects by an immense collectivity, which is described in the essay as "seated at their heart, working through their hands, predominating in all their being" (260). Does Emersonian self-reliance simply reprise a version of the dilemma along the lines described by Tocqueville, so that the imperative to think for oneself culminates in submission to a higher power?

Certainly some have thought so, even to the point of alleging that self-reliant individualism underwrites various forms of inequality such as imperialism, corporate capitalism, or racial supremacy.[15] In context, though, these studies make clear that Emerson betrays the ideals of self-reliance and not the other way around. They follow Mill, that is to say, in assuming that individual dissent ideally serves as a "corrective and counterpoise" to some larger dominant power, the only difference being that the voice of dissent in this particular case has been "co-opted" by that higher power. It's worth emphasizing the fundamentally different nature of Tocqueville's skepticism in that he is not particularly interested in how dissent and freedom of thought are compromised by ideological interests or institutional powers; he is interested in how the passion for equality itself, the true "absolute power" (436) of democratic culture, enshrines and *valorizes* individual dissent and freedom of thought to such an extent that these values are at risk of being trivialized and, in effect, shunned – outwardly embraced but in actuality rendered inert and meaningless. The paradox whereby equality of conditions generates as much as it undercuts the demand for intellectual independence is worth pondering if only because it has been eclipsed by the much more prevalent assumption that freedom and equality are at odds or incompatible, a famous conundrum often associated with Tocqueville's work and which would reappear as an especially stark, uncompromising opposition pivotal to the liberalism espoused by *On Liberty*.[16]

Our previous discussion of "Friendship" and "Love" would seem to suggest that instead of capitulating to democratic authoritarianism Emerson's prose tends to subject it to an ongoing, seemingly interminable process of negotiation and adjudication, as if conceding its inevitability but exploring offsetting considerations. Such a practice is hardly unique to these two essays, as the following passage from "The Over-Soul" makes clear, in which the self's independence is found and lost and found again.

One mode of divine teaching is the incarnation of the spirit in a form, – in forms, like my own. I live in society; with persons who answer to thoughts in my own mind, or express a certain obedience to the great instincts to which I live. I see its presence to them. I am certified of a common nature; and these other souls, these separated selves, draw me as nothing else can. They stir in me the new emotions we call passion; of love, hatred, fear, admiration, pity; thence comes conversation, competition, persuasion, cities, and war. Persons are supplementary to the primary teaching of the soul. In youth we are mad for persons. Childhood and youth see all the world in them. But the larger experience of man discovers the identical nature appearing through them all. Persons themselves acquaint us with the impersonal. In all conversation between two persons, tacit reference is made, as to a third party, to a common nature. That third party or common nature is not social; it is impersonal; it is God. (390)

The excerpt condenses a story told over and over again in the *Essays*. The spirit descends, consciousness dawns, the other draws out, the other hems in, the ego shakes free. Superintending this last development is the emergence of "That third party or common nature." Emerson says it is "not social," though to the extent that it is decidedly a social context (e.g., a conversation) in which this "common nature" manifests itself and to the extent that the affirmation "it is God" is not especially helpful given the apparent absence of any moral content in this "divine teaching," it is difficult to resist the impression that what Emerson is describing here is simply the thematizing of the social as such. Children and youth may see the world in terms of mere parts, their faculties mirrored and drawn out by the presence of other separate beings, but true elevation consists in rising to an awareness of the Soul among souls, the Mind among minds. The emergence of "that third party" is best understood as the discovery of a social *relation* so that the presence of the other to my imagination is superseded by the presence of that third thing, the spirit of likeness that subsists between myself and the other.

Here, as throughout transcendentalist discourse more generally, conversation is the preferred mode for making such discoveries, not least because the conversation succeeds so well in honoring both the self-reliant imperative for the individual to work through and possess his or her thoughts and the spontaneous revelations of the whole. Naturally Emerson prefers to mythologize this position instead of arguing for it. Continuing the paragraph where we left off, he invests conversations among one's peers with a divine aura even as he appears to fall prey to Tocqueville's worst fear:

And so in groups where debate is earnest, and especially on high questions, the company become aware that the thought rises to an equal level in all bosoms, that all have a spiritual property in what was said, as well as the sayer. They all become wiser than they were. It arches over them like a temple, this unity of thought, in which every heart beats with nobler sense of power and duty, and thinks and acts with unusual solemnity. All are conscious of attaining to a higher self-possession. It shines for all. There is a certain wisdom to humanity which is common to the greatest men with the lowest, and which our ordinary education often labors to silence and obstruct. The mind is one, and the best minds, who love truth for its own sake, think much less of property in truth. They accept it thankfully everywhere, and do not label or stamp it with any man's name, for it is theirs long beforehand, and from eternity. (390)

Once again we see how the prohibition against identifying with the other, already stigmatized as mere infatuation, draws individuals into identifying with a higher power. "It arches over them like a temple," says Emerson of the "thought" possessing all, as if in confirmation of Tocqueville's judgment that, "no matter what political laws men devise for themselves, it is safe to foresee that trust in common opinion will become a sort of religion, with the majority as its prophet" (436).

And yet the individuals in this passage become the instruments of a common thought, not a common opinion. As a general rule, Emerson's Universal Minds and Over-souls have no other purpose than alluding to an abstract commonality. Because their role is "to embody every faculty, every thought, every emotion which belongs to the [human spirit]" ("History," *Essays*, 237), they do not signify a meaning, much less channel it in any particular direction. They don't *do* anything outside of signaling the standing possibility of equal relations. From the standpoint of Tocqueville's critique, this reverencing of an abstract "unity of thought" devoid of content is of course likely to be of small comfort; somehow for Emerson, though, the mere revelation of the workings of equality suffices, as a sheer formalism, to ennoble and empower "every heart," the "greatest" along with the "lowest." On the other hand, if we ask what is being transcended in this passage – what is being set aside or moved beyond – the answer is less enigmatic. What is being transcended is precisely the proprietary relation to one's beliefs that accompanies appeals to a self-reliant individualism – the claim of possession and exclusive ownership that makes my ideas and opinions unmistakably mine.

"The root and seed of democracy is the doctrine Judge for yourself," Emerson had written in his journal.[17] Asking us to imagine what happens when everybody takes this doctrine to heart, Tocqueville finds the root and seed of democratic credulity, culminating, one may suppose, in a nation of proud nonconformists, with their bumper stickers proclaiming the need to "Question Authority." But in Emerson's fantasy of speakers and listeners rising to the same level, the self-reliant call to take possession of knowledge and make it one's own is transfigured into a "higher self-possession" that makes the metaphor of ownership appear not just inappropriate but pernicious. Selves retain their separateness but in a way that is meant to be chastening; the company, wiser than they know, sees that it cannot see – sees, that is to say, the limits of agency without necessarily forfeiting it. It's as though the priority accorded to judging for oneself had triggered its own counter-narrative wherein this fiction is left behind. Where "all have a spiritual property" in thought, there is no point in thinking of truth as belonging to anyone.

It is the capacity to thematize relatedness or the spirit of likeness that defines the essence of Emerson's "divine teaching," which protects the democratic subject against a dual threat. In the end his "separated selves" no more identify with each other than with a higher power. Conjuring a public without an opinion and imagining a mode of instruction without an instructor, Emerson confidently declares that "the action of the soul ... broods over every society, and [its membership] unconsciously seek for it in each other" (391). Just as the principle of relatedness or "that third party" retains its impersonality as a matter of definition, so too does truth, which, crucially for Emerson, does not make one wise but instead makes one wiser than one knew. ("We know better than we do," he writes in the same paragraph, repeating one more time for good measure, "we are wiser than we know" [391].) Just as one cannot identify with a "common nature" but only betray one's connection to it, one cannot possess the truth but only submit to it. The dovetailing of the true and the common, each "certified" by the other, may identify exactly what inspires dread in the author of *Democracy in America*, but it moves the author of "The Over-soul" to joy and wonder. By steering a course that avoids the extremes of a naïve faith in self-possession and an uncritical yielding or dispossession before a higher power, Emerson offers a kind of pedagogy, wherein one learns to submit, not to society, but to the "idea" or "thought" that is relatedness itself.

Tocqueville, as we saw at the outset of this section, begins Volume Two of *Democracy* with a meditation not on what the democratic subject believes but how he or she believes – their "method." The impression he conveys is that democracy has no content to speak of; to the extent that it begins and ends with the affirmation that individuals are free and equal, it unavoidably limits itself to the how and not the what of belief. Not telling anyone what to do, democracy mistrusts all forms of authority even as it represents the apotheosis of an extreme formalism. Likewise Emerson's self-reliant individualism combines an extreme hostility to all outward forms of authority with a veneration of Form. It alternates Man Thinking with "unity of thought," the appropriative power of first-person authority with the empty formalism of the third party.

To put the point in this way is not to criticize, much less disparage Emerson's vision when set beside Tocqueville's analysis. As we've seen in the case of the latter, independence among equals fills the democratic subject with pride and confidence in his own thought only to leave him "isolated and weak" in reality. "In this extremity he naturally turns his eyes toward that huge entity which alone stands out above the universal level of abasement. His needs, and even more his longings, continually put him in mind of that entity, and he regards it as the sole and necessary support of his individual weakness" (672). In Emerson's mythologizing of the one mind or common thought we find neither religious doctrine nor engagement with political issues in any direct or immediate sense. What we do find is a struggle to sort through the paradoxes of a democratic authoritarianism much along the lines imagined by Tocqueville, a struggle that suggests that it is time to rethink the common perception that "for Emerson, individual freedom is always prior to social equality."[18]

CHILDREN OF ONE SPIRIT

"By man I mean both man and woman," Margaret Fuller explains in the Preface to *Woman in the Nineteenth Century* (1845), "these are two halves of one thought."[19] Near the end of the volume she reiterates the same point, saying that "the growth of man is two-fold, masculine and feminine" (99). That being the case, "the development of the one cannot be effected without that of the other" (5). Like the familiar claim in anti-slavery discourse that bondage corrupts the master as much as the slave, the suggestion that man and woman are so interdependent that neither can grow without the other is a key premise of *Woman in the Nineteenth Century*. The perspective it adopts is "man considered as a whole"; and "as this whole has one soul and one body, any injury or obstruction to a part … affects the whole" (99). Corrupted by the force of habit and petty vanity, men have failed to grasp that "woman was half himself, that her interests were identical with his, and that, by law of their common being, he could never reach his true proportions while she remained in any wise shorn of hers" (99). As the author explains at the outset, her "highest wish" is to make this simple truth "distinctly and rationally" (5) understood.

By the same token, forceful as it is in pressing the point that "Woman" is "the other half of the same thought" present to "Man" (12), *Woman in the Nineteenth Century* periodically gives the impression that certain features of human beings lend themselves to being considered as more distinctively "female" than "male." Thus its discussion of "that especially female element, spoken of as Femality" takes it for granted that "the especial genius of woman" is to be "electrical in movement, intuitive in function, spiritual in tendency" (68). "The electrical, the magnetic element in woman has not been fairly brought out at any period," we are told a few pages earlier, "everything might be expected from it; she has far more of it than man" (61). In man the reader also encounters a variety of dispositions that come naturally to the sex, from "hard intellectuality" (31) and "a low materialist tendency" (65) to base submission to "his lower self" (90). As "children of one spirit" (68), the man and the woman may be inextricably linked, so that elevating one is sure to elevate the other while debasing one is sure to debase the other. And yet, even if "all soul is the same" it is nevertheless "modified in her as a woman, it flows, it breathes, it sings, rather than deposits soil or finishes work, and that which is especially feminine flushes, in blossom, the face of the earth, and pervades, like air and water, all this seeming solid globe, daily renewing and purifying its life" (68).

     To such observations, however, the text consistently applies its own disclaimers. "Nature provides exceptions to every rule," Fuller writes directly after her meditation on "Femality," [s]he sends women to battle and ... enables the man, who feels maternal love, to nourish his infant like a mother" (69). In truth, male and female are "perpetually passing into one another. Fluid hardens to solid, solid rushes to fluid. There is no wholly masculine man, no purely feminine woman" (68–69). If at one point Fuller ventures the suggestion that it is "more native [for woman] to inspire and receive the poem, than to create it" (68), she elsewhere mocks the same notion: "Woman the poem, man the poet! Woman the heart, man the head! Such divisions are only important when they are never to be transcended" (47). Significantly, what prevents both parties from appreciating the full extent of their symbiosis is "the interposition of artificial obstacles" (27) and "the slavery of habit" (71). Dualisms such as the head and heart are, needless to say, precisely the sort of constructions that have been instrumental in the subjection of women, a point made vivid early in the text in the colloquy with "the irritated trader," whose pieties about domestic contentment are deflated by Fuller's satiric wit (15–16). Summing up her position near the conclusion of the text, she declares simply: "[t]he growth of man is two-fold, masculine and feminine ... Energy and Harmony. Power and Beauty. Intellect and Love. [t]hese two sides are supposed to be expressed in man and woman, that is, as the more and less, for the faculties have not been given pure to either, but only in preponderance. There are also exceptions in great number, such as men of far more beauty than power, and the reverse" (99).

As these formulations imply, however, it would be a mistake to view this alternating emphasis on sameness and difference as somehow tactical on Fuller's part. Even in summarizing her position, she continues to generalize on certain characteristics "in woman as woman" such as "a native love" for "moderation," which is explicitly distinguished from an historically acquired "reverence for decorums and limits inherited and enhanced from generation to generation, which many years of other life could not efface" (102). Perplexed by the apparent tendency simultaneously to demystify and invoke fixed differences in gender, a number of interpreters have followed the model of one-step-forward, two-steps-backward when treating Fuller's feminism, finding in its very exposure of "the limits of the progressive rhetoric of Western culture" the persistence of "a deeper cultural bias at work in her thinking."[20] In a different vein, Julie Ellison asks that we regard these mixed messages "not as contradictions or paradoxes" but as "theoretical surpluses": "she wants women," Ellison suggests, "both to discover their special powers as women and, in her 'let them be sea-captains' mood, to claim equal opportunities with men. She oscillates, therefore, between honoring divination, which proceeds out of the natural law of sexual difference, and celebrating the manifold exceptions to gender typologies."[21]

But of course, however we choose to characterize such an oscillation doesn't necessarily bring us closer to explaining why it occurs. Why should it matter that women be made aware of their "special powers?" The extensive review of mythologies and folklore from cultures going back to antiquity that occupies the middle sections of the book is meant to establish that "no age was left entirely without a witness of the equality of the sexes in function, duty and hope" (101). Fuller's survey of the goddesses, queens, women warriors, and politicians from the past offers many illustrations of women's power, but does not have much to say along the lines of women's special power, which would seem to imply that such an interest is a later development, at least in Fuller's historical sense of things. And that in fact appears to be the point behind one of her contrasts between the pre-modern and modern periods: "in slavery, acknowledged slavery, women are on a par with men. Each is a work-tool, an article of property" (36), whereas in "perfect freedom ... there is no marrying nor giving in marriage, each is a purified intelligence, an enfranchised soul" (37). In times of inequality, the capacity to differentiate is disallowed; women and men, both slaves, are on the same level. In times of equality, where people are set free, the difference that gender makes becomes an issue worth foregrounding. This is why Fuller understands contemporaries who renounce "the feminine element" altogether to be pursuing a false ideal: "Were they free, were they fully to develop the strength and beauty of woman," she argues, "they would never wish to be men or man-like." Casting aside this sort of misconceived equality, Fuller envisions an ideal where "unison in thought, congeniality in difference" (32) may flourish.

Democracy, says Tocqueville, often gives its citizens "extremely contradictory instincts" (672), and the politics of difference is certainly a case in point. Difference is to be eradicated inasmuch as it is an instrument of oppression and a denial of equality; difference is to be embraced inasmuch as it is a mark of self-determination and a validation of equality. A victim of difference, the daughter imagined by Fuller whose father would deny her an education simply because she is a girl (71) may grow up to be a celebrant of difference, finding in books like *Woman in the Nineteenth Century* the inspiration for pursuing "the law of growth that speaks in us and [that] demands the perfection of each in its kind, apple as apple, woman as woman" (104). Or to make the same point while reversing the terms, sameness is an indispensable sign of equality (man and woman being two halves of the same thought) and a threat to equality (in each lie dormant certain predispositions and tendencies setting one apart from the other). On various occasions Fuller makes it sound as though such an alternating emphasis were simply a result of contrasting perspectives; envisioning an ideal of "unison in thought [and] congeniality in difference" (32), she explains that at times she speaks from the vantage point of the soul and at others from the vantage of society (70). But the judgment that "union is only possible to those who are units" (71) has little to do with the switching of rhetorical registers. To be equal is to overcome and therefore insist upon difference. Claiming their equality with men, "women must leave off … being influenced by them, but retire within themselves, and explore the groundwork of life till they find their peculiar secret" (72).

From this standpoint, Fuller's tendency to deprecate even as she indulges in claims regarding the "natural law" of gender or women's "special powers" owes less to her idealism, wishful thinking, or the persistence of "cultural bias" than to her commitment to what she calls "a religious recognition of equality" (42). Indeed, with the concept of "Femality" we have something that initially looks as though it were an ingenious fusion of essentialist and anti-essentialist tendencies – the sensibility whose defining trait is to have no defining trait. As "the intellect, cold, is ever more masculine than feminine," the feminine betrays "the electrical, the magnetic element," whose mere presence operates as "the conductor of the mysterious fluid" charged by "an impassioned sensibility" (61). This emphasis on feminine susceptibility and receptivity calls to mind Fuller's immersion in European

Romanticism, to say nothing of her more general ties to a culture where the pairing of womanhood and sympathetic identification was entirely conventional, but it turns out that Fuller has something different in mind. As she is careful to note on more than one occasion, "the electrical element" may repel as much as attract. "Femality" entails a heightened capacity for discerning certain "atmospheric changes, the fine invisible links which connect the forms of life" that even "common women" "will seize and delineate with unerring discrimination" (61), whereas "men of high intellect" are "absolutely stupid" when it comes to registering such subtleties. "Femality," that is to say, is not about the capacity to feel so much as about a preternatural capacity to discern the tone and nuances of feelings in a given social field, what Fuller calls "inspired apprehensiveness" (61). Even more than "men of high intellect," its true antithesis may be found in the "bad or thoughtless" husband who, "liv[ing] carelessly and irreverently so near another mind," is not only oblivious to the "bad influence" he has on his wife but the bad influence she exercises upon him as a result (55). "Femality," in short, idealizes a balance that avoids the twin extremes of a careless absorption in the other or a narcissistic exclusion of the other.

Emerson had thought that friendship demands a "religious treatment"; Fuller, as we've seen, urges a "religious recognition of equality" (42).[22] The point of departure for both is an all-embracing holism: "as this whole has one soul and one body, any obstruction or injury to a part, or to the meanest member, affects the whole" (*Woman in the Nineteenth Century*, 99). As we might expect, this theme of interdependency is matched by an accompanying horror of dependency. Like the interlocutors in Thoreau's cabin, who converse with their backs to the wall, Fuller's aspiring women above all require more space to "retire within themselves." "Let her put from her the press of other minds and mediate in virgin loneliness" (72); once "undisturbed by the pressure of near ties" (58), a habit of "religious self-dependence" (70) will emerge. Fuller's gallery of ideal relationships is telling in this regard: a Teutonic legend chronicling the love of a maiden for a banished prince she will never see again (33); the address of the "Commonwealth's man to his wife" (39) as he climbs the scaffold; the marriage of Calderon's Justina and her lover at the stake; Godwin's gallant defense of his lately departed wife, Mary Wollstonecraft, despite "all that was repulsive in her past history" (43): these and other vignettes pay homage to a marriage of souls in the context of separation and sacrifice. At one point Fuller translates a phrase from Boccaccio – "the form of a union where union is none" (41) – and derides its excessively bleak and dismissive view of marriage. In her catalogue of sublime partnerships, Fuller is neither bleak nor dismissive, but the implication that nothing brings out "the heroism of a true woman, and the purity of love, in a true marriage" (51) so well as moments when the partners are forced apart is nevertheless unmistakable.

This is not to overlook Fuller's outspoken attacks on prostitution and slavery, her bitter comments on the double standard that honors self-reliance in men and deplores it in women, and, more generally, her indictment of the way men speak and think about women. But a specifically feminist critique is not her intent. Access to power, political or otherwise, is of secondary importance. It would please Fuller if women were to find their voice and speak and write but it would also be acceptable were they to remain silent, as they have for ages, provided that silence is dictated by "divine command" (47). An ardent believer in "the continual development ... of human destiny" (13), she declares "the noble thought" that "all men be born free and equal" to be "a golden certainty" (13). Somewhat in the manner of Douglass, Walker, and other abolitionists discussed in Chapter One, Fuller maintains that concepts such as freedom and equality ride on the momentum of their own promulgation, for "that which is clearly conceived in the intelligence cannot fail sooner or later to be acted out" (14). As for the causes driving sexism, the author cites a petty wish for power (23) and "the slavery of habit" (72). The enemy is not malevolence or economic self-interest so much as a lazy cynicism: "No! man is not willingly ungenerous ... [h]e cries, with sneering skepticism, Give us a sign. But if the sign appears his eyes glisten, and he offers not merely approval but homage" (25).

Thus for Miranda, one of Fuller's many alter egos, the special difficulty of life is not simply coping with male condescension but working through what it means to be "affectionate without passion, intellectual without coldness" (21). Raised by a father who "cherished no sentimental reverence for woman, but a firm belief in the equality of the sexes," Miranda learns "to depend upon [her]self as the only constant friend" (21, 22). Here, as throughout *Woman in the Nineteenth Century*, the key issue is not securing power and agency but the manner in which they are secured. "It is not woman but the law of right, the law of growth that speaks in us" that Fuller champions (104), which is to say that it is not man but the denial of that law of growth that speaks within that she condemns. That denial occurs "in every-day life [where] the feelings of the many are stained with vanity" (23). It is the "want of development" that afflicts these victims of vanity while it is the distinction of women like Miranda to be embarked on a quest to "unfold" from within and "naturally develop" their own "peculiar secret" as well as "[their] faith that the feminine side, the side of love, of beauty, of holiness, was now to have its full chance" (23).

"How to achieve the human connection" is of course a perennial topic of concern in discussions of transcendentalism.[23] The at times overweening emphasis on the individual, the opposition of "self" to "society," the temptation to withdrawal or isolation – these are stock themes in the secondary literature. My interest has been to turn this around, arguing that the question is not how to achieve connection but how to manage the problem of a connectedness that cannot be shaken. But the ironies and paradoxes brought about by the logic of equal, but separate selves do not apply to personal relations alone. The next chapter explores how the entangling alliance between interdependence and independence exercised an impact that went well beyond the vicissitudes of friendship or the trials of spiritual companionship.

CHAPTER SIX

The common condition

Near the end of *Woman in the Nineteenth Century*, Margaret Fuller, intrigued by Fourier's "proposing a great variety of employments" in his vision for a redeemed society, calls for "a much greater range of occupation [for women] than they have, to rouse their latent powers."[1] Written in 1845, Fuller's declaration comes in the midst of a newfound interest in the expressive potential of work that would become an increasingly dominant topic of concern through the antebellum period and beyond. The expectation that work, to be truly meaningful, must engage, cultivate, or actualize the "latent powers" of the self (or a group of selves) finds a home in not just the phalanstery but in countless novels and stories that chronicle the odyssey of protagonists seeking to identify their "true place." Within working-class circles, its influence is no less evident in emerging conceptions of class-consciousness, just as, within the literature of labor protest, it is central to developing theories about worker alienation. Older, Protestant notions of the calling had privileged labor as the preferred means for honoring one's obligation to God. But by the second quarter of the nineteenth century it was no longer just a question of honoring one's obligation to God. One needed to honor the obligation to the person God meant one to be. It was not enough for work to be useful. It must be expressive.

Alongside this emphasis on work's expressive role was another, arguably more powerful association. Also beginning in the second quarter of the nineteenth century, work came to be seen as enjoying a privileged relationship to egalitarian principles. In the words of Gustave de Beaumont, traveling companion of Tocqueville in their tour of the United States, "in a society of perfect equality work is the common condition."[2] Although it's doubtful that anyone seriously thought that the United States was such a society – even the French traveler does not fail to note the possible emergence of a "new aristocrat" in the form of the "industrialist" – hailing labor as a democratic talisman was commonplace. The source of sturdy republican virtue, work, it was confidently declared from a variety of different sectors, stands to democracy as idleness to aristocracy. Even as there were widespread disputes as to who could or could not be considered a worker (e.g., did the capitalist count? Was the clerk a true laborer?), the correlation between work and equality was deeply entrenched.

In effect, then, we see a dual development: at the same time it was becoming more common to value work as an expressive activity responsible for bringing forth a special or destined identity, it was also regarded as a mark of "the common condition." Tocqueville, as we've seen, thought that a characteristic feature of democracies was for each member to "choose his own road and go along separately from all the rest."[3] In this chapter I extend and explore the significance of this claim as it effects representations of work in various literary and theoretical texts. Just as friendship was regarded as an instrument for engaging, cultivating, and actualizing the latent powers of personality, so, too, is one's labor. And yet, just as friendship can often be portrayed as impeding the development of those powers, labor too becomes, I suggest, a site of affiliation and repudiation. In the first section I treat this paradox as intrinsic to the pursuit of a "true place" or "true vocation," while in the second section I go on to show its different manifestations in the nineteenth-century accounts of work and equality.

THE CALLING OF THE CALLING

In Hawthorne's story, "The Intelligence Office," a stranger wearing "the characteristic expression of a man out of his right place" appears at the Intelligence Office seeking work. "I want," he announces to the "grave figure" seated behind a desk, "a place!" Taking him at his word, the Man of Intelligence (as he is named in the story) lists a number of openings about town, ranging "from that of a footman up to a seat at the council board, or in the cabinet, or a throne, or a presidential chair." As it happens, though, the applicant doesn't just want a place: he wants, as he impatiently exclaims, "my own place! my true place in the world! my proper sphere! My thing to do, which Nature intended me to perform when she fashioned me ... and which I have vainly sought all my lifetime!" So far as the applicant is concerned, the particular occupation is immaterial; "whether it is footman's duty or a king's" matters less than that the place (whatever it is) be "naturally mine."[4]

Written in 1844, "The Intelligence Office" plays off of that true epic of vocational desire, Carlyle's *Sartor Resartus*, which appeared in 1836. In Hawthorne's story things end unhappily for the applicant; taking his leave from the Intelligence Office, he takes his leave from the story as well, dispatched by the narrator with the comment that "if he died of disappointment he was probably buried in the wrong tomb."[5] This appears to be a sly parody of Carlyle's text, which at one point observes that "many spend their whole term, and in ever-new expectation, ever-new disappointment, shift from enterprise to enterprise … till at length, as exasperated stripling of three-score and ten, they shift into their last enterprise, that of getting buried." Despite the flippant tone, however, *Sartor Resartus* takes seriously "the stern Monodrama" that "every youth of high talent must enact" – so much so, in fact, that he devotes a chapter, entitled "Getting Under Way," to developing a contrast between the sense of "high vocation" acquired through careful "study" of what our "combined inward and outward Capability specially is" and the tyranny of "Professions" that are "pre-appointed us." Because "each is given a certain inward Talent," true fulfillment consists in matching what we do with what we were made to do, while anything less means submitting to "the neck-halter" of "Economic Society."[6]

The joke behind Hawthorne's story is to ensnare Carlyle's "Monodrama" in a hopeless tautology. The miserable applicant evidently finds himself in a bind: the reason he lacks a "true place" is that he lacks a sense of what, exactly, is "naturally mine," and the reason he lacks a sense of what is "naturally mine" is that he lacks a "true place." Although I shall be arguing that this stalemate actually helps account for the appeal behind the quest for one's true calling, we should not allow Hawthorne's satire to seduce us into thinking that this quest was nothing more than a joke – a relic, like footmen and kings, of an aristocratic past, with its quaint notions of proper stations and fixed places. Carlyle's reputation as both pioneering critic of industrialism ("Signs of the Times," 1829) and high priest to the mysteries of the calling (*Sartor Resartus*, 1836; *Heroes and Hero-Worship*, 1840) suggests that the connection between the turn to the vocational ideal and an attack on "Economic Society" need not be deemed frivolous or superficial. On the contrary, resistance to capitalism's "degradation of labor" and similar threats were often spurred by a concern not just for the dignity of work but the growth and development of the worker precisely through and not despite work. One obvious manifestation of this concern may be found in the discourse of the utopian socialists, whether in Saint-Simon's precepts concerning the distribution of tasks and talents, Owenite schemes for labor reform based on "worker satisfaction," or Fourier's blueprint for a renovated society organized around the ideal of "Attractive Industry."

Indeed, in the case of Fourierist doctrine, utopian society is imagined along the lines of one vast Intelligence Office, expressly conceived to service the vocational needs of each one of its clients. "Nothing is more blighting to both mind and body than the monotony of Civilized Industry," observes Fourier's principal American explicator, Albert Brisbane, in *The Social Destiny of Man* (1840). At the mercy of an increasing division of labor "in which the individual is confined monotonously to a single occupation," the fate of "ninety-nine hundredths of men in Civilization" is to be "born in a position in which their natural powers [have] no chance of development." Hence the pathos of "a Raphael or a Newton" who, born as "serfs, slaves, or poor laborers," lack the "favorable circumstances" for the cultivation of their genius, condemned as they are along with "the immense majority of men at present" to "repulsive pursuits or labors … [that] thus practically enslave and degrade them." Making available "careers or fields of action as numerous and as varied as human capacities" is accordingly the solution made possible by a redeemed "industrial organization," whose members are "at full liberty to choose pursuits which are adapted to [their] tastes and talents".[7]

Still, despite appearances to the contrary, this does not necessarily mean that the division of labor has been altogether banished from the phalanstery. On the contrary, it could be said that the whole point of studying what your "inward and outward Capability specially is," to recall Carlyle's phrasing, is not to do away with specialization but to fine tune its responsiveness in what amounts to a bureaucratization of inner potential. (The nadir of this approach, one imagines, may be found in Fourier's argument for assigning the more disagreeable but necessary chores to children on the grounds that such tasks exploit their "inclination for dirt.")[8] The irony here was not lost on Marx, who derides the crusade for "Attractive Industry" precisely for embracing and not eliminating the division of labor. On the account he presents in *The German Ideology* (1846), the objection to rescuing a Raphael or Newton from the ranks of the oppressed by opening "fields of action" for their genius to flourish is that it indeed only leaves society with so many Raphaels and Newtons. In other words, the proper aim of the socialist, utopian or otherwise, shouldn't be to replace a "false" place with a "true" one but get rid of the notion of place altogether. Thus, what Brisbane celebrates as the consummation of the worker's "*real individuality*," Marx denigrates as merely the continuation of "a one-sided, crippled development … of a single quality at the expense of all the rest." On the other hand, once the division of labor has been abolished under a communist dispensation "there [will be] no painters but at most people who engage in painting among other activities."[9]

What's the difference between a painter and someone who, among other things, happens to "engage in painting?" The difference, presumably, has to do with the degree to which the individual is *defined* by a specific social role or activity. It's not that these roles and activities will cease to be specialized in the communist society envisioned by Marx – there will still be hunters, fishermen, shepherds, and critical critics – it's just that these will be occupations that members may follow and leave off as they wish, hunting in the morning, fishing in the afternoon, rearing cattle in the evening, and criticizing after dinner "without ever becoming hunter, fisherman, shepherd, or critic."[10] At bottom the question of the division of labor really comes down to a question of separating being from doing – of maintaining, that is to say, a division between who one is and what one does. And in at least this one respect the realistic socialism of Marx may not be all that far apart from the utopian socialism of Fourier. For if, as Marx complains, in the phalanstery there will be "a minute division of labor," that is not only to "satisfy the strong and legitimate demand in human nature for Individuality" but also to accommodate what Fourier takes to be the even more powerful and equally innate "Social Passion" for "Alternatism," a basic need "the industrial organization" meets by insuring that all workers – even, presumably, Raphael and Newton – will enjoy the opportunity of "changing occupations several times during the day."[11] (Indeed, it was precisely the options presented by Fourier's scheme in "proposing a great variety of employments" that caught, as we've seen, Margaret Fuller's attention.)

So when Marx tells us that the foremost characteristic of alienated labor consists in "the fact that labor is *external* to the worker, i.e., it does not belong to his essential being,"[12] it's apparent that merely striking the negatives from such a description is not going to solve the problem. Elsewhere Marx observes of Milton that "[He] produced *Paradise Lost* for the same reason a silk worm produces silk. It was an activity of *his* nature."[13] According to this description, *Paradise Lost* does belong to Milton's essential being; it is labor internal to the worker. And yet Milton, producing what he was born to produce, can only be a poet, not somebody who happens to engage in poetry among other activities. Without the distance between identity and activity, his producing can only look like an exercise in compulsion – the poet's creative work isn't a very good example of creative work anymore. Evidently, then, for labor to be truly essential to self-development, there must be a sense in which labor is subordinate or even inessential to that self.

In Hawthorne's story the word "place" is taken to mean two different things. To the Man of Intelligence it signifies nothing more than mere work, something to do to get by. To the applicant it signifies his true calling, "my thing to do." In the futures envisioned by Fourier and Marx this distinction breaks down. Once the self is thought to be irreducible to any one livelihood then its only true calling is to have no true calling. This is essentially the thrust of Marx's attack on the very idea of place, a distaste Fourier shares, albeit somewhat less explicitly. The choice between experiencing labor purely as an instrumental necessity and experiencing it as an expressive ideal has become a choice nobody will have to make because the very commitment to that ideal combines both options. With no true calling, the worker is at liberty to sample many different callings; sampling many different callings, the worker finds the attraction in "Attractive Industry" to consist in its pure instrumentality.

The point here is not to criticize or dismiss this logic as esoteric or improbable – just the opposite. What Fourier and Marx anticipate as a future state of affairs was, to some degree, already becoming commonplace in certain sectors of mid-nineteenth-century America. Along these lines consider Louisa May Alcott's, *Work: A Story of Experience* (1873), which begins with its hero, Christie Devon, issuing her own declaration of independence on the eve of her twenty-first birthday as she ventures, like so many other young New England women of the time, from the farmhouse where she was raised in order "to find her place in the great unknown world." Over the course of the next twenty years and some four hundred pages, Christie takes employment as a maid, an actress, a nurse, a governess, a sweatshop worker, an independent seamstress, and a hospital attendant, all the while pausing between jobs to reflect that she has yet to "find my true place and work."[14] Throughout the novel, the implication is that while yearning for "work I can put my heart into" and that "does me good" (9) may be useful in pointing out the wrong path, it isn't much help in pointing to the right one; remarkably successful as an actress, for example, Christie quits the stage because "[acting] doesn't seem to be my nature" (275) even as she confesses to some perplexity over what that nature is. In practical terms, however, the determination to suit the hidden talent to its chosen task is what allows Alcott's protagonist to retain an ongoing sense of separation between the work she happens to be doing and the person she is destined to be. So while the longing "to find my place and do my duty" (151) is a constant refrain from chapter to chapter, the impression that the jobs Christie holds constitute a series of experiments is equally prevalent. (In fact Alcott's original title for the novel was *Work: Christie's Experiment*.)

Twenty years seems a long time to pursue a quest of any kind, and one might think that after a certain point the law of diminishing returns would have to set in. That's one way of reading *Sartor Resartus*, which chronicles the travails of its hero thrashing about in a perfect "imbroglio of Capabilities" only to end up, after a suitable interval of hair-pulling and inaction, seeking to break the deadlock with frantic exhortations to "Produce! Produce! ... whatsoever thy hand findeth to do, do it with thy whole might."[15] But *Work*, though it features an epigram from *Sartor Resartus* on the title page and equips its heroine with a copy of *Heroes and Hero-Worship* later on, does not opt for the Carlylean cop-out of producing for the sake of producing. True to the bildungsroman tradition, its final chapter shows Christie Devon securing at last "the task which my life has been fitting me for" (430). Attending a public meeting divided between working-class women seeking "justice, sympathy, and help" (425) for their grievances and "accomplished ladies" "rich ... in generous theories [but] poor in practical methods of relief" (426), Christie is seized by "a strong desire to bring the helpers and the helped into truer relations with each other" (427). Her impromptu speech, entirely the result of "a sudden and uncontrollable impulse" (427) on her part, not only makes a minor sensation but makes apparent the "great and noble" mission "to act as interpreter between the two classes" (430) that has been set aside for her all along. And no sooner is this epiphany experienced than Alcott allows her heroine a chance to demonstrate her newfound talent with the arrival of an old acquaintance, Bella Carrol, the wealthy daughter of one of Christie's former employers. As it happens, Bella has heard of Christie's speech and so has sought her out as someone who might aid Bella in locating "something to do in her own sphere, a sort of charity she was fitted for, and with it a pleasant sense of power to give it zest" (439). Hearing Bella's plaintive question "then what should I do?", Christie hears the answer to the "old question" that has been "haunting" (157) her for the past twenty years.

What's notable about the novel's conclusion, in other words, is how fulfilling one's vocational longing consists in passing it along to others. Thus Christie finds her "niche" by setting those like her friend Bella on the way to finding their "niche" ("It may take a little time," Christie explains to Bella, "but I know we shall find your niche if we give our minds to it" [435]). Initially it may seem as though, in going beyond the role of Hawthorne's applicant, Christie takes on the role of the Man of Intelligence – or, in terms of *Work*'s own cast of characters, the role of Christie's friend and benefactor, Reverend Power, for whom there is "nothing pleasanter than to put the right pair of hands to the right task" (212). But while the minister derives "great satisfaction" from "putting the right people in the right places" (218), Christie's "new field of labor" (425) involves a fundamentally different project. It's not the promise of a right place that she offers so much as the allure of that goal – not a calling but the calling of the calling, so to speak. This is the thrust of the climactic speech mentioned a moment ago, a speech that is relayed to us at second hand by the narrator. "What she said she hardly knew," we are told, but "she could tell those who listened that, no matter how hard or humble the task at the beginning, if faithfully and bravely performed, it would surely prove a stepping-stone to something better, and with each honest effort they were fitting themselves for the nobler labor, and larger liberty God meant them to enjoy" (428–29). As *Work* begins by sending its protagonist off to "find her place in the great unknown world" (11), so it ends by awakening the same wish in others. In doing so, it repeats the logic of the phalanstery and the commune. Taking to heart the ideal of expressive work (i.e., "the nobler labor" each is one day most fitted to perform) no more cancels out than it is cancelled out by the more instrumentalist outlook (a "stepping-stone" along the way). It is in this spirit that, in the novel's final pages, the "special leadin" which it is Christie's special "duty" to follow is also half-jokingly described by a friend as her "next job"; and while Alcott means for us to join in the "general laugh[ter]" that brings the book to a close, with its major characters gathered around a table for a final farewell – "a loving league of sisters old and young, black and white, rich and poor" (442) – the further irony is that *Work* gives us little reason to suspect that there is any real incompatibility between the two descriptions. Finding her "true place" by preaching the gospel of finding one's "true place," Christie prepares her listeners for their "next job."

To some extent this paradox might be seen as the result of a compromise, with the old-fashioned idiom of "place" and "proper sphere" accommodating itself to the new realities of a changing labor market. "Changes of fortune come so abruptly," Lucy Larcom observes in a memoir recounting her experiences as factory worker in the Lowell mills during the 1830s and 1840s, "that the millionaire's daughter of to-day may be glad to earn her living by sewing and sweeping tomorrow."[16] Although this particular example states the exception far more than the rule (from a historical standpoint it would be more accurate to say that those who sew today will be sweeping tomorrow), the general point is that, given the fluctuations of a capitalist economy, lifelong attachment to a single calling is hardly a sure thing. Forced by financial necessity to go to Lowell when she is only twelve, Larcom spends the next decade in and out of the factory, a fate shared by most of her co-workers. "None of us," she reminds her readers on more than one occasion, "had the least idea of continuing at that kind of work permanently" (222; 200–01). At the same time, Larcom counts herself as another one of New England's "country girls" who have left home and quit domestic service in search of a "freer kind of work" (200) that would bring out "a dormant strength of character" (199); and so, like Christie Devon's story, this too is organized around the pursuit of "something to do; it might be very little, but still it would be my own work" (193). As readers of the nineteenth century would know, this work will turn out to be writing poetry, although it is important to note that Larcom would object to this way of putting it, however much she encourages the inference. For just as she views her poems as heirlooms that are "not purchasable" (10), she views her "literary career" as something other than a career. Indeed, "I never had a career," she explains to a "youthful aspirant" (274), which is simply to say that "the path leads to the place, and the place, when we have found it, is only an opening into another path" (195). Writing poetry, in other words, is an "occupation" (160) that teaches the transitory character of occupations – its true subject being, here again, not a calling but the calling of the calling: "Having fitted ourselves to our present work in such a way as this, we are usually prepared for better work, and are sent to take a better place" (185).

Yet something more seems at stake here than making a virtue of necessity. Marx thought that the workers of the antebellum United States, by "transfer[ring] from one labour to another," had reached a point "where the specific kind [of labor] is a matter of chance for them, hence of indifference." Indeed, workers in the US had come to treat labor more or less in the same way as the modern economist had been treating it – purely as an abstract category, as nothing more than "'labour as such', labour pure and simple."[17] In effect, now that labor has "ceased to be organically linked with particular individuals in any specific form," it has "become the means of creating wealth in general."[18] But as a description of texts we have been discussing this is not altogether satisfactory. In accepting her destined role as a "mediator" for improved understanding between the classes, it's not as if Christie Devon expects to make a killing – it will be a few decades before this sort of role is recognized as a distinct profession and even longer before someone like Christie will be accepted as a member. Nor can it be said of Larcom's "working-girls" who tend the looms by day and discuss Carlyle by night ("few persons could have welcomed those early writings of Carlyle more enthusiastically than some of us working-girls did" [243]) that their interest in self-improvement and self-unfolding is just a ruse to mask their preoccupation with money-making. The so-called "casualization" of labor was no doubt a massive reality in the nineteenth-century United States, but this particular development is not really acknowledged as significant in either narrative, not even one organized around the experience of working at the country's first major industrial operation at the Lowell mills.

Marx himself suggests a more promising lead when he frames his remarks on the alleged "indifference" of the worker to the content of work by saying that, logically, "the most general abstractions arise only ... where one thing appears as common to many, to all."[19] For Lucy Larcom, as for most Americans in the nineteenth century, that one common thing is "honest work," esteemed as "one of the foundation-stones of the Republic" (201). As noted previously, work and equality enjoy a privileged relationship, at least in a conceptual sense. This is why, in the case of the utopias imagined by Marx and Fourier, renovating society and its pernicious inequities is first and foremost a matter of renovating labor and the conditions under which it is experienced. It is why Whitman's verse, in championing democratic themes, assigns pride of place to the laborers of "these States" – why, for that matter, Alcott has Christie begin her speech with the announcement "I have been and mean to be a working-woman all my life" (428). What makes the speech successful to "the anxious seamstresses, type-setters, and shop-girls" in the audience (426) is its "spirit of companionship," and what makes that companionship credible is the perception that "its speaker was one of them" (429). Obviously not everyone would welcome such fellowship, notwithstanding Marx's comments about the American worker's "indifference" to the particular "content" of work. As Alcott explains, "there are many Christies willing to work, yet unable to bear the contact with coarser natures which makes labor seem degrading" (148). But so long as the refusal to work is taken to be an assertion of superiority (as it had been for centuries), the correlation between work and equality is bound to remain intact. The notion that work was equality's talisman is in fact one of the great truisms of the age.

In recalling the logic that commands difference to emerge from sameness, we can see more clearly why work should become a site of identification and disavowal for the worker. It is a site of identification in the sense that accepting one's status as a worker means accepting equality – hence it is through work and work alone that Lucy Larcom, along with millions of others, shall realize her "peculiar capabilities" (157). It is a site of disavowal in the sense that accepting equality also mean insisting on self-differentiation – it's not just that Larcom's "capabilities" are "peculiar" in being uniquely hers but that they are capabilities that arise *despite* and not because of her labor. For becoming a mere extension of one's work is like becoming a mere extension of one's friend, a mark of dishonor. So while it is important to pay tribute to the inherent dignity of work even to the point of romanticizing its character-building attributes, we can also see how the desire to realize the self through work serves to reinforce a sense of separation between them. To adapt Marx's phrasing while altering his intent, we can say that the more that labor, as a pure abstraction or general category, is valorized as a token of commonality, the less likely it will be valued because it is "organically linked" to particular individuals.

Although published well after the Civil War, both *Work* and *A New England Girlhood* are very much products, in theme and subject matter, of an earlier age. The recurring presence of Carlyle indicates as much, as does Christie's uncle who, at the beginning of his niece's pilgrimage, jeers at her "redic'lus notions about independence and self-cultur" (8). Alcott would of course have known first hand many of the apostles of "self-culture" – her Reverend Power, for example, is modeled on Theodore Parker – while Larcom's enthusiasm for both Carlyle and German Romanticism is manifest throughout her memoir. No doubt the most authoritative text on these issues is "Self-Culture" (1838) by William Ellery Channing, foremost Unitarian of his day and a mentor of sorts to figures like Emerson and Fuller. He was also moved, toward the end of his life, to begin commenting on controversial issues of the time such as slavery or the labor question. Delivered to an audience composed "chiefly by those who are occupied by manual labor," his essay encapsulates with particular clarity the logic I've been describing, although not without some revealing modifications along the way.

THE WORK OF SELF-IMPROVEMENT

Channing defines self-culture as "the care which every man owes to himself, to the unfolding and perfecting of his nature."[20] Work is praised as "this honorable mark, set on us all" – indeed, "I rightfully belong to the great fraternity of working men" – but it takes second place to "the work of self-improvement," which is "to see in ourselves germs and promises of a growth to which no bounds can be set, to dart beyond what we have actually gained to the idea of Perfection as the end of our being" (227). Here the idea that one's place should never be confused with one's identity becomes a matter of open policy. Taking labor to be an indisputable sign of commonality, linking the good minister to his audience of manual tradesmen, Channing also insists "the laborer is not a mere laborer"; "a trade is plainly not the great end of his being, for his mind cannot be shut up in it; his force of thought cannot be exhausted on it" (226). The sober character formed by honest toil so admired by Channing's Puritan forbears here metamorphoses into a character intent on watching this formation take place, a character who, in the words of Theodore Parker, does not simply pursue "his daily business" but makes of "his daily business ... a school to aid in developing the whole man."[21] By learning to see yourself as something more than a mere laborer, you will learn to see what you do as mere labor – learn, once again, to mark the difference between what it is you do and who you were meant to be.

Considering that his address came on the heels of one of the worst financial depressions in United States history, the Panic of 1837, one can only wonder how Channing's audience of masons and carpenters responded to his bromides on self-improvement and spiritual uplift. To the degree that it is remembered at all, his discourse is generally taken to be an exercise in middle-class escapism typical of politicians and clergymen alarmed at the militancy of Jacksonian rhetoric and labor union activism. Indeed Channing's horror of class conflict is made even more apparent in the sequel to "Self-Culture," "Lecture on the Elevation of the Laboring Classes" (1840), which deploys the same binary logic as its predecessor in associating the laboring body with limitation, inertia, and anonymity while recommending a transcendent, universalizing "grandeur of the spirit." Of course, to describe Channing's essays in these terms is also to see that, in addition to registering an antipathy to class politics, their logic also renders "a class hierarchy based on the distinction between manual and mental labor ... so profoundly inarguable that it passes into the realm of common sense."[22]

And yet it seems a mistake to reduce self-culture's stance toward labor, manual or otherwise, to repudiation or bad faith. Curiously, when Channing looks for examples to make his case that "the laborer is not a mere laborer," he turns to labor to illustrate his thesis. Thus the structures reared by "artisans and other laboring men" that are giving "comfort and enjoyment" to the people of Boston will continue to do so for generations to come; the "houses, furniture, markets, public walks, and numberless accommodations" all manifest a "vast usefulness" (246) that staggers the imagination. In Channing's eyes, then, whatever reward Boston's carpenters and masons may think they derive from their toil, it can never be as great as the satisfaction they unknowingly produce. The "germs and promises" of a boundless growth that had been described as a latent force within the artificer are now matched by the "germs and promises" of a boundless magnanimity described as a latent force within the artifact. Convinced that "there is something greater within him than the whole material creation" (239), the artisan is directed back to that "material creation" for signs of "this sublime capacity." Portraying its listeners as unwitting philanthropists, "Self-Culture" urges them to take a "disinterested joy" (246) in labors that are thought to possess exactly this attribute. In one sense a trap for identity, toil is in another a beckoning model for identity.

The paradox here is that labor's intrinsic moral worth shines forth only to those who have learned to see themselves as something more than "a mere laborer." For it is not just joy but a *disinterested* joy that Channing wants to encourage. If this takes us back to the political critique of the clergyman intent on defusing class consciousness, it should also take us back further to Marx's vision of people who are not painters but at most people who, among other things, happen to paint. In both cases, the sanctification of labor is accompanied by the abstraction of labor – by the need to de-individualize it. As if they were artists standing back in order to marvel at productions that "shall live for a century or more after [their creators] sleep in the dust" (246), Channing's artisans discern in their labor the "illuminations, inward suggestions" (245) of an "idea of Perfection" that places them beyond the role of just another laborer. By way of contrast, we might cite the words of Henry Clarke Wright, who achieved a modicum of fame in his own time as an abolitionist, reminiscing about his apprenticeship as a hatter in upstate New York during the early years of the nineteenth century: "I felt real satisfaction in being able to make a hat, because I loved to contemplate the work when finished and because I felt a pleasure in carrying it through the various stages."[23] What the hatter likes about hatting is hatting, the sheer pleasure of a job well done. The whole point of self-culture and its mantra that "progress is the very end of our being" (228), on the other hand, is to convert the hatter's pride in his craft into wonder at the "holy and disinterested principles" (225) immanent to the work but external to the worker.

Ultimately, Channing's self-culture, like Emerson's friendship, Fuller's feminism, or Marx's utopia, is incoherent without the logic of identitarianism. Rather than the sum of one's beliefs and actions, identity in the texts we've been discussing is precisely that which precedes or is irreducible to action. Only those who are vigilant about marking a distinction between who they are and what they do may be deemed free and equal. The saga of setting out to discover one's true place presupposes this separation as a matter of course insofar as it is committed to telling the story of a self that's not yet come into existence. Of course, there's no reason why this story should be confined to individuals; in the concept of class-consciousness, for example, it is presumed that both work and the specific conditions of production under which it is experienced are decisive considerations in the formation of *group* identity, even if that identity has not yet fully taken shape or not yet been fully embraced by the workers themselves. (It is indeed precisely because of its reliance on an expressive, identitarian model that many latter-day Marxist theorists have jettisoned the concept.[24]) Lest it seem as though I am exaggerating the importance of the vocational quest, perhaps it's worth reviewing briefly a well-known story in the course of summing up its significance to my own study.

One reason why Marx considered capitalism a necessary stage in the advance toward socialism is that it made work hateful to the worker. The capitalist mode of production shattered the original symbiosis between worker and work that was thought by Marx to have prevailed in handicraft culture and in the pre-modern period more generally. But by doing so it also destroyed the stultification that generations of producers had endured – or more precisely had never known they had endured. Like the "mere laborer" imagined by Channing "shut up" in his trade, Marx's pre-capitalist workers are "merged" in the conditions of their labor to a point which precludes any experience of a meaningful conflict between their identity and their calling. But with capitalism the de-skilling of the worker "wipes out specialists and craft idiocy." In this painful but necessary process of disenthrallment, what had been all too meaningful now becomes utterly meaningless; the ongoing division of labor into smaller and more monotonous tasks paradoxically erodes specialization as "individuals pass easily from one type of labour to another, the particular type of labour being accidental to them and therefore irrelevant." In Marx's view, this development is "most pronounced in the United States, the most modern form of bourgeois society."[25]

It is a moving story, in its way, even if it is driven to conjure a mythical "worker" who, like one of Hegel's supra-individual subjects, spans centuries, experiencing needs and enduring challenges across time. But what's worth noting for my purposes is the contrast to Tocqueville, another thinker preoccupied by the transition from the pre-modern to the modern world. Whereas for Marx it is the experience of exploitation and radical economic inequality that frees the worker from his work, ideally setting him or her on a path that will eventually result in the abolition not just of exploitation but social roles as such, for Tocqueville it is the reality of an imagined equality that instills in people a wish "to choose [their] own road and go along separately from all the rest" (635). On his reading, the alienation experienced by the Christie Devons and Lucy Larcoms of the world is no more oppressive than liberating; rather, their distance from the meaningfulness of their work equips them with a way of believing themselves to be part of the whole without being sacrificed to or absorbed by the whole. If this seems an utterly fanciful interpretation of how the real world works in the twenty-first century, it at least has the virtue of helping us to understand the fiction that grew out of the process of imagining equality in the nineteenth.

Notes

INTRODUCTION

1 Arguably, the recent surge of interest in hemispheric or trans-national studies of the Americas constitutes one exception to the generalizations in this paragraph. And indeed in their introduction to a recent collection of essays on the topic in *American Literary History*, Caroline F. Levander and Robert S. Levine make a point of suggesting that the contributors to the volume are "less concerned with documenting the tangible, net effects of US power – the inclusion, exclusion, appropriation, marginalization, domination, exploitation, and invasion of other 'neighbor' nations" than with "recognition of the nation as historically evolving and contingent," thus shifting the critical focus "from the terms under which various constituencies are included or excluded within an already established US governing body to how those seemingly other constituencies actually operate as dynamic parts of multiple nations, some of which deny their presence." The immediate concern here is that so long as scholars continue simply to expose US exceptionalism they will be compelled to retain the US as "the default center of comparativist analysis"; such an approach, the editors explain, "too often reproduces the same totalizing structures of US privilege that include 'others' only to subordinate them to US interests." Thus "the importance of doing literary and cultural history from the vantage point of a polycentric American hemisphere" is that there is "no dominant center." This is not the place to assess the merits of this line of reasoning but merely to note that equality, manifest in the concern for inclusiveness and dread of hierarchy, continues to trump all other considerations when it comes to formulating methodological goals and judging interpretive validity. (Caroline F. Levander and Robert S. Levine, "Introduction: Hemispheric American Literary History," *American Literary History*, 18 [2006], 401, 400.)

2 Another candidate might be Raymond Williams's concept of "structures of feeling" as described in *Marxism and Literature* (Oxford University Press, 1977), pp. 128–34. To the extent that these structures are something more than strictly personal but something less than the reflex of ideological conditioning, they seem to approximate the phenomenon Tocqueville has in mind when alluding to "equality of conditions." On the other hand, to the extent that Williams defines these structures as "affective elements of consciousness and relationships" poised at "the very edge of semantic availability" (132) he is

explicitly thinking of something that is emergent and not fully codified by social practice – something, that is to say, which "*escapes*... from the fixed and the explicit and the known" (131; original emphasis). Needless to say, this attempt to reconcile the demands of a class-based, "materialist analysis" with the more Utopian leanings of Marxist critique engages an entirely different set of preoccupations from what we encounter in Tocqueville's social psychology. For a general discussion of the latter, particularly as it diverges from standard features of Marxist methodology, see Raymond Boudon, *Tocqueville Aujourd'hui* (Paris: Odile Jacob, 2005).

3 Alexis de Tocqueville, *Democracy in America*, trans. George Lawrence (New York: Harper and Row, 1969), p. 256.

4 F. R. Ankersmit, *Aesthetic Politics: Political Philosophy Beyond Fact and Value* (Stanford University Press, 1996), pp. 294–343; Claude Lefort, *Democracy and Political Theory*, trans. David Macey (Minneapolis: University of Minnesota Press, 1988), pp. 9–20, 183–209; Sheldon Wolin, *Tocqueville Between Two Worlds: The Making of a Political and Theoretical Life* (Princeton University Press, 2001). In addition to these studies, my understanding of Tocqueville is especially indebted to Francois Furet, "Preface: Le Systeme Conceptuel De La Democratie en Amerique," *De La Democratie en Amerique* (Paris: Flammarion, 1981), pp. 7–46 and Pierre Manent, *Tocqueville and the Nature of Democracy*, trans. John Waggoner (London: Rowman and Littlefield, 1993).

5 In Jon Elster's opinion, "there is no other great thinker who contradicts himself so often and on such central questions" (112) as Tocqueville. To prove his point he conducts a rather daunting inventory of the various contradictions, defects, and critical omissions in *Democracy in America* that takes up nearly one hundred pages. (Jon Elster, *Political Psychology* [Cambridge University Press, 1993], pp. 101–91.) At the other extreme, Ankersmit and Wolin applaud the apparent lack of rigor as a principled declaration of an anti-theoretical stance on Tocqueville's part that refuses to stand outside of democracy in order to propound a comprehensive, systematic account of its workings. (Ankersmit, *Aesthetic Politics*, p. 295; Wolin, *Tocqueville Between Two Worlds*, pp. 96, 117.)

6 Pauline Maier, *American Scripture: Making the Declaration of Independence* (New York: Knopf, 1997), p. 193.

7 Manent, *Tocqueville and the Nature of Democracy*, pp. 126, 32; Furet, "Preface," *De La Democratie en Amerique*, pp. 28–36. The opposition of formal equality to actually existing inequalities is of course a centerpiece of critiques of liberal abstraction. In the area of antebellum studies, see, for example, Wai Chee Dimock, *Residues of Justice: Literature, Law, Philosophy* (Berkeley: University of California Press, 1996); Lauren Berlant, *The Queen of America Goes to Washington City: Essays on Sex and Citizenship* (Durham, NC: Duke University Press, 1997); Russ Castronovo, *Necro Citizenship: Death, Eroticism, and the Public Sphere in the Nineteenth-Century United States* (Durham, NC: Duke University Press, 2001); and Russ Castonovo and Dana D. Nelson, eds., *Materializing Democracy: Toward a Revitalized Cultural Poetics* (Durham, NC: Duke University Press, 2002).

8 Tocqueville, *Democracy in America*, p. 538.
9 Herman Melville, *Moby-Dick*, ed. Harrison Hayford and Herschel Parker (New York: Norton Critical Edition, 1967), p. 105.
10 Tocqueville, *Democracy in America*, p. 589. Though not necessarily conceived as such, the best intellectual history of the identification of nature and equality is David Brion Davis, *The Problem of Slavery in Western Culture* (Ithaca: Cornell University Press, 1966). The sheer diversity of ideologies and interests covered by Davis's study makes clear the impossibility of extrapolating a coherent political orientation from the practice of naturalizing equality. So while I go on to emphasize the importance of this practice to the anti-slavery movement in the nineteenth century, there is no reason why someone might not see it as equally instrumental to, say, American military adventurism of the twenty-first century, where foreign countries are occupied in the expectation that, once tyrants are deposed and tribalism swept away, democracy will spring spontaneously into being, the utterly natural outgrowth of dormant hopes and long-suffering dreams.
11 Meredith McGill, *American Literature and the Culture of Reprinting, 1834–1853* (Philadelphia: University of Pennsylvania Press, 2003).
12 I am thinking of studies such as Eric Lott, *Love and Theft: Blackface Minstrelsy and the American Working Class* (New York: Oxford University Press, 1993) and David Roediger, *The Wages of Whiteness: Race and the Making of the American Working Class* (London: Verso, 1991).
13 Jurgen Habermas, *The Structural Transformation of the Public Sphere: An Inquiry into a Category of Bourgeois Society*, trans. Thomas Burger (Cambridge, MA: The MIT Press, 1989), pp. 132–40. It should be added that Mill and Tocqueville are merely two examples of a more general hostility to public opinion among nineteenth-century intellectuals that Habermas is describing at this point in his book.
14 Especially telling in this regard is the contrast to Mill, whose enthusiasm for experts and professional advisors to intervene in the public sphere and help to educate the masses does suggest that rationality was indeed the critical concern for him. For Tocqueville, on the other hand, the masses do not portend irrationality or anarchy but banality, a malaise brought on by a form of paternalism that emerges because of, not despite, equality of conditions. For further discussion of this last point, see Wolin, *Tocqueville Between Two Worlds*, pp. 349–78. I return to the contrast between Mill and Tocqueville in Chapter Five.
15 For an excellent treatment of this theme and its importance to Tocqueville's project, see Joshua Mitchell, *Fragility of Freedom: Tocqueville on Religion, Democracy, and the American Future* (University of Chicago Press, 1995).

PART I: BY NATURE EQUAL

1 Alexis de Tocqueville, *Democracy in America*, trans. George Lawrence (New York: Harper and Row, 1969), p. 628.

2 *Ibid.* pp. 398, 514.
3 Edward Pessen, *Jacksonian America: Society, Personality, and Politics* (Urbana, IL: University of Illinois Press, 1985), pp. 325–26; Arthur M. Schlesinger, Jr., "Individualism and Apathy in Tocqueville's Democracy" and Sean Wilentz, "Many Democracies: On Tocqueville and Jacksonian America," in *Reconsidering Tocqueville's Democracy in America*, ed. Abraham S. Eisenstadt (New Brunswick, NJ: Rutgers University Press, 1988), pp. 94–109; 207–28.

1 INDESTRUCTIBLE EQUALITY

1 Harriet Beecher Stowe, *Uncle Tom's Cabin Or, Life Among the Lowly*, ed. Ann Douglas (New York: Penguin, 1981). All references in parenthesis are cited from this edition.
2 Philip Fisher, on the other hand, takes Marie's many failings to be a sign of her buried guilt: "Her set of imaginary illnesses, her need for comfort and soothing, act as a kind of moral noise to drown out and preempt the actual suffering and needs of others" (*Hard Facts: Setting and Form in the American Novel* [New York: Oxford University Press, 1985], p. 103. See also, p. 127.) Although I find this interpretation unconvincing – "the idea that [Marie's servants] had either feelings or rights had never dawned upon her, even in distant perspective" (242), Stowe tells us directly – those who do find it convincing are likely to view the book's moral consensus as even more pervasive than I do here.
3 The reader may wish to object that being against slavery is not necessarily the same thing as being for equality. How this slippage occurs and why it is significant are questions taken up in the final section of this chapter.
4 Frederick Douglass, "What to the Slave is the Fourth of July?" in *Frederick Douglass: Autobiographies*, ed. Henry Louis Gates, Jr. (New York: Library of America, 1994), pp. 432, 433. Subsequent references to Douglass will be cited from this edition in parenthesis unless otherwise noted. Douglass is of course exaggerating about the statute books of the slaveholders and what they affirm about black manhood, but the main idea remains that he consistently portrays the slavocracy as self-contradictory or incoherent. For further examples, see Maurice S. Lee, *Slavery, Philosophy, and American Literature, 1830–1860* (Cambridge University Press, 2005), pp. 121–28.
5 The quotation appears in an extract from Weld's *American Slavery As It Is: The Testimony of a Thousand Witnesses* that serves as the Appendix to Sojourner Truth's *Narrative*. See William L. Andrews and Henry Louis Gates, eds., *Slave Narratives* (New York: Library of America, 2000), p. 662. Also worth noting is Harriet Martineau's report that "among the many hundreds" of individuals she met in the slave states, she encountered "only one, a lady, who defended the institution altogether" while everyone else thought either that "it was indefensible in every point of view" or that the only reason for its continued existence was the difficulty of figuring out a way to get rid of it (*Society in America*, ed. Seymour Lipset [New Brunswick, NJ: Transaction, 2000], p. 189).

6 *Minutes of the Fifth Annual Convention for the Improvement of The Free People of Color* (Philadelphia: William P. Gibbons, 1835), p. 29. Reprinted in *Minutes of the Proceedings of the National Negro Conventions 1830–64*, ed. Howard Holman Bell (New York: The Arno Press, 1969).

7 *North Star*, July 16, 1848; cited in Patrick Rael, *Black Identity and Black Protest in the Antebellum North* (Chapel Hill, NC: University of North Carolina Press, 2002), p. 192. For further examples of this optimistic strain in black anti-slavery literature, see Rael, *Black Identity*, pp. 53, 182, 206, 257, 270.

8 *Maria W. Stewart, America's First Black Woman Political Writer: Essays and Speeches*, ed. Marilyn Richardson (Bloomington: Indiana University Press, 1987), p. 37. For the argument that black activists of the early 1830s were constrained to adopt white strategies of resistance, particularly from the immediatists, in order to gain a hearing before they could craft their own distinctive rhetoric of resistance, see Daniel Yacovone, "The Transformation of the Black Temperance Movement, 1827–1854: An Interpretation," *Journal of the Early Republic*, 8 (1988), 282–97. Concern that black activism was in some sense "co-opted" by white vocabularies of dissent faded to a significant extent over the 1990s, however, as a number of studies emphasized the importance of understanding the ways in which black and white abolitionism evolved through a process of mutual influence, both in agreement and dissent. On this point, see, for example, James Oliver Horton and Lois E. Horton, *In Hope of Liberty: Culture, Community, and Protest Among Northern Free Blacks, 1700–1860* (New York: Oxford University Press, 1997), p. xii. For examples of comparative treatments, see Philip Goodman, *Of One Blood: Abolitionism and the Origins of Racial Equality* (Berkeley: University of California Press, 1998), or, more recently, John Stauffer, *The Black Hearts of Men* (Cambridge, MA: Harvard Univerity Press, 2004). I have also benefited from Elizabeth McHenry's important study, *Forgotten Readers: Recovering the Lost History of African American Literary Societies* (Durham, NC: Duke University Press, 2002). For a useful summary of developments in the scholarship on anti-slavery, I am indebted to Richard S. Newman, *The Transformation of American Abolitionism: Fighting Slavery in the Early Republic* (Chapel Hill, NC: University of North Carolina Press, 2002), pp. 86–106.

9 David Walker, *Appeal in Four Articles to the Colored Citizens of the World*, ed. Sean Wilentz (New York: Hill and Wang, 1995), p. 10 (text's emphasis; subsequent references from this text cited in parenthesis).

10 Goodman, *Of One Blood*, p. 29.

11 Quoted in Dan McKanan, *Identifying the Image of God: Radical Christians and Non-violent Power in the Antebellum United States* (New York: Oxford University Press, 2002), p. 53.

12 *Thomas Jefferson: Writings*, ed. Merrill Peterson (New York: Library of America, 1984), p. 269.

13 *Ibid.* p. 289. The full extent to which Walker mimics and, through sheer repetition, breaks off key phrases from Jefferson's text to incorporate as his own has not been sufficiently recognized by Walker's readers. Expressions like

"actuated by sordid avarice" (e.g., pp. 3, 4, 17, 29) or "attribute of justice" (12, 42) or "inferior and distinct race of beings" (19) come to seem like so many particles spun off of Jefferson's text that are made to career and collide throughout Walker's jeremiad.

14 *Jefferson: Writings*, p. 289.

15 For a useful overview of this specific and indisputably important convergence of themes, see McKanan, *Identifying the Image of God.*

16 Frederick Douglass, "On the Claim of the Negro Ethnologically Considered: An Address Delivered in Hudson, Ohio, on 12 July 1854," in *The Frederick Douglass Papers, Series One: Speeches, Debates, and Interviews*, ed. John W. Blassingame *et al.* (New Haven: Yale University Press, 1982), p. 507.

17 For an illuminating discussion that likewise engages "the ethical and political significance of [Douglass's] pre-literate moral feelings" (p. 114) as they emerge in *My Bondage and My Freedom*, see Gregg D. Crane, *Race, Citizenship, and Law in American Literature* (Cambridge University Press, 2002), pp. 104–30.

18 "I knew nothing of my condition then as a slave," writes Henry Bibb on the first page of his *Narrative*, recalling his early years as a child (Andrews and Gates, eds., *Slave Narratives*, p. 441). The incompatibility of the child's consciousness and servitude is emphasized in a number of slave narratives. See, for example, Harriet Jacobs, *Incidents in the Life of a Slave Girl* (Andrews and Gates, eds., *Slave Narratives*, p. 751) and Lunsford Lane's *Narrative* in William L. Andrews, ed., *North Carolina Slave Narratives* (Chapel Hill, NC: University of North Carolina Press, 2003), p. 101.

19 The ineptitude of Southern preaching is a running joke throughout black anti-slavery writings of the time. See, for example, Walker, *Appeal*, pp. 39, 76; William Wells Brown, *Clotel: Or, the President's Daughter*, ed. Robert S. Levine (New York: Bedford, 2000), pp. 113–15; Jacob Green, *Narrative of the Life of Jacob D. Green*, in Andrews and Gates, eds., *Slave Narratives*, pp. 954–55; and Lunsford Lane, *Narrative*, in Andrews, ed., *North Carolina Slave Narratives*, p. 109. Going beyond satire, Henry Bibb angrily comments that, "hav[ing] no confidence at all in the[ ] preaching" they receive, the slaves become so cynical over the hypocritical character of their religious instruction that they are "driven into … infidelity" (Andrews and Gates, eds., *Slave Narratives*, p. 446).

20 Robert Levine, *Martin Delany, Frederick Douglass, and the Politics of Representative Identity* (Chapel Hill, NC: University of North Carolina Press, 1997), pp. 99–143. To underscore further the somewhat one-sided nature of Douglass's response, it's worth noting that one historian reports "thirty-five percent of all slave rebellions in the British Caribbean took place at Christmastime," when "slaves were spared hard labor" and "the carousing easily turned violent." Moreover, in eighteenth-century South Carolina patrols were actually mustered during the Christmas holidays "for fear that slaves would stage another rebellion" in the wake of the Stono Rebellion of 1739. (Jill Lepore, *New York Burning: Liberty, Slavery, and Conspiracy in Eighteenth-Century Manhattan* [New York: Knopf, 2005], p. 160.)

21 William L. Andrews, *To Tell A Free Story: The First Century of Afro-American Autobiography, 1760–1865* (Urbana and Chicago: University of Illinois Press, 1986), p. 103.

22 Henry Louis Gates, *Figures in Black: Words, Signs, and the 'Racial Self'* (New York: Oxford University Press, 1987), p. 97; Houston Baker, *Blues, Ideology, and Afro-American Literature: A Vernacular Theory* (University of Chicago Press, 1984), pp. 39–50.

23 Eric Sundquist, *To Wake the Nations: Race in the Making of American Literature* (Cambridge, MA: Harvard University Press, 1993), p. 111. Others expressing a preference for the second over the first autobiography include David Leverenz, *Manhood and the American Renaissance* (Ithaca, NY: Cornell University Press, 1989), pp. 108–34; Priscilla Wald, *Constituting Americans: Cultural Anxiety and Narrative Form* (Durham, NC: Duke University Press, 1995), pp. 73–105; and Russ Castronovo, *Necro Citizenship: Death, Eroticism, and the Public Sphere in the Nineteenth-Century United States* (Durham, NC: Duke University Press, 2001), pp. 50–61.

24 Ross Posnock, *Color and Culture: Black Writers and the Making of the Modern Intellectual* (Cambridge, MA: Harvard University Press, 1998), p. 53; Paul Gilroy, *The Black Atlantic: Modernity and Double Consciousness* (Cambridge, MA: Harvard University Press, 1993), p. 69. Of course, not all responses to Douglass speak with one voice. For accounts that stress the limits of his anti-foundationalism from a feminist perspective, see Deborah McDowell, "In the First Place: Making Frederick Douglass and the Afro-American Narrative Tradition," in *Critical Essays on Frederick Douglass*, ed. William L. Andrews (Boston: G. K. Hall, 1991) and Jenny Franchot, "The Punishment of Esther: Frederick Douglass and the Construction of the Feminine," in *Frederick Douglass: New Literary and Historical Essays*, ed. Eric Sundquist (Cambridge University Press, 1990), pp. 134–58. For an account that probes the same limits from a class perspective, see Xiomara Santamarina, *Belabored Professions: Narratives of African American Working Womanhood* (Chapel Hill, NC: University of North Carolina Press, 2005), pp. 16–17; 98.

25 The perceived incompatibility between a universalizing belief in basic human equality and a contextualist commitment to the particulars of historical contingency is a staple of commentary on Douglass. Thus even if the author of *My Bondage and My Freedom* explicitly celebrates freedom as "the natural and inborn right of every member of the human family," we should nevertheless see, according to Russ Castronovo, that the text "opposes this ideology of freedom, contesting its naturalness and innateness by encumbering the slave and freeman's story with an awareness of history that makes freedom seem 'natural' and the material conditions that make it seem 'inborn'" (*Necro Citizenship*, pp. 55, 58). For Robert Fanuzzi, Douglass, despite appearances to the contrary, likewise opposes "the pretense of abstraction" to "the corporeality of the black male" (*Abolition's Public Sphere* [Minneapolis: University of Minnesota Press, 2003], p. 114). The suspicion that current notions of epistemological correctness control such readings more than "history" or

"corporeality" extends back to Gilroy's influential *The Black Atlantic*. Although widely acclaimed for its pathbreaking attention to an anti-national, transcultural framework, it treads warily around the topic of Douglass's religious universalism, at one point conceding that "Douglass's own Christianity may have formed the center of his political outlook, but he was emphatic that the best master he ever had was an atheist." The nadir of this sort of evasiveness is reached a few pages later when Gilroy cites the famous anecdote of Sojourner Truth reproaching Douglass after an especially militant speech ("Frederick, is God dead?") and goes on to associate it "with another Frederick (Nietzsche) [who] was pondering the philosophical and ethical implications of the same question" (*The Black Atlantic*, pp. 59, 64).

26 Alexis de Tocqueville, *Democracy in America*, trans. George Lawrence (New York: Harper and Row, 1969), p. 481.

27 Pierre Bourdieu, *Distinction: A Social Critique of the Judgment of Taste*, trans. Richard Nice (Cambridge, MA: Harvard University Press, 1984), p. 462.

28 Frederick Douglass, "A Nation in the Midst of a Nation: An Address Delivered in New York, New York, on 11 May 1853," in *The Frederick Douglass Papers, Series One: Speeches, Debates, and Interviews*, ed. John W. Blassingame, *et al.* (New Haven: Yale University Press, 1982), pp. 426, 438.

29 Rael, *Black Identity and Black Protest*, p. 52.

30 *Collected Works of Abraham Lincoln*, ed. Roy P. Basler, 11 vols. (New Brunswick, NJ: Rutgers University Press, 1953–), III, p. 376. For arguments concerning the irreducibly religious underpinnings of basic human equality, see John E. Coons and Patrick M. Brennan, *By Nature Equal: The Anatomy of a Western Insight* (Princeton University Press, 1999), and Jeremy Waldron, *God, Locke, and Equality: Christian Foundations in Locke's Political Philosophy* (Cambridge University Press, 2002).

31 Bernard Williams, "The Idea of Equality," in *In the Beginning Was the Deed: Realism and Moralism in Political Argument*, ed. Geoffrey Hawthorn (Princeton University Press, 2005), p. 104. The essay was originally published in 1962.

32 To take one prominent example of protest against colonization in the South: regarded by historians as a turning point in pro-slavery discourse, Thomas R. Dew's pamphlet, *Review of the Debate in the Virginia Legislature of 1831 and 1832* (Richmond: T. W. White, 1832), was written in opposition to both emancipation and colonization. See also Mia Bay, *The White Image in the Black Mind: African-American Ideas about White People, 1830–1925* (New York: Oxford University Press, 2000), p. 22.

33 Henry Clay, *An Address Delivered to the Colonization Society of Kentucky at Frankfort, December 17, 1829*; quoted in Michael Lind, *What Lincoln Believed: The Values and Convictions of America's Greatest President* (New York: Doubleday, 2004), p. 86.

34 Lind, *What Lincoln Believed*, p. 86.

35 *Collected Works of Abraham Lincoln*, III, pp. 302, 305.

36 Lind, *What Lincoln Believed*, p. 86.

37 *Collected Works of Abraham Lincoln*, III, pp. 145–46, 301 (text's emphasis).

38 I borrow the phrase from Winthrop Jordan, *White Over Black: American Attitudes Toward the Negro 1550–1812* (Chapel Hill, NC: University of North Carolina Press, 1968), p. 363.

39 Hosea Easton, *A Treatise on the Intellectual Character, and Civil and Political Condition of the Colored People of the U. States; and the Prejudice Exercised towards Them: With a Sermon on the Duty of the Church to Them* (Boston: I. Knapp, 1837), reprinted in George R. Price and James Brewer Stewart, *To Heal the Scourge of Prejudice: The Life and Writings of Hosea Easton* (Amherst: University of Massachusetts Press, 1999), pp. 63–123. Subsequent references from this text are cited in parenthesis.

40 Frederick Douglass, "An Antislavery Tocsin," in *The Frederick Douglass Papers, Series One,* p. 261; text's emphasis.

41 Bruce Dain, *A Hideous Monster of the Mind: American Race Theory in the Early Republic* (Cambridge, MA: Harvard University Press, 2002), p. 183. In *The White Image in the Black Mind*, Mia Bay agrees that Easton's analysis of the racism of his own time is "incisive," but also argues that his *Treatise* elsewhere "reenvisions racial differences rather than repudiating them" (p. 47). Evidence for this centers upon Easton's juxtaposition of the black descendants of Ham, whose creation of Egypt became the cradle for Western civilization, with the white descendants of Japhet's son Javan, the father of the Greeks, whose rapacity and deceit largely destroyed it. But while it's true that Easton characterizes "almost every nation in Europe, and especially Americans," in terms of "their innate thirst for blood and plunder," he also says that their "superior development of intellectual faculties" is "solely owing to the nature of the circumstances into which they were drawn" by precisely this thirst (*A Treatise*, p. 81). The confusing admixture of innatism and environmentalism speaks more to what, from a modern perspective, seems a conceptual disarray with regard to ideas about race circa 1837 than to any determination to establish "racial differences." For similar cautions concerning the unsettled nature of racial discourse at the time, see Dain, *A Hideous Monster of the Mind*, pp. 113–14.

42 Price and Stewart, *To Heal the Scourge of Prejudice*, pp. 16–19.

43 Sarah J. Hale, *Liberia; or, Mr. Peyton's Experiment* (Philadelphia: Harper & Brothers, 1853), pp. 69–70, 68.

44 *Collected Works of Abraham Lincoln*, III, p. 146.

45 "The Anti-Slavery Movement," in *Frederick Douglass: Selected Speeches and Writing*, ed. Philip S. Foner (Chicago: Lawrence Hill Books, 1999), p. 313. Douglass's speech was first delivered on March 19, 1855.

46 I allude to the procedure used by Samuel Morton, father of the American ethnologists, to establish the cranial capacities of various racial groups. The best short overview of his life and research remains William Stanton, *The Leopard's Spots: Scientific Attitudes toward Race in America, 1815–59,* (University of Chicago Press, 1960), pp. 24–44. For an excellent account of responses to Morton and others from McCune Smith and Douglass, see Dain, *A Hideous Monster of the Mind*, pp. 227–63.

2 INEQUALITY IN THEORY

1 George Fitzhugh, *Cannibals All! Or Slaves Without Masters*, ed. C. Vann Woodward (Cambridge, MA: Harvard University Press), 1960, p. 35. Subsequent references cited from this edition in parenthesis with abbreviation CA.

2 *The Ideology of Slavery: Proslavery Thought in the Antebellum South, 1830–1860*, ed. Drew Gilpin Faust (Baton Rouge: Louisiana State University Press, 1981), p. 285. Subsequent references from this edition will be cited in parenthesis with "Faust" followed by the page number. Fitzhugh's essay originally appeared under the title of "Southern Thought Again," *DeBow's Review*, 23 (1857), 449–62.

3 Eugene Genovese, *Roll, Jordan, Roll: The World the Slaves Made* (New York: Vintage Books, 1974), p. 85. In another seminal study, *The Black Image in the White Mind: The Debate on Afro-American Character and Destiny, 1817–1914* (1971; rpt. Middletown, CT: Wesleyan University Press, 1987), George Fredrickson numbers Fitzhugh among those "defenders of a reactionary seigneurialism" (59) who "reject the ideal of equality in general" (61). One problem with this judgment is that it makes Fitzhugh's interest in socialism look nonsensical, to say nothing of his conviction, stated at the outset of *Cannibals All!*, that "the work of the socialists contain the true defence of slavery" (CA, 21). Indeed Fredrickson does not even mention the word in his discussion of Fitzhugh's writings. One suspects that he may have exaggerated Fitzhugh's pretensions to a specifically "aristocratic" form of paternalism in order to heighten the contrast to a supposedly more populist and militant brand of racism evident in the works of John Van Evrie and Josiah Nott, which he goes on to discuss immediately following his account of Fitzhugh.

4 George Fitzhugh, *Sociology for the South* (1854; rpt. New York: Burt Franklin, 1968), pp. 71, 59. Subsequent references cited in parenthesis with abbreviation SFS.

5 Jeremy Waldron, *God, Locke, and Equality: The Christian Foundations of Locke's Political Philosophy* (Cambridge University Press, 2002), p. 18.

6 In this chapter I bypass scriptural arguments on behalf of slavery and offer little more than a passing reference to the so-called "American School" of ethnology. With regard to the first camp, it is interesting to note that, although studies like Stephen Haynes's *Noah's Curse: The Biblical Justification of American Slavery* (New York: Oxford University Press, 2002) provide impressive evidence for the impact of the Bible in shaping antebellum defenses of servitude, this approach is comparatively rare in the literature of the period. Among the rash of novels written in response to *Uncle Tom's Cabin*, for example, only Mary Eastman's *Aunt Phillis's Cabin* enlists scripture to any meaningful degree in justifying slavery (and even there it does so with considerable ambivalence). Tellingly, Stowe herself sees fit to limit her engagement on this score to a brief vignette that features "an honest drover" ridiculing a Southern parson and his transparently self-serving exposition of Noah's curse (*Uncle Tom's Cabin*, 201). As for the second camp, I concur with Kenneth Greenberg's assertion that "neither polygenesis nor the 'scientific' evidence of black inferiority ever dominated the

proslavery argument in public speeches, journals, or in E. N. Elliott's great compendium of proslavery thought published on the eve of the Civil War" (*Masters and Statesmen: The Political Culture of American Slavery* [Baltimore: Johns Hopkins University Press, 1988), pp. 89–90]). I focus on the "positive good" or class-based defense of slavery primarily because it appears to have commanded the most attention among Southern intellectuals from 1830 to 1860.

7 John M. Grammer, *Pastoral and Politics in the Old South* (Baton Rouge: Louisiana State University Press, 1996), p. 116.

8 For example, see also James Henry Hammond, "The Mud-sill Speech," in *Defending Slavery: Proslavery Thought in the Old South*, ed. Paul Finkelman (Boston: Bedford/St. Martin, 2003), p. 86.

9 For acknowledgement of his "peculiar" views, see CA, 7, 10. Faust, *The Ideology of Slavery*, cites the testimony of one contemporary who viewed Fitzhugh as "something of a crackpot." That said, she also notes that "his arguments were basically derived from those of theorists who preceded him and had been developing a general defense of slavery for decades" (Faust, 18). One of the more unmistakable features of pro-slavery discourse is indeed its monotonous recycling of the same handful of themes over many decades, a point vividly demonstrated in the opening pages of Larry Tise, *Proslavery: A History of the Defense of Slavery in America, 1701–1840* (Athens, GA: University of Georgia Press, 1987).

10 I paraphrase the second half of the second lecture from Nott's pamphlet, *Two Lectures on the Natural History of the Caucasian and Negro Races*, excerpts of which are reprinted in Faust, *The Ideology of Slavery*, pp. 208–38. For further discussion, see Fredrickson, *The Black Image in the White Mind*, p. 80.

11 John Van Evrie, *Negroes and Negro "Slavery": The First an Inferior Race, the Second its Normal Condition* (New York: Evrie and Horton, 1861).

12 I rely on the account provided in William Lee Miller, *Arguing About Slavery: The Great Battle in the United States Congress* (New York: Knopf, 1996), p. 439. Fitzhugh's *Cannibals All!*, it's worth noting, was dedicated to Henry Wise.

13 Caroline Lee Hentz, *The Planter's Northern Bride* (Philadelphia: T. B. Peterson, 1854), p. 175. Subsequent references from this text cited in parenthesis.

14 On the pervasiveness of this theme, especially in relation to the issue of social progress, see Eugene Genovese, *The Slaveholder's Dilemma: Freedom and Progress in Southern Conservative Thought, 1820–1860* (Columbia, SC: University of South Carolina Press, 1992).

15 Finkelman, ed., *Defending Slavery*, p. 86.

16 A. T. Holmes, "The Christian Duty of Masters to their Slaves," in Finkelman, ed., *Defending Slavery*, p. 99.

17 Finkelman, ed., *Defending Slavery*, p. 87; text's emphasis. Likewise extolling the improving effects of slavery, Louisa McCord maintains that "the slave-negro of our United States, in spite of his inferiority of race, stands higher in the scale of being, is better informed in the duties of life, more polished and humanized by association – in short, is the higher man – than the wretched off-casts of a nobler race which crowd the streets and lanes of every densely populated metropolis"

(*Louisa M. McCord: Political and Social Essays*, ed. Richard Lounsbury [Charlottesville: University of Virginia Press, 1995], p. 308).

18	The point here is not that such a development necessarily occurred but that paternalist logic required a softening of patriarchal authority to a degree that allowed its adherents to believe it had. For accounts that emphasize the judicial enlargement of women's property rights together with the tightening of cultural restrictions in the antebellum South, see Peter Bardaglio, *Reconstructing the Household: Families, Sex, and the Law in the Nineteenth-Century South* (Chapel Hill, NC: University of North Carolina Press, 1995) and Elizabeth Fox-Genovese, *Within the Plantation Household: Black and White Women of the Old South* (Chapel Hill, NC: University of North Carolina Press, 1988).

19	Greenberg, *Masters and Statesmen*, pp. 85–103. "Boisterous passions" and "odious peculiarities" appear in Jefferson's famous description of the slaveholder's "intemperance of passion" in *Notes on the State of Virginia* (*Thomas Jefferson: Writings*, ed. Merrill Peterson [New York: Library of America, 1984], p. 288).

20	*Louisa S. McCord, Political and Social Essays*, p. 308; emphasis in original.

21	*Ibid.* p. 308.

22	Quoted in William Sumner Jenkins, *Pro-Slavery Thought in the Old South* (Chapel Hill, NC: University of North Carolina Press, 1935), p. 112. Further instances of this contractualism are cited in Greenberg, *Masters and Statesmen*, pp. 93–97.

23	George Eliot's comment appears in her review of *Dred*, which is reprinted in *Critical Essays on Harriet Beecher Stowe*, ed. Elizabeth Ammons (Boston: G. K. Hall, 1980), p. 43. For general reviews of the outpouring of "anti-*Tom*" fiction published in the wake of Stowe's novel, I have relied primarily on Sarah Meer, *Uncle Tom Mania: Slavery, Minstrelsy, and Transatlantic Culture in the 1850s* (Athens, GA: University of Georgia Press, 2005), pp. 75–101; Joy Jordan-Lake, *Whitewashing Uncle Tom's Cabin: Nineteenth-Century Women Novelists Respond to Stowe* (Nashville: Vanderbilt University Press, 2005); and Barrie Hayne, "Yankee in Patriarchy: T. B. Thorpe's Reply to *Uncle Tom's Cabin*, *American Quarterly*, 20 (1968), 180–95.

24	Martha Haines Butt, *Antifanaticism: A Tale of the South* (1853; rpt. New York: AMS Press, 1973), pp. 16–17; 24–26.

25	Caroline Rush, *The North and South: Or, Slavery and its Contrasts: A Tale of Real Life* (1852; rpt. New York: Negro Universities Press, 1968), p. 128. Subsequent references from this text cited in parenthesis.

26	For claims to this effect, see Rhoda Ellison's introduction to her edition of the novel (Chapel Hill, NC: University of North Carolina Press, 1970), pp. vii–xii; Elizabeth Moss, *Domestic Novelists in the Old South* (Baton Rouge: Louisiana University Press, 1992), p. 112; and Cindy Weinstein, *Family, Kinship, and Sympathy in Nineteenth-Century American Literature* (Cambridge University Press, 2004), p. 76.

27	Betina Entzminger, *The Belle Gone Bad: White Southern Women Writers and the Dark Seductress* (Baton Rouge: Louisiana State University Press, 2002), p. 66. See also Michael O'Brien, *Conjectures of Order: Intellectual Life and the*

American South, 1810–1860, 2 vols. (Chapel Hill, NC: University of North Carolina Press, 2004), II, p.770. For further details on Hentz's background, see Mary Kelley, *Private Woman, Public Stage: Literary Domesticity in Nineteenth-Century America* (New York: Oxford University Press, 1984), pp. 31–32. The paths of Hentz and Stowe briefly crossed in the 1830s, when both were members of a literary society, the Semi-Colon Club, in Cincinnati. See Joan Hedrick, *Harriet Beecher Stowe: A Life* (New York: Oxford University Press, 1994), p. 83.

28 See Eugene Genovese, 'Our Family, White and Black': Family and Household in the Southern Slaveholders' World View," "Toward a Kinder and Gentler America: The Southern Lady in the Greening of the Politics of the Old South," and the other contributions collected in *In Joy and In Sorrow: Women, Family, and Marriage in the Victorian South*, ed. Carol Bleser (New York: Oxford University Press, 1991), pp. 69–88, 125–35. Genovese's *Roll, Jordan, Roll* remains the classic treatment of paternalism and its importance to the Old South.

29 Maria McIntosh, *The Lofty and the Lowly; Or, Good in All and None All-Good*, 2 vols. (New York: D. Appleton and Company, 1853), I, p. 16. Subsequent references cited in parenthesis.

30 I am not the first to notice this. See also Michael O'Brien, *Conjectures of Order*, II, p. 771.

31 T. B. Thorpe, *The Master's House: A Tale of Southern Life* (New York: T. L. McElrath, 1854), p. 350.

32 *Ibid.* pp. 378, 379, 390, 391.

33 *Ibid.* p. 158.

34 Mary H. Eastman, *Aunt Phillis's Cabin; Or, Southern Life As It Is* (1852; rpt. New York: Negro Universities Press, 1968), p. 111. Subsequent references from this text are cited in parenthesis.

35 G. M. Flanders, *The Ebony Idol, by a Lady of New England* (New York: D. Appleton, 1860), p. 69.

36 Quoted in Meer, *Uncle Tom Mania*, p. 75.

37 O'Brien, *Conjectures of Order*, II, p. 991.

38 Harriet Beecher Stowe, *A Key to Uncle Tom's Cabin: Presenting the Original Facts and Documents Upon which the Story is Founded. Together with Corroborative Statements Verifying the Truth of the Work* (Boston: John P. Jewettt, 1853), p. 35.

39 Robert A. Dahl, *Democracy and its Critics* (New Haven: Yale University Press, 1989), pp. 37–79.

40 Eugene Genovese, *The Southern Tradition: The Achievement and Limitations of an American Conservatism* (Cambridge, MA: Harvard University Press, 1994), pp. 50–51.

PART II: THE MANY IN THE ONE

1 Alexis de Tocqueville, *Democracy in America*, trans. George Lawrence (New York: Harper and Row, 1969), p. 485.

2 *Ibid.* pp. 508, 507.
3 Thomas Hobbes, *Leviathan*, ed. C. B. Macpherson (New York: Penguin, 1968), p. 83.
4 Tocqueville, *Democracy in America*, p. 484.

3 THE PRECISE SPIRIT OF THE AVERAGE MASS

1 "Miss Huntley's Poetry," *North American Review*, 1 (1815), 111–21. Quotes may be found at pp. 120, 121.
2 Nina Baym, "The Rise of the Woman Author," *Columbia Literary History of the United States*, ed. Emory Elliott (New York: Columbia University Press, 1988), p. 197.
3 *Ibid.* p. 197.
4 I have in mind especially Theo Davis, *Formalism, Experience, and the Making of American Literature in the Nineteenth Century* (Cambridge University Press, 2007); Meredith McGill, *American Literature and the Culture of Reprinting 1834–1853* (Philadelphia: University of Pennsylvania Press, 2003); and Virginia Jackson and Yopie Prins, "Lyrical Studies," *Victorian Literature and Culture*, 7 (1999), 521–29.
5 Quoted in Richard Ruland, ed., *The Native Muse: Theories of American Literature* (New York: Dutton, 1972), p. 111. Consistent with this same logic, Knapp goes on to remark: "the places which we have long frequented are the props of our memory: – it fails, and the mind misses its fullness of ideas, when we are absent from them" (p. 111).
6 Quoted in Robert Spiller, ed., *The American Literary Revolution, 1783–1837* (New York: Anchor Books, 1967), p. 160.
7 Ruland, ed., *The Native Muse*, p. 120.
8 Robert Streeter, "Association Psychology and Literary Nationalism in the *North American Review*, 1815–1825," *American Literature*, 17 (1945), 243–54; 247.
9 William Cullen Bryant, "Redwood, A Tale," *North American Review*, 20 (1825), 245–73, 272.
10 *Ibid.* 247.
11 Streeter, "Association Psychology and Literary Nationalism," 250.
12 Henry Homes, Lord Kames, *Elements of Criticism*, ed. Peter Jones (Indianapolis: Liberty Fund, 2005), p. 21. The most authoritative general review of the Scottish influence on the letters of the early United States remains William Charvat, *The Origins of American Critical Thought, 1810–1835* (Philadelphia: University of Pennsylvania Press, 1936). Also helpful are Terence Martin, *The Instructed Vision: Scottish Common Sense Philosophy and the Origins of American Fiction* (Bloomington: Indiana University Press, 1961) and James D. Wallace, *Early Cooper and His Audience* (New York: Columbia University Press, 1986), pp. 1–29.
13 Theo Davis, *Formalism, Experience, and the Making of American Literature*, pp. 29, 53. For a similar approach to Kames that emphasizes the importance of "emotional extravagance" and its vexed connection to epistemological issues, see

Adela Pinch, *Strange Fits of Passion: Epistemologies of Emotion from Hume to Austen* (Stanford University Press, 1996), pp. 4–7; 50.

14 *North American Review*, 5 (1817), 103. For further discussion of these and related passages, see Charvat, *The Origins of American Critical Thought*, pp. 23–26.

15 *North American Review*, 16 (1823), 24.

16 *American Monthly Review*, 1 (1832), 300.

17 Quoted in Charles H. Brown, *William Cullen Bryant: A Biography* (New York: Scribner's, 1971), p. 144.

18 *Poems of William Cullen Bryant* (London: Oxford University Press, 1914), p. 11. The lines cited are 1–9.

19 Bryant, "Redwood, A Tale," 272.

20 Alexis de Tocqueville, *Democracy in America*, trans. George Lawrence (New York: Harper and Row, 1969), p. 485.

21 *Ibid.* pp. 487, 486. The story of how print acquired political legitimacy in the colonial United States by virtue of its anonymity or apparent authorlessness is told in Michael Warner, *The Letters of the Republic: Publication and the Public Sphere in Eighteenth-Century America* (Cambridge, MA: Harvard University Press, 1990). Grantland S. Rice, *The Transformation of Authorship in America* (University of Chicago Press, 1997) offers a different account of the same phenomenon while McGill, *American Literature and the Culture of Reprinting* carries the exploration of print culture and its ideologies into the nineteenth Century.

22 Charvat, *The Origins of American Critical Thought*, p. 92.

23 Archibald Alison, *Essays on the Nature and Principles of Taste* (New York: G. & C. & H. Carvill, 1830), p. 27.

24 Lydia Sigourney, *Select Poems* (1841; rpt. Philadelphia: Parry & McMillan, 1857), p. 110. Subsequent references from this text will be cited in parenthesis as SP. Initially known simply as *Poems* on its first appearance in 1834, *Select Poems* offers some of the more popular pieces published previously in periodicals and would eventually go through more than twenty-five editions in Sigourney's lifetime. The primary text used for most of the discussions to follow is the eleventh edition of *Select Poems*.

25 Jerome J. McGann, *The Poetics of Sensibility: A Revolution in Literary Style* (Oxford: Clarendon Press, 1996), p. 105. Nina Baym similarly observes: "for Sigourney, to write as a woman meant to remain chiefly in the emotive realm, to be engrossed in immediate personal relations and above all in motherhood" ("The Rise of the Woman Author,", p. 297.)

26 Eliza Richards, *Gender and the Poetics of Reception in Poe's Circle* (Cambridge University Press, 2004), p. 71. The trend in the scholarship has been to turn away from the elegiac writing and focus on Sigourney's interest in history, nationalism, and pedagogy, a turn respectively exemplified in Nina Baym, "Reinventing Lydia Sigourney," in *Feminism and American Literary History* (New Brunswick, NJ: Rutgers University Press, 1992), pp. 151–36; Mary Louise Kete, *Sentimental Collaborations: Mourning and Middle-Class Identity in Nineteenth-Century America* (Durham, NC: Duke University Press, 1999), pp. 103–33; and

Mary Loeffelholz, *From School to Salon: Reading Nineteenth-Century American Women's Poetry* (Princeton University Press, 2004), pp. 32–64. Baym has been the most outspoken in thinking that the elegies have overshadowed the more public concerns of her poetry and that indeed they only constitute a small portion of her total output as a writer ("Re-inventing Lydia Sigourney," p. 152). Unlike Baym, I don't think that the elegies should be written off as a total loss and therefore don't think that posterity played a dirty trick on Sigourney in tying her reputation to them. For a fuller discussion of Baym's position and its shortcomings, see Richards, *Gender and the Poetics of Reception in Poe's Circle*, pp. 67–69.

27 Gordon S. Haight, *Mrs. Sigourney: The Sweet Singer of Hartford* (New Haven: Yale University Press, 1930), p. 92.

28 Lydia Sigourney, *Poems* (1854; rpt. New York: Leavitt and Allen, 1860), p. 158. Subsequent references from this text will be cited in parenthesis as P.

29 Carolyn Steedman, *Strange Dislocations: Childhood and the Idea of Human Interiority, 1780–1930* (Cambridge, MA: Harvard University Press, 1994).

30 Lydia Sigourney, *Pocahontas and Other Poems* (New York: Harper and Brothers, 1841), p. 52.

31 Ann Douglas, *The Feminization of American Culture* (1977; rpt. New York: Avon, 1978). See especially pp. 240–49 for commentary on Sigourney.

32 See, for example, Karen Sanchez-Eppler, *Dependent States: The Child's Part in Nineteenth-Century American Culture* (University of Chicago Press, 2005).

33 Sigourney, *Pocahontas and Other Poems*, p. 134.

34 In keeping with the conventions of the time, Sigourney is frequently drawn to the metaphor of the mother inscribing or imprinting her influence or image on the child. The hand of the father may guide and protect his "shrinking plants," but it is "that blessed Mother's name" that cannot be "erased" from "their infant hearts" ("A Father to his Motherless Children" [SP, 283, 284]). Similarly, "Filial Claims" urges the man who was once a son to "turn back from the book of life / To its first page," where he shall find the "deep trace" left by *"Lines from a Mother's pencil"* (original emphasis, SP, 252). But while the irresistible power of the Mother is often characterized in terms of a hidden text inscribed in the child's soul, it is important to distinguish this maternal imprinting from the writing of divine judgment. As Patricia Crain notes in her discussion of the mother as a "source of alphabetic learning," the "mother imprints whether she wants to or not." The imprinting, impressing, or enstamping of her influence is an involuntary, non-intentional activity, entirely different from Sigourney's descriptions of God's writing and its "impress" of each agent's acts for eternity (Patricia Crain, *The Story of A: The Alphabetization of America from The New England Primer to The Scarlet Letter* [Stanford University Press, 2000], pp. 130, 129). For a more general discussion of Sigourney's contributions to ideas about mothering and literacy, see Sarah Robbins, *Managing Literacy, Mothering America: Women's Narratives on Reading and Writing in the Nineteenth Century* (University of Pittsburgh Press, 2004), pp. 38–73.

35 Alison, *Essays on the Nature and Principles of Taste*, p. 26. The formative influence of Alison on Bryant's writings is discussed in William Palmer Hudson, "Archibald Alison and William Cullen Bryant," *American Literature*, 12 (1940), 59–68. Also relevant here is Kames's contention that objects represented through speech, writing, or painting can achieve an "ideal Presence" of such immediacy that the spectator is carried off into a kind of reverie. For further discussion, see Pinch, *Strange Fits of Passion*, p. 115, Theo Davis, *Formalism, Experience, and the Making of American Literature*, p. 154, and McGann, *The Poetics of Sensibility*, p. 131.

36 Quoted in Douglas, *The Feminization of American Culture*, p. 247. Though she does not cite a source for the deathbed remark, Douglas is careful to point out that it surfaces in a "sentimentalized biographical sketch" published by Sigourney nearly thirty years previously. For an interesting comparison of Sigourney's views on genius and impersonality with those of Emerson, see Victoria Olwell, " 'It Spoke Itself': Women's Genius and Eccentric Politics," *American Literature*, 77 (2005), 33–63.

37 Walt Whitman, "A Backward Glance O'er Travel'd Roads," in *Leaves of Grass: Norton Critical Edition*, ed. Sculley Bradley and Harold W. Blodgett (New York: Norton, 1973), pp. 566–67.

38 The citations are drawn respectively from Angus Fletcher, *A New Theory for American Poetry: Democracy, the Environment, and the Future of Imagination* (Cambridge, MA: Harvard University Press, 2004), p. 9; David Reynolds, *Walt Whitman's America: A Cultural Biography* (New York: Knopf, 1995), p. 175; and Michael Moon, *Disseminating Whitman: Revision and Corporeality in Leaves of Grass* (Cambridge, MA: Harvard University Press, 1991), p. 4.

39 *Walt Whitman's Leaves of Grass: The First (1855) Edition*, ed. Malcolm Cowley (New York: Viking, 1959), p. 13. All references to the Preface and "Song of Myself" are taken from this edition and are cited in the text in parenthesis.

40 Oscar Wilde "The Gospel According to Walt Whitman," in *The Artist as Critic: The Critical Writings of Oscar Wilde*, ed. Richard Ellman (New York: Viking, 1969), p. 125.

41 Fletcher, *A New Theory for American Poetry*, pp. 106, 109.

42 Reynolds, *Walt Whitman's America*, pp. 13, 19.

43 Robert Martin Adams, *Strains of Discord: Studies in Literary Openness* (Ithaca, NY: Cornell University Press, 1959), p. 181.

44 Moon, *Disseminating Whitman*, pp. 11, 60, 14.

45 *Ibid.* pp. 46, 45.

46 *Ibid.* p. 52.

47 Fletcher, *A New Theory of American Poetry*, p. 112.

48 See, for example, Jurgen Habermas, *Legitimation Crisis*, trans. Thomas McCarthy (Boston: Beacon Press, 1975), pp. 107–08.

49 This is essentially the recommendation made by Mark Maslan, who attempts to extrapolate from *Leaves of Grass* a theory of democratic politics that is *not* dependent on renouncing the practice of representation, in *Whitman Possessed: Poetry,*

Sexuality, and Popular Authority (Baltimore: Johns Hopkins University Press, 2001), pp. 92–141.

50 Ralph Waldo Emerson, "The Poet," in *Ralph Waldo Emerson: Essays and Lectures*, ed. Joel Porte (New York: Library of America, 1983), p. 448.

51 Ralph Waldo Emerson, "The Over-soul," in *Essays and Lectures*, p. 396.

4 COMPARATIVELY SPEAKING

1 Alexis de Tocqueville, *Democracy in America*, trans. George Lawrence (New York: Harper and Row, 1969), pp. 310, 57. Subsequent references from this text are cited in parenthesis.

2 John Rawls, *A Theory of Justice* (Cambridge, MA: Harvard University Press, 1971), p. 534; Ronald Dworkin, *Sovereign Virtue: The Theory and Practice of Equality* (Cambridge, MA: Harvard University Press, 2000), pp. 65–119; Wallace Stevens, "Extracts from Addresses to the Academy of Fine Ideas," in *The Palm at the End of the Mind: Selected Poems and a Play*, ed. Holly Stevens (New York: Vintage, 1971), p. 179.

3 Fredric Jameson, *The Political Unconscious: Narrative as a Socially Symbolic Act* (Ithaca: Cornell University Press, 1981), p. 268. Jameson goes so far as to argue that "the theory of 'ressentiment,' wherever it appears, will always be the expression and the production of 'ressentiment' " (268). This idea of envy and its associates recoiling back upon the theorists who deploy them is pursued in Sianne Ngai, *Ugly Feelings* (Cambridge, MA: Harvard University Press, 2005), pp. 126–73.

4 Frances Ferguson, "Envy Rising," *ELH*, 69 (2002), 889–905.

5 Cited in Helmut Schoeck, *Envy: A Theory of Social Behavior* (Indianapolis: Liberty Press, 1987), p. 208.

6 Caroline Kirkland, *A New Home, Who'll Follow?*, ed. Sandra Zagarell (New Brunswick, NJ: Rutgers University Press, 1989), p. 5. Subsequent references cited in parenthesis are from this edition.

7 For an interesting discussion of these genteel neighbors as doubles of Kirkland herself, see David Leverenz, *Manhood and the American Renaissance* (Ithaca, NY: Cornell University Press, 1989), pp. 151–64. Noting that the original idea for *A New Home* was drawn from Kirkland's letters to friends and family in the east, Annette Kolodny interprets the text as ultimately appealing to a pastoral ideal formed around a community of pioneer women inculcating the virtues of middle-class gentility (*The Land Before Her: Fantasy and Experience of the American Frontiers, 1630–1860* [Chapel Hill, NC: University of North Carolina Press, 1984], pp. 131–48).

8 For a reading that emphasizes the eventual affirmation of "communal interdependence" (xl) precisely along these lines, see Zagarell's Introduction to Kinkland, *A New Home*, pp. xi–xlvi.

9 Quoted in Kolodny, *The Land Before Her*, pp. 148 49.

10 Mikhail Bakhtin, *Problems of Dostoevsky's Poetics*, trans. Caryl Emerson (Minneapolis: University of Minnesota Press, 1984), p. 6. The argument that

modern literature, by eschewing omniscience and denying superior knowledge in its construction of a point of view, creates an epistemic equality built upon fallibility and skepticism is pursued in Stewart Justman, *Literature and Human Equality* (Evanston, IL: Northwestern University Press, 2006).

11 Nathaniel Hawthorne, *The House of the Seven Gables*, ed. Robert Levine (New York: Norton, 2006), pp. 192, 24. Subsequent references from this text will be cited in parenthesis.

12 Bakhtin, *Problems of Dostoevsky's Poetics*, p. 71.

13 For an excellent treatment of this connection, see Meredith McGill, *American Literature and the Culture of Reprinting, 1834–1853* (Philadelphia: University of Pennsylvania Press, 2003), pp. 233–69. I agree with McGill that the tendency to see *The House of the Seven Gables* as allegorizing Hawthorne's anxieties about the literary marketplace or mass culture more generally obscures the true extent of the author's investment in both. Indeed, on my reading, the integral role played by envy in the narrator's rendition of the story points to an aggressive, if somewhat opportunistic populism that accounts of the novel routinely overlook.

14 A. N. Kaul, *The American Vision: Actual and Ideal in Nineteenth-Century Fiction* (New Haven: Yale University Press, 1963), p. 192. For readings of the novel that stress the importance of its use of gossip and rumor, see Susan Mizruchi, *The Power of Historical Knowledge: Narrating the Past in Hawthorne, James, and Dreiser* (Princeton University Press, 1988), pp. 128–34; Edgar Dryden, "Hawthorne's Castle in the Air: Form and Theme in *The House of the Seven Gables*," *ELH*, 38 (1967), 294–317; and Richard Poirier, *A World Elsewhere: The Place of Style in American Literature* (New York: Oxford University Press, 1966), pp. 106–09.

15 Michael T. Gilmore, *American Romanticism and the Marketplace* (University of Chicago Press, 1985), p. 111. See also Marcus Cunliffe, "*The House of the Seven Gables*," in *Hawthorne Centenary Essays*, ed. Roy Harvey Pearce (Columbus: Ohio State University Press, 1964), p. 64. In an influential essay, Walter Benn Michaels reads the novel as engaging "the anxiety about ownership," with the ending taken to signify a hopeful withdrawal from the vicissitudes of the market (*The Gold Standard and the Logic of Naturalism* [Berkeley: University of California Press, 1987], pp. 87–112; quote at p. 89). My own sense is that when Hawthorne tells us that the Judge's only chance of attaining true "self-knowledge" is through the immediate "loss of his property and reputation" (164), it's not (or not just) "anxiety" about the market that is foremost in his mind.

16 Max Scheler, *On Feeling, Knowing, and Valuing: Selected Writings*, ed. Harold J. Bershady (University of Chicago, 1992), p. 122. The original italics in Scheler's sentence have been removed.

17 Among the many discussions of Phoebe as a paragon of middle-class domesticity, particularly noteworthy are Gillian Brown, *Domestic Individualism: Imagining Self in Nineteenth-Century America* (Berkeley: University of California Press, 1990); Joel Pfister, *The Production of Personal Life: Class,*

Gender, and the Psychological in Hawthorne's Fiction (Stanford University Press, 1991). Critics tend to sentimentalize Phoebe more than Hawthorne does; for one exception, see McGill, *American Literature and the Culture of Reprinting*, p. 254.

18 Ralph Waldo Emerson, *Essays and Lectures*, ed. Joel Porte (New York: Library of America, 1983), p. 259.

19 *Ibid.* pp. 260, 263, 276.

20 *Ibid.* pp. 265, 262, 263, 264, 309.

21 *Ibid.* p. 259.

22 T. Walter Herbert, *Dearest Beloved: The Hawthornes and the Making of the Middle-Class Family* (Berkeley: University of California Press, 1993), p. 105; 105–06. See also Amy Schrager Lang, *The Syntax of Class: Writing Inequality in Nineteenth-Century America* (Princeton University Press, 2003), pp. 34–41.

23 Harriet Wilson, *Our Nig; or, Sketches from the Life of a Free Black, in a Two-Story White House, North. Showing that Slavery's Shadows Fall Even There*, with a New Preface, Introduction, and Notes by Henry Louis Gates, Jr. (New York: Vintage, 2002), p. 3 (original emphasis). Subsequent references from this text are cited in parenthesis.

24 William Andrews, *To Tell a Free Story: The First Century of Afro-American Autobiography, 1760–1865* (Urbana: University of Illinois Press, 1986), pp. 239–63. It is important to note that Harriet Wilson's Preface to *Our Nig* does explicitly "appeal to my colored brethren universally for patronage" (3), a point emphasized by Hazel Carby and Xiomara Santamarina. On the other hand, Patricia Wald has wondered how extensive, practically speaking, assistance from this quarter could be, while others have suggested that, to the extent that Wilson's novel attracted attention at all, it was from white readers. See Hazel Carby, *Reconstructing Womanhood: The Emergence of the Afro-American Woman Novelist* (New York: Oxford University Press, 1987), p. 44; Xiomara Santamarina, *Belabored Professions: Narratives of African American Working Women* (Chapel Hill, NC: University of North Carolina Press, 2005), p. 65; Priscilla Wald, *Constituting Americans: Cultural Anxiety and Narrative Form* (Durham, NC: Duke University Press, 1995), p. 157; Barbara White, "Afterword," in Wilson, *Our Nig*.

25 Harriet Jacobs, *Incidents in the Life of a Slave Girl*, ed. Jean Fagan Yellin (Cambridge, MA: Harvard University Press, 1984), p. 52. For the specific comparison between the two passages, see Wald, *Constituting Americans*, p. 160; more generally, it has not been uncommon to find Wilson's novel and Jacob's slave narrative considered together, as in Carby, *Reconstructing Womanhood*, pp. 43–61; Harryette Mullen, "Runaway Tongue: Resistant Orality in *Uncle Tom's Cabin, Our Nig*, and *Incidents in the Life of a Slave Girl*, and *Beloved*," in *The Culture of Sentiment: Race, Gender, and Sentimentality in Nineteenth-Century America*, ed. Shirley Samuels (New York: Oxford University Press, 1992), pp. 244–64; and Carla Peterson, *"Doers of the Word": African-American Women Speakers and Writers in the North (1810–1880)* (New York: Oxford University Press, 1995), pp. 151–56.

26 *The Essential Kierkegaard*, ed. Howard V. Hong and Edna H. Hong (Princeton University Press, 1997), p. 258.

27 For example, see Wilson, *Our Nig*, pp. 50, 72, 83.

28 Santamarina, *Belabored Professions*, pp. 87–88; Robert Reid-Pharr, *Conjugal Union: The Body, the House, and the Black American* (Baltimore: Johns Hopkins University Press, 1999), pp. 105, 107, 109. See also Lang, *The Syntax of Class*, pp. 63–68.

29 White's findings appear in the Afterword to the re-issue of Henry Louis Gates's edition of Wilson, *Our Nig*, pp. iii–liv.

30 J. R. Pole, *The Pursuit of Equality in American History* (Berkeley: University of California Press, 1978), p. ix. The argument that all group feeling is sublimated envy may be found in Sigmund Freud, *Group Psychology and the Analysis of the Ego*, trans. James Strachey (New York: Bantam, 1965), p. 67. See also Schoeck, *Envy: A Theory of Social Behavior*, p. 305, for further discussion.

PART III: EQUAL BUT SEPARATE

1 Frederick Douglass, *Autobiographies*, ed. Henry Louis Gates, Jr. (New York: Library of America, 1994), p. 414.

2 Harriet Beecher Stowe, *Dred: A Tale of the Great Dismal Swamp*, ed. Robert S. Levine (New York: Penguin, 2000), p. 101. Subsequent references cited in parenthesis.

3 Douglass, *Autobiographies*, p. 198.

4 Interrogations of the limits of sympathy in *Uncle Tom's Cabin* may be found in Lauren Berlant, "Poor Eliza," *American Literature*, 70 (1998), 635–68; Elizabeth Barnes, *States of Sympathy: Seduction and Democracy in the American Novel* (New York: Columbia University Press, 1997); Laura Wexler, "Tender Violence: Literary Eavesdropping, Domestic Fiction, and Educational Reform," in *The Culture of Sentiment: Race, Gender, and Sentimentality in 19th Century America*, ed. Shirley Samuels (New York: Oxford University Press, 1992), pp. 9–19; Amy Kaplan, "Manifest Domesticity," *American Literature*, 70 (1998), 581–606.

5 TRANSCENDING FRIENDSHIPS

1 *Ralph Waldo Emerson: Essays and Lectures*, ed. Joel Porte (New York: Library of America, 1983), p. 237. Subsequent references are cited from this text.

2 See, for example, John Carlos Rowe, *At Emerson's Tomb: The Politics of Classic American Literature* (New York: Columbia University Press, 1997), pp. 1–41; Christopher Newfield, *The Emerson Effect: Individualism and Submission in America* (University of Chicago Press, 1996); and Russ Castronovo, *Necro Citizenship: Death, Eroticism, and the Public Sphere in the Nineteenth-Century United States* (Durham, NC: Duke University Press, 2001), pp. 62–98.

3 Henry James, "Ralph Waldo Emerson," in *Literary Criticism: Essays on Literature, American Writers, English Writers*, ed. Leon Edel (New York: Library of America, 1984), p. 245.

4 "Emerson speaks of his friends too much as if they were disembodied spirits. One doesn't see the color in the cheeks of them and the coats on their back." (James, "Ralph Waldo Emerson," p. 246.)

5 Caleb Crain likewise observes that "in Emerson's hands, literature aspired not to describe or disguise but to *be* the relationship between two men" (*American Sympathy: Men, Friendship, and Literature in the New Nation* [New Haven: Yale University Press, 2001], p. 153; emphasis in original). In a searching analysis of "Friendship," Crain develops the idea that Emerson, "the architect of an impersonalized person," authored works that bear "not just the weight of recording a relationship but the weight of being a relationship" (*American Sympathy*, p. 173). Ultimately, Crain treats this investment in impersonality as a sign of sexual repression and escape, particularly so far as his attraction to other men is concerned. While my own reading does not necessarily contradict Crain's psychobiographical reading, it does suggest that the motives involved in Emersonian impersonality extend well beyond the personal.

6 Henry David Thoreau, *Walden and Civil Disobedience*, ed. Owen Thomas (New York: Norton Critical Edition, 1966), p. 94. Subsequent references cited in parenthesis.

7 Perry Miller, *The Transcendentalists: An Anthology* (Cambridge, MA: Harvard University Press, 1950), p. 14.

8 George Kateb, *Emerson and Self-Reliance* (Thousand Oaks, CA: Sage Publications, 1995), p. 102.

9 Richard Poirier, *Poetry and Pragmatism* (Cambridge, MA: Harvard University Press, 1992), pp. 79–128. There is general agreement among commentators that self-reliance is best understood as "essentially a method of intellect" (Kateb, *Emerson and Self-Reliance*, p. 10) – not a set of propositions about how to act in the world but a framework for evaluating one's beliefs. As such, it is above all concerned with "the *manner* rather than the *content* of action" (Howard Horwitz, *By the Law of Nature: Form and Value in Nineteenth-Century America* [New York: Oxford University Press, 1991], p. 75; original emphasis).

10 The full quotation reads: "People enjoying [freedom of the press] become attached to their opinions as much from pride as from conviction. They love them because they think them correct, but also because they have chosen them; and they stick to them, not only as something true but also as something of their very own" (Alexis de Tocqueville, *Democracy in American*, trans. George Lawrence [New York: Harper and Row, 1969], p. 186). Subsequent references cited in parenthesis.

11 Emerson wrote two speeches on Brown, one delivered shortly before his execution and the other shortly after. They are collected in *Emerson's Anti-Slavery Writings*, ed. Len Gougeon and Joel Myerson (New Haven: Yale University Press, 1995), pp. 117–24. Emerson's description of Brown's idealism may be found on p. 118 and his reference to the admiration of Southern politicians for Brown's heroic bearing during his trial may be found on pp. 118–19.

12 *Ibid.* p. 122.

13 John Stuart Mill, *On Liberty* (New York: Penguin, 1974), p. 132. Mill reviewed the first volume of *Democracy in America* for the *London and Westminster Review* in October 1835 and the second for the *Edinburgh Review* in October 1840.

14 Mill, *On Liberty*, p. 132.

15 Quentin Anderson (*The Imperial Self* [New York: Knopf, 1971]) and Myra Jehlen (*American Incarnation: The Individual, the Nation, and the Continent* [Cambridge, MA: Harvard University Press, 1986]) treat the Emersonian project of self-authorization and its appeals to a god within as leading to a sacrifice of relation and conquest of the natural world, while David Simpson (*The Politics of American English* [New York: Oxford University Press, 1986]) links this project to westward expansion. Christopher Newfield (*The Emerson Effect*) views Emerson's superpersonal minds and souls as harbingers of corporate capitalism and Emerson himself as an apologist for the liberal state. On the other hand, Anita Patterson finds that Emerson becomes increasingly disenchanted with liberalism as a viable form of democratic cohesion and so turns to race in order to consolidate national identity (*From Emerson to King: Democracy, Race, and the Politics of Protest* [New York: Oxford University Press, 1997]).

16 Tocqueville's discussion of freedom and equality and their possible tensions leads off Part 2 of *Democracy in America*, Volume II. Mill's perception that the tyranny of the majority is essentially the tyranny of mass society is plainly indebted to Tocqueville, and thereby sets the stage for the struggle of individual independence against collective opinion that is the dominant concern in *On Liberty*. I am suggesting, nevertheless, that the discussion of self-reliance that leads off Part 1 of Tocqueville's volume implies a different understanding of this fabled conflict.

17 *The Journals and Miscellaneous Notebooks of Ralph Waldo Emerson*, ed. William H. Gilman *et al.*, 16 vols. (Cambridge, MA: Harvard University Press, 1960–82), IV, p. 342.

18 Lawrence Buell, *Emerson* (Cambridge, MA: Harvard University Press, 2003), p. 63.

19 Margaret Fuller, *Woman in the Nineteenth Century*, ed. Larry Reynolds (New York: Norton Critical Edition, 1998), p. 5. Subsequent references cited in parenthesis from this text.

20 Christina Zwarg, *Feminist Conversations: Fuller, Emerson, and the Play of Reading* (Ithaca, NY: Cornell University Press, 1995), pp. 164, 170. For Zwarg, *Woman* "attempts to address the lethal fatality that made democracy and equality dependent or conditional on the subordination and conquest of those who reveal themselves to be strange or Other" – though not without moments that "appear to blunt the radical edge of her feminism" (pp. 169, 172). Margaret Vanderhaar Allen claims that *Woman* betrays "ambivalence" with regard to "the issues of women and power" on account of its author's "deeply felt though ill-defined personal need to yield to superior masculine authority" (*The Achievement of Margaret Fuller* [University Park, PA: Pennsylvania State University Press, 1979], p. 142). The assumption that Fuller's progressivism is anticipated by *Woman* but not fully realized until she left the United States for

Europe is common. See, for example, Larry Reynolds, *European Revolutions and the American Literary Renaissance* (New Haven: Yale University Press, 1988), pp. 62–78.

21 Julie Ellison, *Delicate Subjects: Romanticism, Gender, and the Ethics of Understanding* (Ithaca, NY: Cornell University Press, 1990), p. 271.

22 For thoughtful discussions of the competing definitions of friendship held by Emerson and Fuller – where they overlap, where they diverge – see Crain, *American Sympathy*, pp. 177–237 and Charles Capper, *Margaret Fuller: An American Romantic Life: The Public Years* (New York: Oxford University Press, 2007), pp. 66–73.

23 Crain, *American Sympathy*, p. 191.

6 THE COMMON CONDITION

1 Margaret Fuller, *Woman in the Nineteenth Century*, ed. Larry Reynolds (New York: Norton Critical Edition, 1998), p. 102.

2 Gustave de Beaumont, *Marie or, Slavery in the United States*, trans. Barbara Chapman (Baltimore: The Johns Hopkins University Press, 1999), p. 107.

3 Alexis de Tocqueville, *Democracy in America*, trans. George Lawrence (New York: Harper and Row, 1969), p. 635.

4 *Hawthorne: Tales and Sketches*, ed. Roy Harvey Pearce (New York: Library of America, 1982), p. 874.

5 *Ibid.* p. 875.

6 Thomas Carlyle, *Sartor Resartus: The Life and Opinions of Herr Teufelsdrockh* (Indianapolis: Bobbs Merrill, 1937), pp. 119, 120.

7 Charles Fourier, *The Social Destiny of Man, or the Theory of the Four Movements*, ed. Albert Brisbane (New York: Dewitt, 1857), pp. 155, 156. As Carl J. Guarneri points out, Brisbane was primarily drawn to Fourierism on the basis of its ideas about "Attractive Industry" (*The Utopian Alternative: Fourierism in Nineteenth-Century America* [Ithaca, NY: Cornell University Press, 1991], pp. 29–41).

8 Guarneri, *The Utopian Alternative*, p. 126.

9 Karl Marx and Frederick Engels, *The German Ideology*, ed. C. J. Arthur (New York: International Publishers, 1970), pp. 105, 109. In a reading not too different from my own, G. A. Cohen suggests that Marx envisions here the abolition of social roles as conventionally understood. The point behind allowing people to paint without becoming painters is not to encourage part-time painters or even hobbyists but to enable "individuals to face one another and themselves 'as such', without the mediation of institutions" (*Karl Marx's Theory of History: A Defence* [Princeton University Press, 1979], pp. 132–33.) The quote about "real individuality" may be found in Fourier, *The Social Destiny of Man*, p. 155.

10 Marx and Engels, *The German Ideology*, p. 53.

11 Fourier *The Social Destiny of Man*, pp. 144, 149, 152.

12 Karl Marx, *The Economic and Philosophic Manuscripts of 1844*, ed. Dirk J. Struik (New York: International Publishers, 1964), p. 110.

13 Karl Marx, *Theories of Surplus Value*, 2 vols. (London: Lawrence and Wishart, 1972), I, p. 401.

14 Louisa May Alcott, *Work: A Story of Experience* (New York: Schocken Books, 1977), p. 58. Subsequent references cited in parenthesis are from this text.

15 Carlyle, *Sartor Resartus*, pp. 119, 197. Of course, the question-begging nature of this "solution" does not preclude starting up the same quest all over again. When the pattern of enchantment and disenchantment is repeated often enough, the result is something like the first half of Orestes Brownson's aptly named autobiography, *The Convert*, first published in 1859. As the young Brownson moves from one calling to the next (Presbyterian, Universalist, Owenite socialist, Unitarian, working-class reformer, and so on), the oppressive sense that "I must have something to do, to prevent my activity from recoiling upon itself" (p. 63) spurs fresh expectations of a true place at the same time that it incurs fresh disappointments. Brownson even has a name for the syndrome, calling it a case of "running without being sent". See *The Convert, or Leaves from My Experience* (New York: D. & J. Sadlier, 1889), p. 110.

16 Lucy Larcom, *A New England Girlhood* (Gloucester, MA: Peter Smith, 1973), p. 200. Subsequent references cited in parenthesis are from this text.

17 Karl Marx, *The Grundrisse*, in *The Marx-Engels Reader*, ed. Robert C. Tucker (New York: Norton, 1972), pp. 240–41. See also *Capital*, Vol. 1, trans. Ben Fowkes (New York: Vintage, 1977), pp. 1014, 618.

18 Karl Marx, "Introduction to a Critique of Political Economy," in Marx and Engels, *German Ideology*, p. 144.

19 *The Marx-Engels Reader*, p. 240.

20 *William Ellery Channing: Selected Writings*, ed. David Robinson (New York: Paulist Press, 1985), p. 226. Subsequent references cited in parenthesis are from this edition.

21 Theodore Parker, "Thoughts on Labor," *Dial*, 1 (1841), 501.

22 Nicholas K. Bromell, *By the Sweat of the Brow: Literature and Labor in Antebellum America* (University of Chicago Press, 1993), p. 26. For similar critiques, see Carolyn Porter, *Seeing and Being: The Plight of the Participant Observer in Emerson, James, and Faulkner* (Middleton, CT: Wesleyan University Press, 1981), p. 88 and Andrew Delbanco, *William Ellery Channing: An Essay on the Liberal Spirit* (Cambridge, MA: Harvard University Press, 1981), pp. 67–69.

23 Henry Clarke Wright, *Growing Up in Cooper Country: Boyhood Recollections of the New York Frontier*, ed. Louis C. Jones (Syracuse University Press, 1965), p. 167. Clarke Wright's statement is often quoted by labor historians as a summary of pre-capitalist, handicraft culture, as in Susan Hirsch, *Roots of the Working Class: The Industrialization of Crafts in Newark, 1800–1860* (Philadelphia: University of Pennsylvania Press, 1978), p. 9; Michael H. Frisch and Daniel Walkowitz, eds., *Working-Class America: Essays on Labor, Community, and American Society* (Urbana: University of Illinois Press, 1976), p. 25; and Bruce Laurie, *Artisans into Workers: Labor in Nineteenth-Century America* (New York: Hill and Wang, 1989), p. 35.

24 Louis Althusser, *For Marx* (1965; rpt. London: Verso, 1990); Nicos Poulantzas, *Political Power and Social Classes* (London: New Left Books, 1973), p. 62; Fredric Jameson, *The Political Unconscious: Narrative as a Socially Symbolic Act* (Ithaca, NY: Cornell University Press, 1981), p. 294. The influence of such dismissals of class consciousness as unduly "essentialist" or "subjectivist" should not be overstated, however. For a defense of the concept in a work that continues to be one of the more widely respected labor histories of the period, see Sean Wilentz, *Chants Democratic: New York City and the Rise of the American Working Class, 1788–1850,* (New York: Oxford University Press, 1984), p. 18.

25 My summary distills passages from *The Communist Manifesto* and *The Grundrisse*. It draws heavily on G. A. Cohen's discussion, "The Dialect of Labor in Marx," from *History, Labour, and Freedom: Themes from Marx* (Oxford University Press, 1988), pp. 183–208.

Index

Index

Made in the USA
Middletown, DE
25 August 2015